In an Outpost
of the Global Economy

In an Outpost of the Global Economy

Work and Workers in India's Information Technology Industry

Edited by

Carol Upadhya and A.R. Vasavi

Routledge
Taylor & Francis Group

LONDON AND NEW YORK

First published 2008
by Routledge

2 Park Square, Milton Park, Abingdon, Oxfordshire OX14 4RN
52 Vanderbilt Avenue, New York, NY 10017

Routledge is an imprint of the Taylor & Francis Group, an informa business

First issued in paperback 2019

Transferred to Digital Printing 2008

Typeset by
Star Compugraphics Private Limited
5-CSC, 1st Floor, Near City Apartments
Vasundhara Enclave
Delhi 110 096

British Library Cataloguing-in-Publication Data
A catalogue record of this book is available from the British Library

ISBN 978-0-415-45680-7 (hbk)
ISBN 978-0-367-17613-6 (pbk)

Contents

Preface   7

1. Outposts of the Global Information Economy:
   Work and Workers in India's Outsourcing Industry   9
   Carol Upadhya and *A.R. Vasavi*

2. Producing the Knowledge Professional: Gendered
   Geographies of Alienation in India's New High-tech
   Workplace   50
   Sanjukta Mukherjee

3. Betwixt and Between? Exploring Mobilities in a
   Global Workplace in India   76
   Marisa D'Mello and *Sundeep Sahay*

4. Management of Culture and Management through
   Culture in the Indian Software Outsourcing Industry   101
   Carol Upadhya

5. The Scientific Imperative to be Positive:
   Self-reliance and Success in the Modern Workplace   136
   Sonali Sathaye

6. Software Work in India: A Labour Process View   162
   P. Vigneswara Ilavarasan

7. Empowerment and Constraint: Women, Work and the
   Family in Chennai's Software Industry   190
   Chris Fuller and *Haripriya Narasimhan*

8. 'Serviced from India': The Making of India's Global
   Youth Workforce   211
     A.R. Vasavi

9. Work Organisation, Control and 'Empowerment':
   Managing the Contradictions of Call Centre Work   235
     Babu P. Remesh

Editors   263
Contributors   264
Index   267

Preface

Several chapters collected in this volume were written for an International Conference on 'New Global Workforces and Virtual Workplaces: Connections, Culture, and Control', held at the National Institute of Advanced Studies (NIAS), Bangalore, on August 12–13, 2005. The conference was organised as part of a research project entitled 'Indian IT Professionals in India and the Netherlands: Work, Culture, and Transnationalism', which was conducted at NIAS between November 2003 and March 2006. The aim of the conference was to bring together researchers working on various aspects of India's rapidly growing information technology industry, especially from sociological and anthropological perspectives. While all the papers presented were of high quality, for various reasons it is not possible to include all of them here. We are grateful to all those who contributed papers to the conference, as well as to the discussants and other participants, whose comments helped us to revise the papers and think through the issues discussed in this volume.

The NIAS research project and the conference were conducted with financial support from the Indo–Dutch Programme on Alternatives in Development (IDPAD), a joint programme on development research of the Indian Council of Social Science Research (ICSSR), New Delhi, and Science for Global Development (WOTRO), The Hague. We are very grateful to IDPAD for their support. Peter van der Veer of the University of Utrecht, The Netherlands, was our research partner, and we are grateful to him for his contributions and support. Sahana Udupa and Sarita Seshagiri worked as Research Associates on the project and played a major role in the organisation of the conference. We thank Dr. Sanchita Dutta of IDPAD, New Delhi, for her unstinting support for our project and for the conference, and to the International Institute of Asian Studies, Amsterdam, for hosting us as Visiting Fellows in 2004 and 2006. We express our gratitude as well to the Director of NIAS, Dr. K. Kasturirangan, and Prof. Dilip Ahuja, then Dean of the School of Social Sciences, NIAS, for their constant encouragement and support for our work.

We would also like to thank several friends and colleagues who have acted as sounding boards during the course of our study and/or who have read and commented on our papers in this volume: Sarah Joseph, Narendar Pani, M. Vijaybaskar, Solomon Benjamin, Gautam Sonti, Janaki Nair, Madhava Prasad, Mary John, Satish Deshpande, Supriya Roy-Choudhury and Lata Mani. Our colleagues and students at NIAS have also contributed to this project in various ways, not least by patiently listening to presentations of our research on more than one occasion, and asking penetrating and at times uncomfortable questions!

Carol Upadhya and *A.R. Vasavi*

1

Outposts of the Global Information Economy: Work and Workers in India's Outsourcing Industry

Carol Upadhya and *A.R. Vasavi*

Over the past two decades, India has become a major outpost of the global economy, as the recipient of outsourced technology-based and mediated work mainly from the post-industrial economies of the West. The emergent information technology (IT) and IT enabled services (ITES) industries have become emblematic of India's entry and integration into the global economy and have put India at the centre of discourses about globalisation.

The emergence of these 'high tech' offshore industries in India is one manifestation of the latest phase in the development of global capitalism. Aided by the spread of sophisticated computer and tele-communications technologies, systems of production are becoming ever more geographically dispersed and an increasing array of economic activities are being outsourced and offshored to new destinations, leading to the establishment of new 'knowledge' industries in countries that were formerly labelled 'Third World'. Today, China and India are continually under the gaze of international media, and the apparent unstoppable outflow of jobs from the US to these and other 'developing' countries has sparked public outcries in the West. Although the IT and ITES industries still constitute a very small part of India's economy as a whole and employ an insignificant proportion of the working population, they have substantially enhanced India's visibility and reputation in the global cultural economy. The country's prowess in the IT field has been widely celebrated even as Indian software engineers and call centre agents are blamed for stealing American and European jobs (as seen in the use of term 'Bangalored' to refer to the loss of American jobs to India).

While the state, the media and IT industry leaders hail this new sector as a model for development that will enable India to 'leapfrog' into a post-industrial economy (and hence provide an opportunity to become a world superpower), and although the industry has received substantial media and academic attention, there has been till recently relatively little research on these developments from sociological or anthropological perspectives. There is substantial literature on the history, growth and structure of India's IT-ITES industries,[1] but few critical analyses of the nature of work in this sector, the new work-forces that have been created, or their significance for India's overall social and economic development. For instance, we know little about the organisational structures and work processes that have developed in these industries—are they culturally distinctive or do they simply replicate the features of their Western parent or client companies? Have IT-ITES companies introduced new forms and cultures of work into India, and if so, what are the implications of these changes? What are the characteristics of the new workforces that have been produced to cater to these industries, and how does working 'virtually' in the global economy affect the lives and identities of workers? Has the IT-ITES sector provided employment to a broad cross-section of the population, expanding India's 'new middle classes' (Deshpande 2003; Fernandes 2000) or only reinforced existing caste-class-gender divisions by drawing primarily on the existing educated middle class for its workforce?

An additional set of questions concerns the wider cultural and social repercussions of the rapid growth of these offshore industries in India and the emergence of a distinctive category of global 'know-ledge workers'. In cities where IT activity is concentrated, such as Bangalore, Chennai, NOIDA and Hyderabad, the transformations that have been wrought by this industry are starkly visible. Most IT and ITES companies are housed in hypermodern glass-and-steel structures that are often jarring against the background of their more traditional urban or semi-rural surroundings. IT professionals too have become a highly visible segment of the new middle class that has emerged in liberalising India: with their high salaries and opportunities for travel abroad, they can afford fairly luxurious lifestyles at relatively young ages, thus forming a new elite professional class. IT and ITES jobs have become the most sought after career options for Indian youth, significantly altering their educational choices and social trajectories.

Moreover, due to their sudden rise and social significance, the IT and ITES industries have been subjected to excessive media attention, and this has produced a range of popular images about these new workplaces and their workers. Narratives circulating in the media and other public spheres have helped to create the high level of visibility that these industries and their workers enjoy, and are central to the construction of a specific discourse about IT and its significance for India's development. For all these reasons, there is a need to match the dynamics of these fast evolving industries with solid academic research, deploying a sociological gaze to scrutinise them and their employees, and especially to understand the ways in which outsourced IT work leaves its imprint on workers and the larger society.

The chapters in this volume explore some of the questions outlined above. The IT-ITES industries are quite new in India and research on them and their workforces is at a preliminary stage. All the chapters presented here are based on field research and are situated within current theoretical debates, but the volume as a whole is exploratory. More field-level and empirical research needs to be done to develop a comprehensive understanding of the transformations that have been set in motion by this phase of globalisation in India. Nonetheless, we believe that these essays make a significant contribution to what promises to be a growing and important field of study in India as well as more broadly to the anthropological and sociological literature on globalisation.

In this introductory chapter, we situate the essays within the broad contours of current debates on cultural and social processes of globalisation, the nature of work in the 'new economy' and the emergence of new categories of global workers. But first, in the following section we provide the context to these studies by briefly reviewing the history and political economy of the Indian information technology industry.

Political Economy of the Indian IT Industry

As already noted, the emergence of the Indian IT-ITES industries is directly linked to the process of global economic restructuring that has been underway since the 1980s. In the first phase, the shift from 'Fordist' mass production to 'post-Fordist' networked flexible production forged new links among countries and economies across the globe (Larry and Urry 1987; Castells 1996). Under the regime of 'flexible accumulation' that emerged (Harvey 1989), economic activity was increasingly organised through complex transnational production networks rather than through vertically integrated multinational companies.[2] Since the 1980s, the regime of flexible accumulation has been taken a step further. Work is increasingly performed through the manipulation of symbols in computer systems rather than of material objects—what Zuboff (1988) has called textualisation of work. As a result, production and services have become 'dematerialised', disembodied, and divided among workers located in geographically distant sites. Modern information and communication technologies (ICTs) have facilitated the vertical disintegration of the production process within large companies, which are then reaggregated into specialised industries and relocated in various global production centres (Huws 2003; Lash and Urry 1987).

The globalisation of services is a key feature of this phase in the development of global capitalism (Castells 1996). The 'servitisation' of the advanced economies and increasingly sharp competition have led companies to prioritise customer service and satisfaction even while they attempt to reduce their costs by centralising and outsourcing routine services such as customer support. These shifts, together with the integration and spread of new digital and communication technologies, have given rise to global commodity chains of service provision. While in the earlier stage of globalisation manufacturing jobs moved from the industrialised economies to low-cost locations in the 'Third World', now it is primarily service jobs that are migrating—both 'high tech' professional jobs such as computer programming and software development as well as 'low-end' back office services such as insurance claims processing and telemarketing (IT-enabled services and business process outsourcing or BPO). Thus, a range of white and 'pink collar' work has been outsourced or offshored to sites where cheaper labour enables large amounts of clerical work to be carried out round the clock. Work carried out in these dispersed sites is managed and coordinated through the use of the new ICTs. These economic shifts have created a global 'informational economy' (Castells 1996) based on complex production and services networks that create and support information technology systems and provide remote backend services, linking together workers, managers, and customers located across multiple sites and borders. In this 'new economy', information or 'knowledge' has become the key resource and factor of production as well as the primary product.

The emergence and growth of India's IT industry coincided with an acceleration in the internationalisation of the production, distribution, and management of goods and services in the 1990s (Castells 1996: 116). Companies located in the advanced industrial economies are outsourcing and offshoring an increasing proportion and range of their business activities to places where skilled human resources are more easily available and at lower cost. India has seen the setting up of offshore software development centres by MNCs (multinational corporations) and the burgeoning of international call centres and other back office operations. In tandem with these developments has been the emergence and spectacular growth of Indian-owned IT services companies (now being transformed into transnational corporations) to cater to the global demand for these services. India now accounts for 65 per cent of the global market for offshore IT services and 46 per cent of global business process outsourcing (NASSCOM 2005, 2006). The Indian software and services industry (often simply referred to as the 'IT industry')[3] grew at a rate of about 50 per cent per year in the 1990s and in 2005–06 generated total earnings of $17.8 billion. Riding on the back of the software industry's success, ITES (which includes BPO or business process outsourcing and call centres) has become the new boom industry, generating revenues of $7.2 billion in 2005–06 (NASSCOM 2007). Although accurate employment figures are difficult to obtain, current official estimates place total direct employment generated by the industry at 1.3 million in 2005–06—representing a rapid expansion from the figure of 284,000 in 1999–2000.[4]

While global economic restructuring provided the space for the emergence of the IT-ITES industries in India, their rapid growth can also be attributed to specific political and economic processes that have unfolded in the country since the 1980s. These include the deepening policy of liberalisation that has exposed India to global economic forces; the push towards technological modernisation, especially in the computer and telecom sectors, that began under Rajiv Gandhi's regime; and the emergence of a class of indigenous 'middle class' entrepreneurs in the IT sector who represent a new model for Indian business (Upadhya 2004). The IT industry right from its inception has enjoyed significant state support, both directly and indirectly, and at both national and state levels.[5] In addition, it has drawn on the large pool of skilled manpower (especially engineering graduates) that was produced during the long period of Nehruvian state-led development policies. The industry's requirement for a steady supply of 'knowledge workers' has shaped both public policy and the production of the IT workforce in particular ways (Upadhya 2006a).

The export-oriented nature of the IT-ITES industries in India also has significant implications for the nature of work and the modes of organisational control employed. Despite frequent claims that it is 'moving up the value chain' towards the provision of end-to-end software development, consultancy and 'knowledge process outsourcing', the IT industry continues to rely on labour cost arbitrage (Balakrishnan 2006). Its profitability is based largely on its ability to marshal sufficient and well-qualified human resources, to deploy them onto projects as and when needed, and to maximise labour productivity. Similarly, the ITES industry needs to hire and manage large numbers of English-speaking educated youth. The labour market and modes of control over the labour process are largely structured by the need to recruit, deploy, and manage this army of 'knowledge workers'.

Work and Workers:
Flexibility, Virtuality and Mobility

Software engineers, BPO workers and others employed in IT-related occupations constitute new categories of global technical workers or 'knowledge professionals' in India. In several ways, the characteristics of these workforces and the nature of work are distinctly different from those in 'old economy' companies as well as traditional service and professional occupations. These differences flow primarily from the specificities of the outsourcing business.

First, while Indian software engineers are physically mobile within the global economy, the growth of offshoring is immobilising labour in new ways as work is increasingly performed 'virtually' and online, reducing the need for the physical migration or circulation of labour. Although this labour is disembodied and deterritorialised, the fact that workers across the globe are connected in dispersed networks of production or services '… retemporalises labour by introducing a register of instantaneousness … [altering] the cultural frame of labour, restructuring it in shapes that are not readily discernible' (Poster 2002: 340). This in turn alters the very experience of work and hence the subjectivity of the worker in significant ways. Although parallels may be drawn with the earlier phase of globalisation which was marked by the geographical dispersal of manufacturing, the way in which IT-based offshore workforces are linked into the global economy is substantially different from export-oriented manufacturing industries. Workers in offshore factories in Malaysia or Brazil produce goods destined for the global market but have no connection with the ultimate consumers of these goods, or usually even with the multinational companies which market them under their brand names. In contrast, many offshore software engineers and telematics workers are in direct and frequent contact with customers, colleagues, or managers located in their employers' head offices or client sites. Outsourced service work thus requires a significant level of interaction and collaboration across borders, bringing to the fore issues of cross-cultural communication that are addressed by companies through myriad training and orientation programmes.

Second, many of the features of service or 'knowledge' work that have been discussed in the literature on the 'new economy' in the West are also found in the Indian IT industry. For instance, *culture*, in various ways, has become central to the management of work and workers, as in the 'new economy' generally (du Gay and Pryke 2002; Ray and Sayer 1999), and this in turn shapes the subjectivities of employees, who are expected to mould themselves to meet the demands of the 'new workplace'. But some characteristics of management and labour are perhaps unique to the Indian industry because of the requirements of the outsourcing relationship. For instance, customer service is a key value in many companies, and this together with the constant need to shore up the bottom line, leads to the long working hours that are typical of this industry. Similarly, IT companies privilege labour flexibility and promote a new 'global corporate culture' based on worker individualisation and self-management, but they also employ exacting and top-down forms of control in order to extract the maximum work out of employees.

In the following sections, these features of work, the workplace and workers in the IT-ITES industries are discussed in more detail, with a focus on their specificities in the Indian context. We elaborate on several inter-related processes that we see as central to India's out-sourced economy: the processes through which these new workforces are produced; the flexibilisation, despatialisation and disembodiment of labour; and the emergence of new forms of labour mobility, both physical and virtual, as well as the immobilisation of labour.

Before turning to this discussion, it should be emphasised that software and IT enabled services are very different kinds of business, offering distinctive kinds of jobs and employing different types of workers. However, in India, for historical and ideological reasons, they are categorised together under the 'IT' label—not least because both come under the ambit of NASSCOM (the National Association of Software and Service Companies), the major industry body. We have chosen to cover both sectors in this volume because of the fact that they are linked together in the Indian context in several ways. For instance, most of the large and medium size Indian IT companies have attempted to enter the ITES market by starting or buying BPO companies and building synergies between IT services and ITES. Also, there is an equation between the two in popular imagination, for instance in the ambition of many call centre workers to get IT jobs.[6] Nonetheless, there are significant differences, which will become clearer in the following section.

Indian IT Workforce: Production and Control

Gaining access to and maintaining control over a sufficient supply of qualified and malleable 'knowledge workers' is a crucial issue for both the software and BPO industries. This concern is reflected in the frequent complaints by industry about the shortage of skilled manpower; the development of strategies by both the state and the industry to augment the supply of qualified workers; and the numerous industry-sponsored conclaves and discussions that are held on HR (human resources) issues. These debates and discussions can be seen as discursive techniques through which the IT-ITES workforce is created, shaped and controlled, as the chapters by Babu Remesh and A.R. Vasavi in this volume suggest. While the industry often represents itself as the victim of IT and ITES professionals' selfish ambitions (who just quit their jobs if they are dissatisfied), IT companies deploy a range of discursive and managerial strategies to produce and control the IT workforce. For instance, the workforce is defined and segmented through a process of social and cultural marking, based on gender (chapter 2), age (chapter 8) and 'Indian culture' (chapter 4).

In addition to these discursive strategies, the IT industry also uses practical tactics to garner qualified workers. For instance, software companies prefer to hire engineering graduates, which India turns out in large numbers. As noted by P. Vigneswara Illavarasan (chapter 6), the type of engineering education these graduates have received is unrelated to the nature of their work. The ready availability of a large technical workforce has made it possible for IT companies to hire people who are over-qualified and often ill-suited for their jobs (in terms of formal degrees) as a strategy for marketing their services to foreign customers. Moreover, the engineering education they receive is often inadequate, and for all these reasons new recruits are put through extended periods of intensive training. This mismatch between the education of most Indian IT workers and the actual work in which they are engaged is linked to the low level of work that is outsourced to India and the fact that ordinary engineering or science graduates can be trained for the job of software engineer within few months. Similarly, Indian call centres and BPOs are able to hire workers who are educationally over-qualified (most are college graduates) compared to their counterparts in the West. This is at once a selling point for the industry and a source of the high 'attrition rates', for most workers plan to move into different careers or pursue higher education after working for one or two years in such jobs.

Ilavarasan's study shows that software engineers in India are quite homogeneous in terms of socio-economic and educational background, in contrast to the class differences that mark different categories of software workers in the US (primarily, between those engaged in design and conceptualisation work versus those who are engaged in the execution of projects). Because of this relative homogeneity, he suggests, most Indian software workers enter the industry at the same level, are given the same training, and then are inducted into similar (managerial) career paths. This contrasts with the situation in the West where software workers tend to be segmented into different kinds of jobs and career paths (high- or low-skilled) on the basis of social class and education. The Indian IT industry also lacks a well-developed 'technical' career path, a fact that is again linked to the nature of most of the work that is outsourced to India. This difference can be attributed to differences in social context, especially the socio-economic class system: in the US low level technical jobs and engineering/managerial occupations draw on distinct social strata for their workforces, while in India all levels and categories of IT jobs are filled by people from similar social backgrounds (urban, educated and middle class). However, there is evidence of some degree of segmentation by social class and educational background in the Indian IT industry as well—for instance, IIT graduates and others from premier institutions tend to corner the best jobs (research, design and higher management positions) in the most prestigious companies (Upadhya 2006a).

Flexibilisation of Labour

The flexibilisation of labour has been identified by many scholars as a key feature of work and employment in the post-industrial era.[7] Harvey (1989: 147), for instance, places flexibility with respect to labour processes and labour markets at the heart of the regime of 'flexible accumulation'. The concept of flexibilisation actually refers to several separate processes: the growth of flexible forms of employment (contract labour and part-time jobs), labour market flexibility, physical and job mobility of workers, and flexibility in the work process and forms of organisation (Benner 2002). While all these processes are evident to some extent in the Indian software industry, the forms of flexible labour that have emerged in this context are somewhat different from those found in the West.

In the post-industrial economies of the West, flexible employment arrangements have transformed work and careers, eroding job security, creating longer working hours and double shifts, and leading to a process of individualisation.[8] In India too, similar changes have taken place since the 1990s under the liberalised economic regime. In place of the paternalism that typified 'traditional' Indian companies and provided some level of protection for workers, a new culture of competitive individualism has entered private sector workplaces.[9] This shift is most visible in the IT-ITES sector where employment relations are more 'flexible' than what was typically found in the 'old economy'. Labour market flexibility is indicated by high 'attrition' rates and lack of job security. Software services companies require a high level of labour flexibility because they are required to deploy large numbers of software engineers ('resources') on projects quickly, send them onsite or bring them back to India as needed, and increase or decrease the size of their workforces as projects come and go. This requirement is met by using temporary contract workers as well as by the practice of maintaining a certain proportion of the workforce 'on the bench' (a term that refers to software engineers who are not assigned to projects and so are not 'billable', but are available for work). Employment in this sector is particularly sensitive to shifts in the global economic scenario, as was witnessed in the aftermath of the 'dot com' bust and '9/11', when contracts dried up and many Indian software workers in India and abroad were laid off. Despite this uncertainty, IT jobs are highly desirable and are usually the first career choice for India's educated youth (Arulmani and Nag-Arulmani 2006) because of the high salaries and opportunities for career mobility and travel abroad that they offer. Indeed, the boom in the IT industry and the Indian economy in general since 2003 has stimulated a significant process of upward mobility for these privileged employees. Yet, as Marisa D'Mello and Sundeep Sahay in this volume (chapter 3) demonstrate, the pervasive sense of insecurity that workers experience takes its toll on their sense of self and their orientation to the future.

The trend towards flexibilisation is more apparent in the ITES sector, which appears to have created the ultimate flexible workforce, as the chapters by Vasavi and Remesh reveal. The ITES workforce is not only malleable because of the youth and inexperience of the majority of workers, and unorganised due to the transient nature of employment and the representation of workers as 'professionals', but is also considered by companies to be dispensable as existing workers are replaced by new ones every year or two. BPO companies have developed a revolving-door system of continuously hiring new recruits, training them quickly and pushing them onto 'the floor', while churning out a large proportion of the workforce each year through both 'voluntary' and 'involuntary attrition' (Upadhya and Vasavi 2006: Chapter 8). Conversely, and perhaps largely for this reason, most workers do not look at a call centre job as a long-term prospect, but rather as a stop-gap arrangement to earn money before moving on to another career or further education.

Another important aspect of labour flexibilisation pertains to the work itself and to the skills of workers. Indian software engineers are known in the global market for their 'flexibility' and adaptability in being able to learn new technologies quickly while on the job, as noted in the chapters by Mukherjee and Upadhya. The large software services companies encourage this kind of flexibility by assigning programmers to different types of projects, platforms and domains, and they prefer to hire 'generic programmers' over those who are highly specialised because they need to execute different kinds of projects. As Ilavasaran notes in his chapter, one reason for this is that the Indian software services business is primarily a numbers game in which success depends on the ability to put a large number of programmers quickly onto a project. This feature of outsourced software work has implications for the way in which workers and work are organised and managed, as well as for the long-term development of skills. He addresses the question of whether this feature of software outsourcing is leading to a process of 'deskilling'.

Despatialisation, Disembodiment and Mobility of Labour

As noted earlier, in the new global economy many arenas of production and services—especially knowledge work—are becoming more transnationalised, such that economic processes lose their fixed spatial attachments. Increasingly we find various kind of work being performed remotely (for instance, as in offshore call centres)—a process that Aneesh (2006: 9) refers to as 'liquifaction of labour'. In this context, while capital is globally organised labour becomes increasingly localised (Beck 2000).[10] Thus, labour is increasingly tied to the locality, but at the same time it is more profoundly affected by the risks of transnational capital flows over which it has little control.

The implications of despatialistation and disembodiment of work in India's offshore economy are explored in several chapters in this volume. D'Mello and Sahay highlight the alterations in the conception and use of space and time in the context of global software outsourcing, while Mukherjee notes the contrast between the 'disembodied' or virtual labour performed by software engineers and the actual embodied experience of work.

In tandem with these processes of deterritorialisation of labour has been the production of a globally networked workforce and a new type of 'high-tech' nomadic worker who is capable of 'being both here and there at the same time, of overcoming the gravity of space' (Beck 2000: 75). The IT-ITES workforce in India exemplifies this: the outsourcing industry requires workers who are flexible and mobile but it also creates new immobilities. Although the Indian IT industry developed on the basis of 'bodyshopping' or mobile labour—in which companies fulfilled their contracts for software services primarily by sending software engineers to the customer site[11]—in recent years an increasing proportion of work has been performed in India, or 'offshore', rather than 'onsite' at the customer's location. While many IT professionals still travel and work abroad for short and long periods of time, the trend toward offshoring has created a new category of networked 'virtual' workers who work primarily from India. In these systems of online, offshore labour, Indian programmers are often logged onto the computer networks of their customers abroad, working on projects as part of 'virtual teams' consisting of colleagues, managers and customers spread across several geographical locations, so that the client is able to monitor progress, check the quality of the work, and communicate with programmers as if they were onsite.[12]

Thus, while the physical mobility or circulation of workers continues to be a significant feature of the Indian software industry, new forms of mobility and immobility have appeared and are becoming central to the way in which the industry operates—especially the mobility of 'knowledge work' minus the body of the worker, or what Aneesh (2001a, 2006) has termed 'virtual migration'.[13] With the shift to offshore, online work, the bodies of workers are immobilised while their labour flows through computer and satellite links to their customers and colleagues on the other side of globe. This phenomenon of virtual migration is most visible in call centres and BPOs, whose agents interact with foreign customers or are engaged in work for clients outside of India on a daily basis. As Gephart notes, digitalisation has facilitated the flexibilisation of labour as well as the virtualisation and rationalisation of the work process, but simultaneously a 'diffuse mode of work and transnational capital flows affect labour that is culturally tied to a given locale' (2002: 331). Offshore business process outsourcing workers are directly linked into dispersed computer networks through which they handle customer service and back office work and can be managed and monitored remotely by managers and customers. In fact, offshore IT and ITES work can be seen as at once disembodied and embodied—while much of it is performed remotely it is also embodied in particular ways, as Mukherjee points out in her article. She highlights the apparent contradictions between virtual work and systems of control and the actual embodied and social nature of software work—for instance in the ways in which work is gendered.

Another significant feature of offshore service work is the centrality of technology to the performance of work itself and to modes of control over the labour process. In this industry as in the informational economy in general, labour is increasingly interpenetrated by information machines. The networked computer has changed the territorial and temporal specificity of labour, altering the organisation of work, and creating new structures and patterns of organisational control (see following section). According to its advocates, the 'symbolisation' of work requires a less rigid system of control and allows more scope for creativity, which makes the new digital economy more 'humanising'. But to its critics, the new economy is one of 'posthumanisation' characterised by a 'deep symbiosis of humans with machines' (Poster 2002: 347). The nature of work in call centres, described in Remesh's chapter, best represents the emergence of such 'cyborg' workers. The close integration of the worker with the information machine shapes the experience of work, as also suggested in Mukherjee's article.

Workplaces: Cultures of Work and Organisational Control

The features of work in the global 'informational economy' outlined above are closely linked to the practices and ideologies of management that have emerged in the post-industrial economies of the West over the last several decades, which are thought to be as very different from those of the Fordist factory regime. Some scholars argue that the 'new workplace' is characterised by flexible and more democratic structures, affording more autonomy to workers (Zuboff 1988), while others suggest that the extensive use of computers and information technology has enabled managements to exert greater control over labour through 'panoptical' forms of surveillance and monitoring (Garson 1988; Thompson and Warhurst 1998).

While there is a burgeoning literature on the 'new workplace' in the West, much less has been written about the new global workplaces that have emerged in the outposts of the information economy—outsourcing/offshore hubs such as the National Capital Region (Delhi), Chennai, Mumbai, Hyderabad and Bangalore in India. Many characteristics of organisation and management in the Indian software and BPO industries are similar to those found in high-tech services and IT industries in the US and elsewhere. However, there are specific features of the outsourcing situation that have produced significant differences in systems of organisational control and work culture.

The 'New Workplace' and the New Worker

According to popular management books as well as some academic literature, the 'new economy' has given rise to a 'new model' corporation that is characterised by a more open and informal work culture and 'flat', flexible organisational structures, in contrast to the hierarchical and bureaucratic systems that typified corporate workplaces in the Fordist era. These new management systems are designed to 'empower' workers and encourage individual initiative, thereby stimulating greater productivity as well as employee satisfaction. Such practices are found particularly in the 'knowledge' industries, where the speed of innovation and production has been increasing steadily and companies attempt to promote innovation and creativity by granting employees a large degree of autonomy. The 'new workplace' is identified especially with the American IT industry: Silicon Valley's informal, individualistic work culture is supposed to have been a key factor fostering the climate of innovation that has been so central to the industry's growth (Benner 2002; Cooper 2000).[14] However, the management ideologies and practices associated with 'soft capitalism' (Heelas 2002) have spread more widely, engendering new cultures of work that have permeated workplaces around the world. What has been called a 'cultural turn' in management ideology and practice[15] has important implications for the subjectivities of workers (Ray and Sayer 1999).

A key feature of the 'new workplace' is that workers and the work process in theory are controlled primarily through indirect or 'subjective' techniques rather than the direct and top-down methods typical of Taylorism.[16] Methods of 'normative' control, such as teamwork and cultural management, are designed to create worker commitment and induce them to manage themselves (Kunda 1992). In the 'new workplace', employees are supposed to internalise management goals, and actively monitor and control their own behaviour and that of co-workers (Gephart 2002: 335). The deployment of subjective mechanisms of control means that the employment relationship is no longer purely economic but involves the shaping of the employee's very sense of self.[17]

A significant consequence of the 'cultural turn' in corporate management, combined with the flexibilisation of labour, is a process of individualisation[18] in the workplace and among workers (Beck 2000; Beck and Beck-Gernsheim 2002). This process can be observed also in the context of the Indian IT-ITES industry, with its flexible labour market, mobile and flexible workforces, and 'new workplace' HR policies that emphasise individual achievement, self-motivation and competition. A central feature of individualisation is the fact that employees do not have a collective identity as workers or as employees, nor do they collectively negotiate with management on common issues. Moreover, due to job insecurity software engineers and other IT employees are constrained to become 'entrepreneurial' workers (Beck 2000) who fashion their own careers through strategies such as job-hopping, self-improvement courses, and constant online and on-the-job learning. Under the new dispensation, workers are responsible for their own economic security and careers by continually re-outfitting themselves with new skills in order to be saleable in the job market. Another aspect of individualisation is the fact that responsibility for completing work or making decisions is devolved to a large extent onto individual employees, who are motivated to perform because they identify (in theory) with the company and its goals. In this context, discipline is enforced as much by self and by peer pressure as by managers. D'Mello and Sahay (chapter 3) describe in detail the personal and social consequences of this demand for individual self-responsibility.

Although normative management techniques are used throughout the corporate world today, they are particularly characteristic of 'knowledge industries' that depend on gaining control over highly educated, and skilled technical and professional workers. But there is a tension between software companies' desire to encourage individual autonomy and innovation, and the need to manage and coordinate the labour and knowledge of workers. In her study of the Australian software industry, Barrett (2001, 2004) found that the work culture focuses on the technical aspects of work, personal opportunities and flexible employee-friendly policies—a strategy of control she terms 'responsible autonomy', an attempt '… to harness the adaptability of labour power by giving workers leeway and encouraging them to adapt to changing situations in a manner beneficial to the firm' (2001: 31). Similar practices are typical of the IT industry across the world and are linked to the promotion of flexibility in labour relations and work. The same ideology of worker autonomy and techniques of normative control are found in the Indian software and ITES industries as well, as described in the articles by Mukherjee, Upadhya, Vasavi and Remesh.

One of primary 'soft' management techniques that is touted by contemporary management theory is the creation and inculcation of a distinctive corporate culture, which is considered to be crucial for the promotion of employee loyalty and the 'alignment' of individual with company goals (Kunda 1992). In the Indian software industry as well, the large companies—both Indian and multinational—have developed their own corporate cultures through which employees are supposed to be incorporated into the collectivity, imbued with common values and oriented to the corporate 'mission'. This is accomplished through induction programmes, social events and soft skills training sessions, among other methods, as discussed in the articles by Sonali Sathaye and Upadhya (see Upadhya and Vasavi 2006).[19] Another important technique of indirect control that is widely employed by IT and ITES companies in India is team-based organisation. As several scholars have argued, this is not merely an organisational strategy but is also a means of indirect control over the work process by using peer pressure and turning workers into unpaid supervisors.[20] But as Mukherjee points out in her article, the ideology of teamwork is contradicted by the competitive individualism that is promoted by other management practices such as individualised performance appraisals and confidential salary negotiations.

The articles by Upadhya and Sathaye focus on the 'cultural turn' in management practice and ideology in the Indian IT industry. Under the new work regime, individualised workers need to plan and manage not only their careers but also their lives. To help them to do this, most software companies offer 'soft skills' training programmes in subjects such as time management, self-actualisation, personality development, assertiveness, emotional intelligence and communication skills. These programmes are aimed at producing self-managing workers who are also goal-oriented, autonomous individuals. In her article, Sathaye focuses on the use of Western psychological concepts and techniques in soft skills training programmes that are intended to improve cooperation at work, promote creativity, and achieve a 'fit' between the organisation and the individual. Desirable personality traits such as 'assertiveness' and 'self-confidence' are taught through supposedly universal psychological categories, invoking 'science' to establish their authority and ignoring the specificity of Indian culture. Psychometric tests are employed to quantify and categorise personality types in order to improve employees' understanding of the self and the other. Moreover, because 'emotional labour' (Hochschild 1983; Taylor 1998) is central to the performance of many service sector jobs, behavioural training is imparted to the employees in IT and ITES companies to improve their performance, and to make them interact with customers and colleagues in ways that are sensitive to their (Western) culture.

Psychological training techniques can be understood as 'technologies of the self' (Foucault 1988) that are deployed to produce the right kind of 'knowledge worker'—one who engages in self-surveillance and continually 'casts a constant rational eye' over his or her personal and professional relationships, and 'works on' him/herself at home and at work (chapter 5). In line with wider trends in the West that have been linked to the process of individualisation—especially the burgeoning of books and programmes aimed at 'self-actualisation', self-help, 'life skills' and success (Howell and Ingham 2001; Rimke 2000)—the soft skills training offered by many software companies in India assure participants that it will help them to 'learn to become themselves'. The valorisation of the modern, individualised subject in the context of these new workplaces raises a number of questions about the cultural adjustments that Indian IT workers are required to make.

While 'cultural management' is a central feature of contemporary management ideology across the globe, in the Indian software outsourcing industry 'culture' has become even more crucial because of the cross-border nature of the business. In her article, Upadhya argues that 'culture' is used as a tool for the management that is deployed both consciously and implicitly. This is seen in the techniques and theories of 'cross-cultural' management that are used to manage and coordinate multicultural 'virtual' teams, in 'cultural sensitivity' training programmes that aim to teach Indian software engineers to communicate effectively with their foreign customers and colleagues, and in the figure of the Indian techie as a global technical professional who is imbued with specific cultural characteristics. In these new global workplaces, national cultures are being redefined and leveraged in specific ways, for instance through the stereotyping of 'Indian work culture' in contradistinction to that of the West (see Upadhya 2006b). Ironically, cultural training programmes highlight and reproduce reified notions of cultural difference, even as the psychological techniques discussed by Sathaye (chapter 5) assume a common human psyche and ride roughshod over difference. Indian software engineers are culturally stereotyped by these discourses while at the same time they are trained to adapt to a singular model of 'global corporate culture' that dominates the space in which they work. Both the 'Indian' and the 'global' can be regarded as cultural categories that are defined and wielded as strategies of control over the IT industry's virtual and mobile workforces. This in turn has significant implications for the production and reconstitution of the cultural identities and subjectivities of workers, which aligns closely with Berking's observation that in the current phase of globalisation, new forms of 'internal ethnicisation' will act as 'a self-regulatory mode of modern societies' (2003: 261).

Routinisation of Software Production and Techniques of Direct Control

While most IT companies operating in India, both Indian and multinational, subscribe to the ideology of 'soft management' discussed above, the exigencies of outsourced software production have also induced them to introduce more direct forms of organisational control. In fact, far from providing employees greater autonomy and flexibility, in large software services companies work is increasingly closely controlled and monitored. This reflects a wider trend in which the process of software development has shifted away from individualised craft-like production towards a more routinised, rationalised factory-like production process (Beirne et al. 1998). The development of structured programming and object-oriented languages that allow for modular programming, and the use of software engineering tools, have led to the emergence of 'software factories' or 'assembly lines' for software development (Barrett 2001: 25). In this system, work is divided into small portions and allocated among engineers within a team and among different teams, and often an individual engineer or team does not know how their component fits into the whole system.

While the rationalisation of software production is a global trend, it has been taken to a new level by major Indian software services companies, which excel at executing large projects expeditiously by assigning large numbers of engineers to execute them. The standard 'global delivery model' involves the coordination of work among several geographically dispersed sites, taking advantage of time differences to work '24/7'. In order to keep control over costs and timelines in such large projects, these companies have introduced exacting systems of monitoring and control. The adoption by many Indian software companies of international quality certifications such as the ISO 9000 and CMM Level 5 has injected an even higher level of 'process orientation' into project management.[21] Some scholars argue that these software quality processes constitute forms of 'panoptical control' and surveillance, in apparent contradiction to the official rhetoric of worker initiative and autonomy (Prasad 1998). These systems go beyond traditional bureaucratic techniques in their ability to instil discipline and consolidate control over the work process. The effectiveness of these techniques of control is further enhanced by the fact that surveillance now takes place primarily through electronic means—what Zuboff (1986) called the 'information panopticon'. The fragmentation of the work process and lack of autonomy for individual engineers are, in Mukherjee's view (chapter 2), among the factors responsible for the 'alienation' of software workers.

The advent of large 'software factories' and the transformation of software production into a highly fragmented and mechanical process has provoked a fresh debate on the 'deskilling' or 'invisible deskilling' of software engineers (Aneesh 2001b; Prasad 1998), following Braverman (1975). In the context of manufacturing industries, Braverman argued that Taylorist strategies of dividing the work process into small parts (task fragmentation), thereby 'deskilling' workers, is aimed not only at increasing productivity and profits but also at enhancing managerial control over labour and especially over the tacit knowledge of workers. The fact that software engineers are often required merely to put together ready-made modules, produce code according to fixed norms, or customise existing applications reduces the scope for creativity or autonomy. This 'deskilling' is exacerbated in the Indian outsourcing industry because it tends to concentrate on projects at the 'low end' of the software services spectrum, such as routine coding, maintenance and testing. Ilavarasan's chapter addresses this issue (chapter 6): he reviews the debate on 'task fragmentation' that has dominated discussions of computer work in the West and then asks whether similar arguments can be made in the Indian context. Based on his survey of work and workers in two Bangalore software companies, he contends that work is not task fragmented because there is considerable overlap among different categories and levels of software workers in terms of the roles and tasks they perform. But if the task fragmentation argument is not entirely applicable to the Indian software industry, this may be linked to the difference in the social composition of the workforce, compared to the West (noted above), and to the position of the industry in the global division of labour as a provider of low-cost and low-end services.

Most accounts of software work in India emphasise the routinised and mechanical nature of much of it, coupled with high levels of stress caused by unrealistic project deadlines and consequent long working hours. Panoptical management techniques introduced to control the work process are combined with the extensive use of indirect or 'soft' management techniques, which are aimed not only at motivating workers to put in extra effort and time but also at alleviating the stress and frustration that is created by the routinisation of the production process. This combination of direct and indirect techniques of organisational control allows companies to extract the maximum work out of their employees and hence to maximise productivity. But it also contains a contradiction: workers are expected to transform themselves into individualised, self-managed and self-directed 'entrepreneurial' employees while at the same time they must perform within a tightly controlled and impersonal management system that tracks their every move and moment. The combination of extreme forms of panoptical control with subjective techniques of 'illusory empowerment' is found to an even greater extent in the IT-enabled services sector.

Panoptical Control and
Worker Resistance in IT-enabled Services

Much of what has been written about the 'new workplace' of the post-industrial 'information economy' is based on the high-tech industries of the US. However, at the other end of the service economy is the vast range of back office and customer service work typical of the IT-enabled services industry. Here, workers are styled as 'knowledge workers' or 'professionals' through designations such as 'customer care executive' and 'business process manager', but in fact most of their work is highly mechanical and unskilled, consisting of little more than remotely performed and technology mediated clerical work.

The techniques of organisational control that are deployed by business process outsourcing companies and call centres are closer to traditional Taylorist systems of direct management than to the 'soft' techniques that are promoted by contemporary management theory. These highly rationalised management systems have been described in the growing literature on call centres as 'electronic panopticons' (Foucault 1995; Sewell and Wilkinson).[22] Digitilised systems of surveillance and control allow management to continually monitor and rate employee performance and thereby extract higher levels of productivity. These systems create ranks of 'cyborg' workers (Poster 2002) who are completely welded to their workstations.[23] Call centre work is widely regarded as representing the latest phase in the development of Taylorism in which the use of information and communication technologies has elevated '... management control to new historical levels by target-setting and monitoring, in "real time", both quantitative and qualitative aspects of employee performance' (Bain et al. 2002: 173). Given the harshness of these 'panoptical' systems of control and surveillance, ITES companies also need to deploy subjective or normative management strategies that are aimed at masking or diverting attention away from the monotonous, closely regulated and stressful nature of work (for instance, by creating a 'party' or 'college' atmosphere), promoting a sense of identification with the company, and socialising workers through teamwork (van den Broek 2004). Soft management is crucial, especially in call centres because of the large element of 'emotional' (Bain and Taylor 2000; Hochschild 1983) or 'affective' labour (Hardt 1999) that is involved in the work.

Carla Freeman's (2000) study of informatics workers in Barbados illustrates the panoptic mechanisms at work where workers are subjected to '... the gaze of computer, the gaze of supervisor, the manager, the fellow production worker, and finally the internal gaze of the self ...' (2000: 258). Similar techniques of direct (as well as indirect) control employed in the Indian call centre industry are described by Remesh (chapter 9) in this volume. The computer-controlled system not only manages the call flow and the entire work process, but also monitors and records the use of each minute by employees and measures their productivity and quality of service by collecting statistics on a variety of 'metrics'. Most companies attempt to mask these Taylorist elements and to reduce stress and monotony through 'soft management' techniques aimed at creating a lively, attractive and 'fun' workplace. Workers are motivated to perform and to stay on the job through a combination of material incentives, strategies of 'illusory empowerment' and implied promises of rapid upward mobility (see Remesh 2004a, 2004b; Upadhya and Vasavi 2006: Chap. 8). As Vasavi points out (chapter 8), call centre work is retailed as entertainment, as education and as empowerment. Middle-class youth are attracted to these jobs because they are represented not as workers but as professionals or executives—a feature that is found in the industry across the world (see van den Broek 2004).

As noted above, much of the critical literature on call centres represent them as 'electronic panopticons' in which control by management over the work process is near-complete and workers have little autonomy or space for manoeuvre. But several scholars consider this to be an overstatement of the power of these surveillance techniques, discounting the scope for resistance by workers (Bain and Taylor 2000; Winiecki 2004). Winiecki argues that we need to go beyond the description of such overt forms of control and investigate the ways in which techniques of measurement and evaluation are '… apparatuses of rationality and rationalisation that act in the production and reproduction of *subjectivities* in technology-mediated tertiary labour' (2004: 81) and also '… provide spaces in which the subject can exert resistance that may allow him or her to alter one's own subjectivity' (2004: 79).[24] Although the concept of resistance is fraught with difficulties, it is indispensable to understanding the dynamics of workplaces and employment relationships. There is as yet insufficient work on the Indian ITES industry that addresses this question. Remesh's study suggests that ITES workers do indulge in small acts of resistance, such as deliberately mishandling calls or making fun of managers. Our study of call centres in Bangalore also points to informal strategies of resistance, ranging from the traditional one of absenteeism and high labour turnover to individualised acts of sabotage and subversion (Upadhya and Vasavi 2006: Chap. 8). As in any other industry, workers find ways to outwit even the most invasive technologies of control, and in a service industry it is particularly difficult to control the emotional labour of workers or to invoke genuine participation in mandated 'fun' activities (Mulholland 2004: 716–18). Still, it appears that in the Indian ITES industry, many workers (especially those who are new on the job) are successfully incorporated as subjects into the cultures of their companies and internalise the norms and values of customer service, at least for some time. This is yet another advantage of using a youth workforce, for they are less likely than older workers to be critical of the work process and resistant to management. At the same time, the very high rates of employee attrition in the Indian ITES industry suggest that companies, for all their investment in new HR 'retention strategies', are not entirely successful in gaining control over their workforces.

Workers: Sociality, Subjectivity and Identity

If the IT industry and its workforce are emblematic of India's entry into the global economy and its latest embrace of modernity, then several sociological questions about IT workers and their altered subjectivities, identities and social worlds must be posed. For example, what is the meaning and impact of the kind of human–machine interaction that is at the centre of IT and ITES work? How do IT workers make sense of their world of work? Will the 'enchantment with technology' (Strathern 2001: 9) rupture or reconfigure the world of work and the cultural canvas of Indian society? What will be the imprint of this enclave economy of high-tech work on a still largely agrarian and developing economy and society?

We may begin to answer such questions by looking closely at the actual experiences of IT workers, at work and outside, and tracing the alterations in subjectivity, identity and sociality that are taking place. As the site of a new kind of intensive, globalised, technology-mediated work, it is likely that the very structure, orientation and functioning of IT organisations have profound consequences for individual workers' sense of self. Delineating the sources and processes of 'subjectification' in the work context calls attention to key questions such as: whether and why workers submit to processes of routinisation and control, and how they respond to them; how gender or racial identities shape or constrain individual opportunities at work; and what strategies of resistance are deployed (O'Doherty and Wilmott 2001). In addition, attention to forms of data collection, monitoring and assessment in the workplace may illuminate the ways in which subjectivities are altered (Winiecki 2004). Focusing on the work context also points to the ways in which organisational culture normalises work regimes, inducing workers to become not only efficient, effective or reliable but also infusing them with a strong sense of belonging to the organisation.

There are several features of IT work that appear to be especially significant in the process of subjectification and in shaping the fabric of social relations. First, the industry's need for a flexible, mobile and disposable workforce; the fast-paced obsolescence of knowledge forms and practices; and the intense periodic training and orientation programmes that workers undergo, all serve to heighten the process of individualisation. This is manifested for instance in employees' competition for new knowledge, the constant lookout for better opportunities in terms of higher salaries and enhanced positions, and the rapid accumulation of wealth. These processes are elaborated by Mukherjee in her article (chapter 2), in which she argues that alienation in the software industry arises not only from the fragmented nature of the work process but also from the extreme competitiveness of the workplace and the consequent individualisation of workers. Moreover, software professionals need to continually reinvent themselves in order to remain competitive in the labour market. While the monetary rewards of working in the IT industry are substantial, employees are unable to make long-term career or life plans, which would depend on having a fairly stable economy and job market— features that are absent in the IT industry and in the global economy in general. Software professionals and BPO workers cannot predict what kinds of jobs will be available in ten years, what they will be doing or where they might be living. This uncertainty, together with the features of labour flexibility described above, coalesce to create novel forms of risk, which workers then need to manage by creating new forms of sociality, developing personal economic strategies or re-orienting their selves in significant ways (Beck 2000).

Second, adding to this sense of insecurity are the various forms of mobility (detailed by D'Mello and Sahay in chapter 3 in this volume) that typify the software industry—geographical, social, economic and 'existential'. The authors highlight the itinerant state of existence in which most IT workers find themselves, which they term as a condition of 'permanent transience', and its effects on their subjectivities, lifestyles and identities. The experience of job insecurity, coupled with high levels of mobility, situate these workers 'betwixt and between', reflecting the networked pattern of the economy itself. Socio-economic mobility creates affluence, new consumption patterns and a new-found confidence, but career mobility gives rise to instability. Older social identities are submerged as new individualised ones are created in the workplace. Long hours at work reduce personal and family time, further destabilising workers' sense of social rootedness. Moreover, periodic workplace mobility means that IT professionals must negotiate among different cultures and face the dilemmas of finding their place in foreign countries. Their transnational existences inflect their sense of identity, sometimes by creating hybrid forms but often by producing 'immobilities of culture' as itinerant workers cling to their roots in the face of this instability.

Third, as Mukherjee points out in her article (chapter 2), the restructuring of work under the regime of flexible accumulation has blurred the boundary between work and non-work, and between production and consumption (Huws 2003), in the process altering the experience of work itself. While Indian software and call centre workers are engaged in 'virtual labour', their work experience continues to be deeply embodied and is linked to their experience as gendered and culturally constituted beings. Mukherjee further suggests that the advent of the IT industry in India has had profound implications for gender relations and for the middle-class women who work in this industry. She highlights the hegemonic discourse of 'women's empowerment' that pervades the Indian IT industry, pointing out that the entry of women into the workforce in large numbers is purveyed as a 'symbol of modernity' that helps to attract investment. IT work is represented as ideal for women because it is 'modern', non-manual and highly skilled labour that is performed in a posh and clean working environment, and because of the 'flexibility' that it is supposed to afford to women who are presumed to be primarily responsible for domestic tasks. Although there is in this discourse a process of gendering of IT work, the work is not apparently exploitative or devalued (as was argued in the earlier literature on the feminisation of labour in the global factories). Yet, as Mukherjee suggests, this gendering takes place precisely because the valorisation of 'flexibility' normalises the social role of women in the domestic sphere. This observation raises the question of whether the ideology of 'empowerment' accords with women's actual work experiences.

Chris Fuller and Haripriya Narasimhan (chapter 7) focus on this question, and their in-depth interviews with a number of women IT employees in Chennai suggests that many do internalise the hegemonic notion of empowerment even as they continue to accept their 'traditional' roles as wives and mothers at home. Their research also indicates that the apparent 'emancipation' of women IT workers has not been matched, in most cases, by liberation in the familial/

domestic sphere. Women IT professionals feel 'empowered' because of their professional status and high earning power, which gives them a degree of bargaining power in the household, but most still give equal or higher priority to their families. The commitment of women to their careers is suggested by the fact that most said that they would like to marry men who will allow them to continue working after marriage, and also prefer to marry other IT professionals because they would understand the demands on their time placed by the industry. At the same time, most women prefer conventional arranged marriages (rather than 'love marriages' that might be opposed by parents) that will ensure that they have the support structures they need to continue working. But because they view it as their duty, they assume more familial responsibilities than men and are more willing to sideline their careers for the sake of children. The chapter thus illustrates the difficulties that women professionals face in juggling family and work and the importance of strong family ties (with parents and parents-in-laws) in striking a balance (especially for child care).

Overall, the cultural consequences of global IT work in India appear to be somewhat contradictory: on the one hand new forms of modernity are emerging (for instance, individualisation of workers and the creation of new middle-class subjects), while on the other hand a process of reaffirmation of 'tradition' is at work as IT workers rediscover 'Indian culture' through discursive process such as cultural sensitivity training and interaction with people of other nationalities in the course of their work. In this context, Indian culture has been redefined in specific, rather simplistic ways (for instance, in terms of 'family values'). A sense of loss and nostalgia for an earlier form of sociality, dense with networks of family, kin and friends, pervades the self-reflective narratives of IT workers and points to a real shift in the nature of sociality in this class (Upadhya and Vasavi 2006: Chap. 7). The peculiar blend of international 'exposure', high incomes and time-challenged lives appears to have the effect of consolidating 'traditional middle class values', albeit within the new consumerist culture (Upadhya, forthcoming).

Further, cultural identity within this group of upwardly mobile professionals is moulded in part by a new discourse about Indian culture and tradition that is circulating within the global cultural economy. This discourse contains several strands: India as an ancient land with a long tradition of science and mathematics, which is invoked to explain its current prowess in the field of IT; India as a rising economic power that (along with China) will soon overtake the West, once it is freed from the vestigial shackles of the planned economy; Indian society as a happy mixture of tradition (adherence to family values and spirituality, to 'Indian culture' itself) and modernity (opening to the world, leading in the development of new technologies); and the new global professional as embodiment of this successful negotiation between the different worlds of the global workplace and home, the customer in the West and the boss in India. But these celebratory narratives about IT—often articulated by IT elites, the media and certain public intellectuals—are at odds with those of many individual IT professionals who are struggling to make sense of the contradictions they face in forming a stable sense of identity in an unstable and rapidly changing world. Indian IT workers, more than most other social groups, are at the 'cutting edge' of globalisation, but their location and movement within different circuits of economic and cultural flows, and their interstitial position between India and the new global economy, have given rise to a new set of still inchoate subjectivities, orientations and dilemmas.

The question of subjectivity and formation of self is perhaps even more acute in the case of ITES workers. As Vasavi details in her article (chapter 8), the creation of a new youth workforce, its management through a combination of extremely rigid Taylorist techniques and 'soft' mechanisms of subjective control, and the redefinition of work as education and entertainment, all work together to produce new social tensions among these workers as they must negotiate between the compulsions of the social norms of families and communities and the new culture generated at the workplace. In the forging of new socialities, identities and subjectivities is situated the core problem of the working identity of this virtual workforce. In her study of 'pink collar' offshore women workers in Barbados, Freeman ponders if the emergence of this type of global high-tech service work signals the rise of a 'newly emergent "class" of workers' (2000: 36). But, as Huws has shown, despite the fact that their work is similar to that in the industrial production line,[25] the subject position and hence the formation of a class-based identity of high-tech service workers as 'workers' is problematic. Their identification as workers is made even more unlikely by their primarily middle class, urban, educated backgrounds and the mediating role of technology. Instead, these 'e-workers' '... may prefer to differentiate themselves by quite other criteria—their educational qualifications, for instance, or their consumption habits, or where they live ...' (Huws 2003: 161). This discussion is relevant to the Indian context, where plush workplaces, the use of sophisticated technologies, interacting on a global terrain and certain management tactics combine to constitute the working identity of ITES employees as 'professionals' rather than as workers. This issue is raised by Vasavi, whose article (chapter 8) details the contexts and bases for the emergence of new work identities among ITES employees, and by Remesh (chapter 9) who notes the lack of collective mobilisation or avenues for redressal of grievances among ITES workers. Similarly, there is little interest in unionisation among software professionals despite long working hours, due to their largely middle class backgrounds and their self-identification as 'professionals' and potential managers.

Finally, we note the linkages between the expansion of global capitalism's consumer culture into India and the imbrication of IT and ITES workers into circuits of consumerism as one of the key sources of new identities and subjectivities. Freeman's (2000) ethnographic account of Barbados' offshore women workers, whose culturally driven gendered identities are amalgamated with their links to the world of new consumer goods, is apposite. She shows how the transnationalisation of work closely ties regimes of production to consumption and image-making in the lives of offshore workers. Using the work site as a place to escape the paternalism of local society, engaging in the world of fashion to craft new statuses, and identifying themselves as professionals, the case of Barbabos' pink collar workers points to the '... disjuncture and contestation between material realities and symbolic appearances, between local paternalism and transnational anonymity, between compliance and resistance, and between alienation and pleasure' (Freeman 1998: 257). Similar observations could be made about the emerging 'call centre culture' in India that has become a distinctive urban subculture linked to the global consumption-oriented youth culture (Upadhya and Vasavi 2006: Chap. 8).

Outposts of Global Information Technology Work: Cultural Refractions and Reflections

Global capitalism's relentless search for new markets, spaces and sources of labour, combined with the marvels of modern communication

and information technologies, have created new worlds of globalised work spaces. Catering to capital's need for 'cost-effective' and
'customer-oriented' IT labour, India has emerged as the premier site
for this outsourced high-tech service work. The gleaming edifices
of software and BPO companies, the gated residential communities
that house their workers, the ever-increasing array of goods that
are available in the new sites of globalised consumption, the public
and private narratives that anticipate the making of another India,
all constitute the new economy and its attendant political and cultural 'assemblages' (Ong and Collier 2005). In the midst of these
celebratory narratives about the successes of the IT industry and its
leaders, it is often forgotten that India's 'informational economy' is an
enclave economy linked primarily to the post-industrial economies
of the West, which has largely failed to spawn an attendant local
'information society'.

As many anthropological studies of globalisation have suggested, the instanciation of the global at the local level is never a one-
way process but works through existing cultural forms and structures
of power (Appadurai 1997; Ong 1999). In the globalisation of the
economy, the agency of local workers and enterprises shape the way
in which global forces are played out 'on the ground'. In the case of
India's IT industry, a range of structures, forms, processes and markers
combine to constitute the work process, the workplace and workers
in forms that are in many ways distinctive. Despite the impress of the
Silicon Valley model of the IT industry, in India both multinational
and Indian companies have had to forge distinctive work cultures and
organisational structures that seek simultaneously to integrate workers
into the culture and collectivity of the organisation and to alter their
working and non-working identities to fit into the global work culture
that they attempt to replicate. In their organisational structures and
processes Indian IT and ITES companies bear a strong resemblance
to their counterparts in the West, but in the process of producing and
managing their workforces a cultural refraction takes place: 'culture',
both local and global, is deployed and articulated to constitute an
efficient and compliant workforce to meet global demands.

Flexible capital has also produced its mirror image in the outsourced
information technology industry: flexible forms of employment,
flexible labour markets, flexible forms of work, and flexible skill
sets have all become part and parcel of the IT work culture and its

production processes. Representing recent developments in the global 'informational economy', such as the despatialisation and virtualisation of work, the labour of IT and ITES workers in India has become disembodied and largely delinked from its social context. The image of the Indian call centre worker with an American accent pursuing credit card defaulters in the US typifies this process. Yet this representation of outsourcing oversimplifies the situation, for the new forms of work and workers that have been created by the outsourcing/offshoring wave are not simply products of 'globalisation', but are interpelleted in complex ways both by their work in the new global economy as well as by the political and economic structures and social and cultural compulsions of their local contexts. In translocating work, mediated through technology, the worker does not merely become a global or a 'glocal' worker but a 'transnationalised' subject (Freeman 2000) formed through both the imperatives of work and the compulsions of local society. Cultures are then doubly refracted—the dominant culture of the industry is refracted by workers to suit their own interests, while the culture of the workers is refracted by the industry to gain legitimacy and control over the workforce.

Management and control over the work process and the workforce in the IT industry hinges on the deployment of a triad of control mechanisms: technology creates an electronic panopticon, measuring, assessing and controlling the work process and the worker; new management strategies seek to integrate the culturally 'other' individual into the work ethos of the global company; and psychological interventions are deployed to deflect the resulting stress and strain and to create an individualised worker responsible for his or her own work destiny. The 'brave new world of work' (Beck 2000) of flexible capital and labour, which places the onus of risk on the individual rather than on the organisation or the state, becomes all the braver in the new outposts of outsourced technology-mediated work. Workers identify themselves as empowered professionals and assume the role of global players, even as their labour is disembodied and 'liquefied' (Aneesh 2006) so that it can flow through the circuits of the global information economy, while they themselves are re-embodied socially as global worker–consumers.

The new technologies have not only enabled the deterritorialisation of IT related work, feeding into the compression of time and space (Harvey 1989), they also allow time and space differences to be leveraged such that work can go on round the clock as it travels across time zones—thereby enhancing the 'speed to market' logic of the new production regime. In this competitive garnering of time we find a new tyranny of the global clock. The new logic of time becomes a key factor in the organisation of production, and workers must submit to this regime (project time, interaction time, conference call time and shift time; see Shih 2004). It would not be out of place to see the world clocks that are proudly displayed on the floors of most IT and ITES companies, showing the times in the different countries and cities to which they are linked, as the totems of this industry—collective symbols around which work is oriented, organised and performed.

What flows between the centre and the periphery of the global informational economy are not merely jobs, capital or technology, but also a range of cultural identities and narratives, each crafted to mark the worker in different ways. The accent that is required of the teleworker in order to be 'customer oriented', the flexible skills and work timings expected of the software engineer, and the constant trainings imparted to workers in order to fit them into the mould of the global workplace, are not merely markers of a certain kind of work but create new orientations and identities which workers are impelled to negotiate.

Future Directions

Pointing to the neglect of Indian industry and labour by sociology, Parry notes: '... the proportion of recent sociological field research that has been devoted to the social processes and consequences of industrialisation is surprisingly small ...' (1999: xi). Within the limited literature on work and workers in India, the key sites of study have been the worlds of agricultural labour and the brick and mortar industries. We have sought to partially fill this gap with this collection of writings on work and workers in the sunrise IT industry, which presents a specific set of issues that flow from the fact that it is at once part of the new 'information economy', an integral part of the global economy, as well as a service industry.

We recognise that many issues, questions and concerns remain unaddressed in this volume, which necessarily presents only some preliminary insights into an industry that is sharply different from earlier ones, and which in its global and yet localised character is a fast evolving and complex subject of study. Much more work in this area remains to be done, which may entail detailed, multi-sited ethnographies; the tracking of the careers and lives of the global knowledge workers and of the transformation in the workforce in tandem with the maturing of the industry; and, not least, keeping a sharp sociological eye on the wider cultural and social implications of the rapid expansion of IT and ITES jobs in India.

In addition to deepening our understanding of the transformations that have been set in motion by the advent of these global offshore industries in India, we hope that this volume will lead to new trajectories in the sociology of work and ethnography of organisations in the Indian context, as well as contribute more broadly to theoretical debates about the nature of globalisation in the 21st century.

Notes

1. There are a number of studies of the history, economics and structure of the Indian software industry. A selected sampling includes Arora and Athreye (2002), Balakrishnan (2006), Chandrasekhar (2005), D'Costa (2003), Heeks (1996), Kumar (2001), Lakha (1994), Millar (2000), Parthasarathy (2000, 2005), Sahay et al. (2003), Saith and Vijayabaskar (2005) and Saxenian (2000). For studies of labour and the workforce in the IT industry see Athreye (2005), Basant and Rani (2004), Krishna and Brihmadesam (2006), Mir et al. (2000), Prasad (1998), Rothboeck et al. (2001) and Xiang (2001, 2002, 2007). On labour in the Indian call centre industry, see Remesh (2004a, 2004b). Only recently have several sociological/anthropological studies of Indian software engineers and the IT industry appeared; see Aneesh (2006), Fuller and Narasimhan (2006, 2007), Upadhya (2005, 2006), Upadhya and Vasavi (2006) and van der Veer (2005).

2. Even large multinational corporations (MNCs) have been restructured into 'network enterprises' composed of semi-autonomous entities that contract out work to one another (Castells 1996: Chap. 3). For instance, MNC software development subsidiaries in India are set up to service 'customers' within the parent organisation.

3. Strictly speaking, the IT industry includes computer hardware as well as software, but in the Indian context what is referred to as the IT industry is almost entirely devoted to software hence, the terms 'software industry' and 'IT industry' are often used interchangeably.

4. NASSCOM, 'Knowledge Professionals–Factsheet, www.nasscom.org. Of the estimated 1,293,000 million IT employees, about 398,000 are in the software exports sector, 415,000 in the ITES–BPO sector and the rest are in the domestic sector, R&D, other services, or are 'in-house' IT professionals. NASSCOM, 'Indian IT Industry—Factsheet, February 2007'. www.nasscom.org.

5. The various technology missions that were initiated under Rajiv Gandhi's government after 1984, as well as the new telecom and computer policies, provided the infrastructural base on which the industry could grow. Growth was further encouraged

by the policy of liberalisation in the 1990s. Further, the IT industry has been specifically promoted through policies such as tax holidays, duty-free import of equipment, provision of free or subsidised infrastructure and land, the establishment of software technology parks (STPs), and the like (Balakrishnan 2006; Parthasarathy 2005).

6. In some ways, ITES has become IT's 'evil twin'—IT represents what call centre workers aspire for, while call centre workers are disparaged by many IT professionals, and call centres perhaps represent to them what they could become if they fail in their IT careers.

7. See Beck (2000), Castells (1996) and Harvey (1989).

8. Benner (2002), Carnoy (2000), Hayes (1989), Hochschild (1997), Sennett (1998) and others have described these changes in detail (especially in Silicon Valley, considered to be the heart of the new economy), as well as their implications for workers, families and communities.

9. It is important to note that these shifts cannot be singularly attributed to the emergence of the IT industry but are also linked to wider transformations that have taken place in the Indian economy in the period of globalisation and liberalisation. However, the IT sector has been a major site where these processes have been observed, and a close study of the changes in this industry may provide pointers to a wider transformation that is taking place in the Indian economy. The discussion in this section draws heavily on Upadhya and Vasavi (2006).

10. This gives rise to the 'paradox of social closeness and geographical distance': '... geographically remote differences and oppositions are lived and experienced as socially proximate, whereas geographical proximity leaves untouched the differentness of social worlds. People can exist in one and the same place as if they were on different planets, while continents merge into a single social space in which people may live together across vast distances' (Beck 2000: 29). This situation is typical of centres of the offshore IT industry such as Bangalore, where IT workers appear to exist in a separate social space that is more closely linked to London and New York than it is to local society.

11. On bodyshopping, see Xiang (2001, 2002, 2007). Although the 'Y2K crisis' of 1998–99 revived the bodyshopping system as software engineers with certain 'skill sets' (such as familiarity with Unix) were in great demand in the US and Europe, now outsourced software projects are increasingly executed 'offshore' rather than 'onsite'. Instead of workers moving to where the jobs are, jobs increasingly are moving to where the workers are located.

12. The magnitude of this shift is shown by the fact that in 1990–91, 90 per cent of Indian software and service export revenues came from onsite work and only 5 per cent from offshore, whereas by 2002–03 the proportion had changed to 39 per cent onsite and 58 per cent offshore (estimated by Basant and Rani 2004: 5318). According to industry sources, at present typically 70 per cent of the work in a software project is performed offshore and 30 per cent onsite. However, most software engineers based in India also travel abroad at intervals for onsite assignments or other kinds of work. Indeed, foreign travel and the 'exposure' to Western countries that it affords is considered to be one of the most attractive and significant perquisites of IT work.

13. He suggests that online software services should be understood as flows of labour akin to the physical migration of workers in the global economy, rather than

trade in goods and services (as it is usually regarded), because the provision of offshore services is basically a technique for supplying labour without the constraints and difficulties of physical migration. This is the crux of the debate on the liberalisation of trade in services under GATT, in which the Indian IT industry and the government have been pushing for the definition of IT-related services as trade rather than labour migration, which would allow companies to send their personnel to foreign locations to work with greater ease.

14. For a sample of the debate on the 'new workplace', see Thompson and Warhurst (1998), Gephart (2002) and Jermier (1998). For a historical overview of shifts in dominant management ideologies in the US, see Barley and Kunda (1992).

15. See du Gay and Pryke (2002), McKinlay and Starkey (1998), Marcus (1998), and Ray and Sayer (1999). For an overview of the debate on the 'cultural turn' in the economy, see O'Doherty and Willmott (2001).

16. According to Gephart (2002), the development of these new management techniques has been facilitated and stimulated by the advent of computer mediated communication and information systems and the consequent digitalisation of the workplace, which has enabled more flexible production systems. These shifts have led to the decentralisation of work systems, the diffusion of power and decision-making within organisations and the proliferation of cultural rather than structural tactics for gaining employee consent.

17. See Ogbor (2001), Kunda (1992), Warhurst and Thompson (1998) and Wilmott (1993).

18. Beck and Beck-Gernsheim (2002) delineate the range of ways in which individualisation is manifested in European (primarily German) society with an emphasis on how life situations, ranging from work to identity, and biographies have been altered in the post-industrial phase of 'second modernity'. That some elements of this are discernable in the new outposts of the global economy is not surprising. The structure and orientation of the IT industry largely reflects such trends in which individualisation and standardisation simultaneously impact individual lives.

19. The corporate cultures and modes of organisational control in three different software companies are depicted in the NIAS–IDPAD film series 'Coding Culture: Bangalore's Software Industry' (*www.codingculture.com*).

20. For critical analyses of management through teamwork and corporate culture, see Ezzamel and Willmott (1998), Ezzy (2001) and Sewell (1998).

21. These quality models prescribe detailed and systematic processes for the organisation of work flows at every stage of the software cycle, the setting of specific productivity goals for each worker and team on a daily and weekly basis, and detailed monitoring, measuring, reporting and evaluation of work completed. Apart from reducing software production to a highly routinised and mechanical process, these systems exert heavy pressure on engineers to meet their production and quality goals in order to maintain their individual and team ratings, which are being constantly measured (Upadhya and Vasavi 2006: 62–67).

22. Much of the growing literature on call centres in various countries is located within 'critical organisational theory' and stresses the Taylorist methods of control and methods of intense surveillance that are employed (Bain and Taylor 2000). See, for example, Winiecki (2004), van den Broek (2004), Bain et al. (2002) and Mulholland (2004). Available accounts indicate that the methods of management employed in Indian ITES companies are similar to those described for the US, UK and other developed countries, from where they originated. On call centres in

India, see McMillin (2006), Ng and Mitter (2005), Remesh (2004a, 2004b), Singh and Pandey (2005), and Taylor and Bain (2005).

23. The significance of the use of computers in offices for surveillance was recognised as early as the 1980s, as was the emergence of 'electronic sweatshops' (Attewell 1987; Zuboff 1982). However, the surveillance of clerical work using electronic means did not begin with computers, only the techniques have become more sophisticated as technology has become more complex. As Attewell (1987) points out, listening in on calls to monitor performance of telephone operators has been reported as long ago as the 1920s. Computers make surveillance easier because they can automatically monitor call times, count keystrokes, record the number of forms processed or note when a worker logs in and out of the system. These systems of electronic surveillance and control have been described especially for the call centre industry, but they are more widespread.

24. Similarly, van den Broek (2004) argues that although in theory subjective management techniques are supposed to promote worker autonomy and self-management, the simultaneous use of 'managerial discipline' contradicts this objective, leading to employee frustration and, at times, resistance. Several other studies also highlight forms of resistance and counter-discourses generated by employees in these industries. For instance, based on her study of an Irish call centre Mulholland (2004) criticises the argument that individualising managerial strategies have eliminated worker resistance and argues that workers in subordinated working conditions engage in a range of informal collective actions that challenge management practices.

25. Huws (2003) details how the work process in technology industries is similar to that in the production of commodities. For example, there is hierarchy in the organisation, much of the work is routinised, the workforce is not permanent, forms of control and management are similar and there is a strong link to new forms of consumption.

References

Aneesh, A. 2001a. Rethinking Migration: On-Line Labour Flows from India to the United States. In W.A. Cornelius (eds), *The International Migration of the Highly Skilled*, pp. 351–70. La Jolla: Centre for Comparative Immigration Studies, University of California, San Diego.

———. 2001b. Skill Saturation: Rationalisation and Post-industrial Work. *Theory and Society* (3)30: 363–96.

———. 2006. *Virtual Migration: The Programming of Globalisation*. Durham: Duke University Press.

Appadurai, Arjun. 1997. *Modernity at Large: Cultural Dimensions of Globalisation*. Delhi: Oxford University Press.

Arora, A. and S. Athreye. 2002. The Software Industry and India's Economic Development. *Information Economic and Policy*, 14(2): 253–73.

Arulmani, Gideon and Sonali Nag–Arulmani. 2006. *Work Orientations and Responses to Career Choices—Indian Regional Survey*. Draft Report. Bangalore: The Promise Foundation.

Athreye, Suma S. 2005. Human Capital, Labour Scarcity and Development of the Software Services Sector. In *ICTs and Indian Economic Development: Economy, Work, Regulation*, A. Saith, and M. Vijayabaskar (eds), 154–74, New Delhi: Sage Publications.

Attewell, Paul. 1987. Big Brother and the Sweatshop: Computer Surveillance in the Automated Office. *Sociological Theory* 5: 87–99.

Bain, Peter and Phil Taylor. 2000. Entrapped by the 'Electronic Panopticon'? Worker Resistance in the Call Centre. *New Technology, Work and Employment* 15(1): 2–18.

Bain, Peter, A. Watson, G. Mulvey, P. Taylor and G. Gall. 2002. Taylorism, Targets and the Pursuit of Quantity and Quality by Call Centre Management. *New Technology, Work and Employment* 17(3): 170–85.

Balakrishnan, Pulapre. 2006. Benign Neglect or Strategic Intent? Contested Lineage of Indian Software Industry. *Economic and Political Weekly* 41(36): 3865–72.

Barley, Stephen R. and Gideon Kunda. 1992. Design and Devotion: Surges of Rational and Normative Ideologies of Control in Management Discourse. *Administrative Science Quarterly* 37(3): 363–99.

Barrett, Rowena. 2001. Labouring under an Illusion? The Labour Process of Software Development in the Australian information Industry. *New Technology, Work and Employment* 16(1): 18–34.

———. 2004. Working at Webboyz: An Analysis of Control over the Software Development Labour Process. *Sociology* 38(4): 777–94.

Basant, Rakesh and Uma Rani. 2004. Labour Market Deepening in India's IT: An Exploratory Analysis. *Economic and Political Weekly* 39(50): 5317–26.

Beck, Ulrich. 2000. *The Brave New World of Work*. Cambridge: Polity Press.

Beck, Ulrich and Elisabeth Beck–Gernsheim. 2002. *Individualisation: Institutionalised Individualism and its Social and Political Consequences*. London: Sage Publications.

Beirne, M., H. Ramsay and A. Panteli. 1998. Developments in Computing Work: Control and Contradiction in the Software Labour Process. In *Workplaces of the Future*, Paul Thompson and Chris Warhurst (eds), 142–61, Hampshire: Macmillan.

Benner, Chris. 2002. *Work in the New Economy; Flexible Labour Markets in Silicon Valley*. Oxford: Blackwell Publishing.

Berking, Helmuth. 2003. Ethnicity is Everywhere: On Globalisation and the Transformation of Cultural Identity. *Current Sociology* 51(3/4): 248–64.

Braverman, Harry. 1975. *Labour and Monopoly Capital: The Degradation of Work in the Twentieth Century*. New York: Monthly Review Press.

Carnoy, Martin. 2000. *Work, Family and Community in the Information Age*. New York: Russell Sage.

Castells, Manuel. 1996. *The Information Age: Economy, Society and Culture*. Vol. 1 of *The Rise of the Network Society*. Oxford: Blackwell Publishing.

Chandrasekhar, C.P. 2005. The Diffusion of Information Technology and Implications for Development: A Perspective Based on the Indian Experience. In *ICTs and Indian Economic Development: Economy, Work, Regulation*, A. Saith and M. Vijayabaskar (eds), 40–92. New Delhi: Sage Publications.

Cooper, Marianne. 2000. Being the 'Go-to-guy': Fatherhood, Masculinity, and the Organisation of Work in Silicon Valley. *Qualitative Sociology* 23(4): 379–405.

D'Costa, Anthony P. 2003. Uneven and Combined Development: Understanding India's Software Exports. *World Development* 31(1): 211–26.

Deshpande, Satish. 2003. *Contemporary India: A Sociological View*. New Delhi: Viking.

du Gay, Paul and Michael Pryke (eds). 2002. *Cultural Economy*. London: Sage Publications.

Ezzamel, Mahmoud and Hugh Willmott. 1998. Accounting for Teamwork: A Critical Study of Group-Based Systems of Organisational Control. *Administrative Science Quarterly* 43(2): 358–96.

Ezzy, Douglas. 2001. A Simulacrum of Workplace Community: Individualism and Engineered Culture. *Sociology* 35(3): 631–50.

Fernandes, Leela. 2000. Nationalising 'the Global': Media Images, Cultural Politics and the Middle Class in India. *Media, Culture and Society* 22: 611–28.

Foucault, M. 1988. Technologies of the Self. In *Technologies of the Self*, L. Martin, H. Gutman and P. Hutton (eds), 16–49. Amherst: University of Massachusetts Press.

———. 1995. *Discipline and Punish: The Birth of the Prison*. New York: Vintage Books.

Freeman, Carla. 1998. Femininity and Flexible Labour: Fashioning Class through Gender on the Global Assembly Line. *Critique of Anthropology* 18(3): 245–62.

———. 2000. *High Tech and High Heels in the Global Economy: Women, Work and Pink-Collar Identities in the Caribbean*. Durham: Duke University Press.

Fuller, C.J. and Haripriya Narasimhan. 2006. Engineering Colleges, 'Exposure' and Information Technology Professionals in Tamil Nadu. *Economic and Political Weekly* 41(3): 258–62.

———. 2007. Information Technology Professionals and the New-rich Middle Class in Chennai (Madras). *Modern Asian Studies* 41(1):121–50.

Garson, B. 1988. *The Electronic Sweatshop: How Computers are Transforming the Office of the Future into the Factory of the Past*. New York: Simon & Schuster.

Gephart, Robert P. Jr. 2002. Introduction to the Brave New Workplace: Organisational Behaviour in the Electronic Age. *Journal of Organisational Behaviour* 23: 327–44.

Hardt, Michael. 1999. Affective Labour. *Boundary* 26(2): 89–100.

Harvey, David. 1989. *The Condition of Postmodernity: An Enquiry into the Origins of Cultural Change*. Oxford: Basil Blackwell.

Hayes, Dennis. 1989. *Behind the Silicon Curtain: The Seductions of Work in a Lonely Era*. London: Free Association.

Heeks R.B. 1996. *India's Software Industry: State Policy, Liberalisation and Industrial Development*. New Delhi: Sage Publications.

Heelas, Paul. 2002. Work Ethics, Soft Capitalism and the Turn to Life. In *Cultural Economy*, Paul du Gay and Michael Pryke (eds), 78–96. London: Sage Publications.

Hochschild, Arlie Russell. 1983. *The Managed Heart: Commercialisation of Human Feeling*. Berkeley: University of California Press.

———. 1997. *The Time Bind: When Work Becomes Home and Home Becomes Work*. New York: Henry Holt and Company.

Howell, Jeremy and Alan Ingham. 2001. From Social Problem to Personal Issue: The Language of Lifestyle. *Cultural Studies* 15(2): 326–51.

Huws, Ursula. 2003. *The Making of a Cybertariat: Virtual Work in a Real World*. New York: Monthly Review Press.

Jermier, John M. 1998. Introduction: Critical Perspective on Organisational Control. *Administrative Science Quarterly* 43(2): 235–56.

Krishna, Anirudh and Vijay Brihmadesam. 2006. What Does it Take to Become a Software Professional? *Economic and Political Weekly* 41(30): 3307–14.

Kunda, Gideon. 1992. *Engineering Culture: Control and Commitment in a High-Tech Corporation*. Philadelphia: Temple University Press.

Kumar, Nagesh. 2001. Indian Software Industry Development: International and National Perspective. *Economic and Political Weekly* 36(45): 4278–90.

Lash, Scott and John Urry. 1987. *The End of Organised Capitalism*. Cambridge: Polity Press.

Lakha, Salim. 1994. The New International Division of Labour and the Indian Computer Software Industry. *Modern Asian Studies* 28(2): 381–408.

Mckinlay, A. and K. Starkey (eds). 1998. *Foucault, Management and Organisation Theory: From Panopticon to Technologies of Self*. Thousand Oaks: Sage Publications.

McMillin, Divya. 2006. Outsourcing Identities: Call Centres and Cultural Transformation in India. *Economic and Political Weekly* 41(3): 235–41.

Marcus, George E. 1998. *Corporate Futures: The Diffusion of the Culturally Sensitive Corporate Form*. 5th ed. Chicago: University of Chicago Press.

Millar, Jane. 2000. Sustaining Software Teletrade in Bangalore: Fostering Market Agility through Economic Competence. *Economic and Political Weekly* 35(26): 2253–62.

Mir, Ali, Biju Mathew and Raza Mir. 2000. The Codes of Migration: Contours of the Global Software Labor Market. *Cultural Dynamics* 12(1): 5–33.

Mulholland, Kate. 2004. Workplace Resistance in an Irish Call Centre: Slammin', Scammin' Smokin' an' Leavin. *Work, Employment and Society* 18(4): 709–24.

NASSCOM (The National Association of Software and Services Companies). 2005. Summary of NASSCOM-McKinsey Report 2005. NASSCOM Newsline No. 50, December . www.nasscom.org.

———. 2006. Indian IT Industry–Factsheet. May. www.nasscom.org.

———. 2007. Indian IT Industry—Factsheet. February. www.nasscom.org.

Ng, Cecilia and Swasti Mitter. 2005. Valuing Women's Voices: Call Centre Workers in Malaysia and India. In *idem* (eds) *Gender and the Digital Economy; Perspectives from the Developing World*, 132–58. New Delhi: Sage Publications.

O'Doherty, Damian and Hugh Wilmott. 2001. Debating Labour Process Theory: The Issue of Subjectivity and the Relevance of Post-structuralism. *Sociology* 35(2): 457–76.

Ogbor, John O. 2001. Critical Theory and the Hegemony of Corporate Culture. *Journal of Organisational Change Management* 14(6): 590–608.

Ong, Aihwa. 1999. *Flexible Citizenship: The Cultural Logics of Transnationality*. Durham: Duke University Press.

Ong, Aihwa and Stephen J. Collier (eds). 2005. *Global Assemblages: Technology, Politics, and Ethics as Anthropological Problems*. Oxford: Blackwell Publishing.

Parry, Jonathan. P. 1999. Introduction. In *The Worlds of Indian Industrial Labour*, Jonathan P. Parry, Jan Breman and Karin Kapadia (eds), ix–xxxvi. New Delhi: Sage Publications.

Parthasarathy, Balaji. 2000. Globalisation and Agglomeration in Newly Industrialising Countries: The State and the Information Technology Industry in Bangalore, India. (Unpublished) Ph.D. dissertation, University of California, Berkeley.

———. 2005. The Political Economy of the Computer Software Indus-try in Bangalore, India. In *ICTs and Indian Economic Development; Economy, Work, Regulation*, A. Saith and M. Vijayabaskar (eds), 199–230. New Delhi: Sage Publications.

Poster, Mark. 2002. Workers as Cyborgs: Labour and Networked Computers. *Journal of Labour Research* 23: 339–54.

Prasad, Monica. 1998. International Capital on 'Silicon Plateau': Work and Control in India's Computer Industry. *Social Forces* 77(2): 429–52.

Ray, L. and A. Sayer (eds). 1999. *Culture and Economy after the Cultural Turn*. London: Sage Publications.

Remesh, Babu P. 2004a. Cyber Coolies in BPO: Insecurities and Vulnerabilities of Non-Standard Work. *Economic and Political Weekly* 39(5): 492–97.

———. 2004b. Labour in Business Process Outsourcing: A Case Study of Call Centre Agents. NLI Research Studies Series No. 051/2004. NOIDA: V.V. Giri National Labour Institute.

Rimke, Heidi Marie. 2000. Governing Citizens through Self-Help Literature. *Cultural Studies*, 14(1): 61–78.

Rothboeck, S., M. Vijaybaskar and V. Gayathri. 2001. *Labour in the New Economy: The Case of the Indian Software Labour Market*. New Delhi: International Labour Organisation.

Sahay, Sundeep, Brian Nicholson and S. Krishna. 2003. *Global IT Outsourcing; Software Development across Borders*. Cambridge: Cambridge University Press.

Saith, A. and M. Vijayabaskar (eds). 2005. *ICTs and Indian Economic Development: Economy, Work, Regulation*. New Delhi: Sage Publications.

Saxenian, AnnaLee. 2000. Bangalore: the Silicon Valley of Asia? Paper presented at the Conference on Indian Economic Prospects: Advancing Policy Reform. Centre for Research on Economic Development and Policy Reform, Stanford University.

Sennett, Richard. 1998. *The Corrosion of Character: The Personal Consequences of Work in the New Capitalism*. New York: W.W. Norton & Co.

Sewell, Graham. 1998. The Discipline of Teams: The Control of Team-based Industrial Work through Electronic and Peer Surveillance. *Administrative Science Quarterly* 43(2): 397–428.

Sewell, G. and B. Wilkinson. 1992. Someone to Watch Over Me: Surveillance, Discipline and the Just-in-Time Labour Process. *Sociology* 26: 271–89.

Shih, Johanna. 2004. Project Time in Silicon Valley. *Qualitative Sociology* 27(2): 223–45.

Singh, Preeti and Anu Pandey. 2005. Women in Call Centres. *Economic and Political Weekly* 40(7): 684–88.

Strathern, Marilyn. 2001. The Patent and the Malanggan. *Theory, Culture and Society* 18(4): 1–26.

Taylor, Phil and Peter Bain. 2005. India Calling to the Far Away Towns: The Call Centre Labour Process and Globalisation. *Work, Employment and Society* 19(2): 261–82.

Taylor, Steve. 1998. Emotional Labour and the New Workplace. In *Workplaces of the Future*, Paul Thompson and Chris Warhurst (eds), 84–103. Hampshire: Macmillan.

Thompson, Paul and Chris Warhurst (eds). 1998. *Workplaces of the Future*. Hampshire: Macmillan.

Upadhya, Carol. 2004. A New Transnational Class? Capital Flows, Business Networks and Entrepreneurs in the Indian Software Industry. *Economic and Political Weekly* 39(48): 5141–51.

———. 2006a. Employment and Exclusion in the Indian IT industry. Paper presented at IDPAD End Symposium on India's Split Development: Reflections on Development Theory and Practice. Hyderabad.

———. 2006b. The Global Indian Software Labour Force: IT Professionals in Europe. Working Paper No. 1. The Hague: The Indo-Dutch Programme on Alternatives in Development (IDPAD).

———. Forthcoming. Rewriting the Code: Software Professionals and the Reconstitution of Indian Middle Class Identity. In *Patterns of Middle Class Consumption in India and China*, Peter van der Veer and Christophe Jaffrelot (eds). New Delhi: Sage Publications.

Upadhya, Carol and A.R. Vasavi. 2006. Work, Culture, and Sociality in the Indian IT Industry: A Sociological Study (Final Report submitted to IDPAD). Bangalore: National Institute of Advanced Studies.

van den Broek, Diane. 2004. 'We have the Values': Customers, Control and Corporate Ideology in Call Centre Operations. *New Technology, Work and Employment* 19(1): 1–13.

van der Veer, Peter. 2005. Virtual India: Indian IT Labour and the Nation-State. In *Sovereign Bodies: Citizens, Migrants, and States in the Postcolonial World*, Thomas Blom Hansen and Finn Stepputat (eds), 276–90. Princeton: Princeton University Press.

Warhurst, C. and P. Thompson. 1998. Hands, Hearts and Minds: Changing Work and Workers at the End of the Century. In *Workplaces of the Future*, Paul Thompson and Chris Warhurst (eds), pp. 1–24. Hampshire: Macmillan.

Wilmott, H. 1993. Strength is Ignorance, Slavery is Freedom; Managing Culture in Modern Organisations. *Journal of Management Studies* 30(4): 515–52.

Winiecki, Donald J. 2004. Shadowboxing with Data: Production of the Subject in Contemporary Call Centre Organisations. *New Technology, Work and Employment* 19(2): 78–95.

Xiang, Biao. 2001. Structuration of Indian Information Technology: Professionals Migration to Australia: An Ethnographic Story. *International Migration* 39(5): 73–90.

———. 2002. Global 'Body Shopping': A New International Labour System in the Information Technology Industry. D. Phil Dissertation, the University of Oxford.

———. 2007. *Global 'Body Shopping': An Indian Labour System in the Information Technology Industry*. Princeton: Princeton University Press.

Zuboff, Shoshana. 1988. *In the Age of the Smart Machine: The Future of Work and Power*. New York: Basic Books.

2

Producing the Knowledge Professional: Gendered Geographies of Alienation in India's New High-tech Workplace

Sanjukta Mukherjee

The emergence of a software services industry over the last decade has rapidly altered India's position in the global imaginary. Since India officially liberalised its economy in 1991,[1] inviting foreign capital, the software industry has grown steadily and has managed to build an international reputation. Popular media in India and abroad are replete with accounts of this growing high-tech industry, the emergence of new urban spaces of consumption and its smart, young, educated, hyper-mobile, albeit largely middle class[2] workforce of 'knowledge professionals'—the beneficiaries of the new globalised economy. The rhetoric around work culture in this industry emphasises a flat organisational structure, camaraderie at the workplace and meritocracy. Work has been redefined as 'intellectual and disembodied labour' and workplaces as flexible and fun. Part of this new image of a modern, progressive and tech savvy India that has embraced open market policies is the increasing visibility of and dependence on educated middle class professional women and a hegemonic discourse of 'empowerment' that is symbolic of the IT (information technology) sector.

The Indian software industry has been highly acclaimed for creating new sources of employment for a significant proportion of engineering and management school graduates. The National Association of Software and Services Companies (NASSCOM) estimated in 2003 that the proportion of women in software firms has been steadily increasing and is likely to rise from 21 per cent in 2003 to 35 per cent in 2005. Celebratory dictums pronouncing the 'High-tech Lift for India's Women'[3] adorn both international and national newspapers, announcing that IT is breaking traditional social barriers of gender. Software companies, acknowledging the significance of women's role—particularly their expertise in 'soft skills'—post frequent advertisements representing women as 'the delivering value face of new India'.[4] Even the Indian state has made special provisions in the Millennium IT Policy to attract women to this growing export sector. In effect, it could be argued that the entry of women into the IT industry has become vital for both the corporate sector and the Indian state as a symbol of modernity, attracting foreign multinationals and justifying a neoliberal reform agenda. But, what attracts women to this industry and why are software workspaces considered ideal places for women? Moreover, is the increased participation and new opportunities of work for software professionals, especially women, leading to progressive social and economic changes in their lives? Does the popular discourse of 'empowerment' resonate with the real lived experiences of women and men in the workplace?

Based on extensive field research conducted in Bangalore in 2003 and 2004, this article draws upon career narratives of software workers and interviews with policy-makers and entrepreneurs in an attempt to answer these questions. This article reveals that while the software industry has created new opportunities for the educated middle class in India, it has simultaneously created new regimes of work and workplace control leading to a heightened sense of alienation. It can be argued that such a sense of alienation, while reminiscent of the Marxist critique of industrial capitalism, must also be understood in relation to the embodied experience of women and men as gendered beings and their identification as a new class of 'knowledge professionals'. As work gets restructured in new ways under flexible regimes of accumulation in the new economy,[5] obfuscating the boundaries between work and non-work, the ensuing sense of alienation is not just a product of capitalist exploitation of people as workers: it is also connected to socially sanctioned gendered norms and relations that simultaneously influence and are influenced by the mutually reinforcing dictates of global capital and hegemonic gender regimes.

The article first examines the changing nature of work in the context of contemporary forces of global capitalism, particularly its implications for labour. It then provides a brief overview of the Indian software industry focusing mainly on the industry's structure, work process, corporate culture and division of labour. Finally, it critically examines the manner in which software work and workplace relationships lend themselves to a gendered analysis of alienation.

Economic Restructuring and Changing Nature of Work

Critics of neoliberal[6] globalisation have argued that economic restructuring has heralded major changes in the nature of work characterised by a proliferation of insecure, short-term, contract-based arrangements. This new regime of accumulation that marks a transition from Fordism to post-Fordism is based on the notion of flexibility—flexibility of workers and workspaces. While the champions of today's neoliberal economy, especially large corporations, celebrate the concept of flexibility (i.e., the ability to change, react to changing demand with little penalty in time, cost, effort or performance), many argue that this is a highly contested and value-laden concept (Benner 2002). On one hand, it has been argued that flexibility is important for firms to remain competitive in today's changing marketplace. Yet, on the other hand corporations' drive for flexibility reflects a desire for decreased regulation so that they can hire and fire employees at will (Pollert 1988), undermining labour laws and pushing for a global race to the bottom. Flexibility has been criticised because it leads to insecurity, declining wages and deteriorating working conditions for a large proportion of working people (Standing 1999).

It has also been argued that flexible labour markets in general and in IT in particular have led to the polarisation of skills such that the poor, women and people of colour predominate in low paid, low skill work (Hanson and Pratt 1995; Marchand and Runyan 2000; Pearson 1993). In fact, it has been long argued that the increasing numbers of women in the formal labour markets since the 1970s and 1980s has heralded the feminisation of labour. Feminisation of labour refers not only to the increasing numbers of women in the labour market but also to the fact that certain kinds of jobs are redefined as female or feminised—whether performed by men or women. To be feminised means to be made extremely vulnerable—able to be disassembled, reassembled, exploited as a reserve labour force, seen less as workers and more as servers. For example, jobs requiring service of any sort, caring and nurturing, such as nursing, hospitality and particular kinds of exotic tourism industries, secretarial jobs and even manufacturing jobs such as microchip manufacture in electronics or assembling labour intensive textile products (requiring 'nimble fingers') are deemed to be more suited to women than men because they rely on certain essentially feminised characteristics of 'women'. Traditionally, the association of (some) women with the private sphere involving unpaid work led to the devaluation of women's waged work. Women's role in the economy was considered to be secondary having led to their inferior status in workplaces. Workplaces are consequently constructed as gendered places. Depending on the nature of work, some workplaces have also been identified as masculine spaces where more value is attributed to essentially masculine characteristics that become the norm governing behaviour patterns (Duncan 1996; Massey 1996; Pringle 1988; Webster 1996). Others, mainly anti-racist feminists, have however maintained that women have always worked in the 'formal' economy irrespective of the fact that they were often unpaid and/or outside wage relations. Poor women of colour and their marginalisation as workers cannot just be explained by their class positions but has to also take into consideration their embodiment as 'racialised' and 'gendered' beings, thus devaluing them as bearers of inferior labour.

Feminisation has occurred in both the global North and the South. In the global North, innovations in telecommunications, computers, and office technology have enabled the separation and relocation of routinised data entry operations such as invoicing, payroll, stock control, accounting, sales records, etc., from the company headquarters in the cities to suburbs. The labour pool consisted of mainly, white, middle class 'housewives' who worked only to supplement their husband's income (Pearson 1991). Further advances in the telecommunication industry, especially satellite communications, enabled companies in the industrialised countries to relocate their data entry facilities offshore to the free trade zones of the Third World, taking advantage of cheap labour costs. Large scale foreign investors such as American Airlines' operations in Barbados and electronic and garment *maquiladoras* in Mexico employ mainly women and people of colour who are paid very low wages, are less likely to unionise, are mostly poor and untrained and are willing to work under unhealthy conditions (Nash and Fernandez-Kelly 1983; Pearson 1993, 1995). The global cities of London and New York have increasingly come to depend on large numbers of immigrant workers, a fact characteristic of a gendered and racialised labour market (McDowell 1997).

However, feminisation has worked in favour of some: middle class women in urban centres of the global North have entered certain jobs previously dominated by men, such as finance and banking. But these service jobs have been reclassified as being better performed by women as they rely on essentialised feminine attributes of caring, nurturing, understanding and empathy (McDowell 1997). Class differences have also been heightened as professional service sector workers have gained at the expense of the working classes as a direct result of economic restructuring (McDowell 2001).

The increased participation of highly educated middle class women in Indian software firms could present an alternative discourse of feminisation, one that is not blatantly linked to financial and physical exploitation or the devaluation of work. But, what attracts women to software work? Does the industry, in more subtle ways, require women and men to conform to a particular gendered performance? For example, women software developers have been more involved in in-house programming and software development than in sales and marketing divisions, which are known to be more competitive and aggressive divisions, requiring greater mobility and intensive travel commitments. Has this resulted in the gendering of software work? While software and computer services are regarded as highly skilled work, there are important differences in the nature of work between software production and services. Close scrutiny of the internal division of labour in software firms and the spatial relocation of software production reveals that 'high-tech' work is not uniform, and is characterised by a polarisation of skills operationalised through gender and class-based differences amongst employees.

Overview of the Indian Software Industry

The Indian software industry is unevenly distributed regionally. Bangalore has emerged as the national hub that houses both Indian and foreign IT companies. The city has grown rapidly over the last decade due to in-migration of workers seeking employment in software and IT firms. The labour market is characterised by a number of large Indian software firms that predominate in overall export revenue (the three giants, Wipro, Infosys and TCS, account for more than US $ 1 billion each), medium and smaller firms, and several multinational IT/software companies such as IBM, Texas Instruments, Lucent and Phillips, which have set up their captive units or in-house IT operations in India. Many of these multinationals have complex subcontracting relationships with Indian firms. Indian software firms are mainly engaged in application development, customisation and maintenance work for customers, which basically translates into writing code, fixing bugs, testing and providing maintenance support. In the international division of labour in software production, Indian programmers primarily provide relatively lower end service functions. Most of the high end designing and packaged production of software is dominated by American and European firms. It is only recently that Indian firms have gained increasing credibility to move towards provision of end-to-end solutions, making new forays into the sphere of consulting.

It is extremely difficult to access information from software companies, especially about organisational structures and employee profiles. Corporate practices are considered to be proprietary issues and fiercely guarded in the competitive environment characteristic of the contemporary global economy. Moreover, it appears that the deregulation and delicensing of the Indian economy has further allowed special privileges to this export services sector, including concessions such as limited or no government inspections and less stringent labour laws, particularly with regard to women's working hours. In addition, there is a complex network of formal and informal workers connected through different overlapping layers of vending relationships, which makes it even more difficult to trace linkages and gather accurate information. The following account of organisational structure is based on the limited information gathered from informants.

Software work is usually tied to individual projects associated with a particular client company that sets up an 'account' with an Indian firm. Software professionals are organised into teams under these accounts. Within these teams there are technical and management streams. Usually Indian firms are structured such that most technical streams coalesce into management streams as one matures in a company; unlike in the US where a software engineer can keep coding for life, in India a coder is expected to become an analyst, a technical or team lead and then foray into project management. Some of my interviewees attributed this to the low level of maturity of the Indian software industry which, compared to Silicon Valley, is in its nascent stage and thus has not become specialised. Others, however, argue that this is a residue of Indian colonial experience, which has produced a bureaucratic mentality and a proclivity towards hierarchical and rigid institutional structures.[7]

The organisational structure of a generic software firm can be broadly divided into management, delivery (the work of software production itself) and HR (human resource/functional) streams. It usually includes a board of directors and CEO at the top, and under them various vertical divisions, each with its own head, such as business development, delivery, industry service/practice, functions/projects, and HR and administration. Under delivery, the technical trajectory starts from an entry-level trainee (usually on six months probation), software engineer (having 0–3 years of experience), programmer analyst/project or module lead (3–5 years), project manager (5–6 years), senior project manager (more than six years) and delivery manager (more than six years). Senior managers generally have more than eight years of work experience. It is also very common to organise personnel under specific business units or 'verticals' such as energy, retail, banking and so on. Some companies have separate sales and marketing teams who work closely with the different business units. A common organisational structure is the organisation of these job categories into four 'bands'. Band A consists of 'individual contributors' (engineers and module leads), Band B of project managers, Band C, account/ technical managers and Band D, business unit heads. The difficulty in comprehending and comparing these titles and job descriptions stems from the fact that they are often loosely defined and lateral movement is highly encouraged; this is actually a corporate strategy to maintain the flexibility of the labour force while projecting a certain veneer of creativity, change and camaraderie.

Towards Gendered Geographies of Alienation

The spatial restructuring of the global software industry and the attendant division of labour and gender relations of work, organisational structures, policies/practices and cultures within workspaces reveal both continuities and disjunctures with Marxian forms of alienation. The redefinitions of work and the embodied experience of women and men as gendered beings have augmented alienation in new ways in the new economy. This embodied experience is a function of particular gendered implications (mediated through subjectivities of race, class and age) of economic restructuring and flexibilisation of work.

Marxist Insights on Alienation and Software Work

Marx in his early writings provided valuable insights on the manner in which capitalism is essentially imbued with inequalities and is based on the alienation of labour, in different forms. Although writing in the context of 19th century industrialisation and mainly focused on factory production, his compelling analysis is still relevant in understanding software work. According to Marx, alienation is a product of capitalist production whereby workers are estranged from the labour process, the products of labour, his/her 'species-being' and other human beings. Alienation from the labour process and from the products of labour ensues from the capitalist division of labour and the deskilling of workers that takes place due to the introduction of machines. This results in workers' disenchantment with repetitive, non-creative and simple tasks that often have no connection to the finished product. Moreover, capitalist control of the labour market and work process due to an incessant search for profit detaches the worker from having any control over the final form, use, distribution or availability of the product (Marx 1964).

The sense of alienation that arises from various stages of software production and the attendant culture of work it generates is reminiscent of industrial capitalism in many ways. Module-based software work leads to atomisation such that the coder/programmer often has a very limited idea of the finished product or the other stages of production involved. According to Rakesh, a very cynical software engineer from one of the largest Indian firms:

A software engineer is nothing but a clerk in any other company. We do the clerical job for the software industry, i.e., grass root level job. That is very preliminary—coding and testing and all that; and we are not in a position to design or visualise the total project, that will take time. ... This kind of position what I am working now, I am not satisfied with that because this has no prestige in this industry, though this is 90 per cent of the industry. Software engineers, coders, developers, they are the major chunk of the industry, but they are not given the prestige and everything. So, it is very important that the work of these people get some value to the company so that you can have power with yourself—both knowledge-wise, technically and monetarily.

Such a fragmented work process, characteristic of the division of labour in these organisational spaces, is particularly applicable to the work of the junior software engineers or 'techies', who constitute the bulk of the workforce.

In addition, the software industry is considered to be very unpredictable due to rapid rate of change in technology and frequent fluctuation of global business cycles. Often projects on which people have invested a lot of time and energy are abruptly cancelled. As Saroj, who had recently been told that the project he had been working on has been pulled by the client abroad, emphasised, 'It is very demoralising when something you have spent days and nights over becomes redundant; and not just for me but it affects the whole team'.

Another source of alienation comes from the perception of work as 'virtual', i.e., disembodied both because there is no tangible finished 'product' and because the satellite-based transmission processes through which codes and applications are sent to clients abroad limits actual one-on-one interaction. The real and embodied nature of workplace interactions, complex organisational structures, and even the very bodily experience of sitting at a computer for long hours get diffused, and hidden behind a series of computer codes and a veneer of digitised work process. One of the contradictions of this industry, however, is the emphasis laid on communication and teamwork. Networking and personal ties are very important for career progression because employee referrals are the most valued and popular recruiting tool. Thus, what appears as depersonalised, intangible and unreal actually involves real, embodied people and their social networks. The issue of embodiment will be discussed in greater detail in the next section.

Drawing on Marx again, the worker is also alienated from other workers and from the capitalists. Alienation from other workers is a result of competition with others for survival in the wage economy. This is rampant in the contemporary software industry but gets manifested in complex and often contradictory ways. Under a superficial veneer of a 'flat' organisational structure and easy camaraderie exists a very competitive work environment, where social networks and 'selling oneself' are key for climbing the corporate ladder. Ramesh, a technical lead in a large software company of 20,000 employees, remarked: 'It is very hard to make your mark and promotions are slow; yearly promotion based on seniority as the norm of traditional industries have been mostly replaced with performance and rating oriented appraisal system.'

Most of the performance evaluation is done on an individual basis, i.e., each individual is evaluated on the basis of his/her performance, which is reflected in various numerical ratings. This is yet another corporate strategy of flexible production. Software companies formulate a statistical scale to normalise the ratings and only a certain number of employees can be allocated to each category, based on the yearly profit. Hence, software professionals often lament that no matter how well one performs somebody or the other has to be allocated to a lower scale to 'fit' into the normal curve. Further dissatisfaction arises from the fact that rating influences compensation, and many feel that such an arbitrary statistical scale robs them of the year-end bonus they deserve. For example, the company may decide that only 8 per cent of employees can get a rating of 1, 27 per cent can get 2, 35 per cent 3, 25 per cent 4 and 5 per cent 5. The higher the rating, greater the 'variable component' (performance-linked) of compensation. Some version of this system is observed in most companies. This individualised performance appraisal system belies the fact that in most of the low level programming jobs, the technical skills needed for work are rather generic. This corporate strategy aids in rewarding a limited number of workers but simultaneously creates animosity and divisiveness amongst the workers at large. One of my interviewees emphasised that performance evaluation in software firms augments the sense of alienation. She remarked, 'Sometimes very good relationships go sour; in March/April people don't speak and have a long face. And then again in May you realise what to do, we have to work in the same team so lets be friends again; and wait for the next year.' In addition, this system of evaluation abstracts the subjective element attempting to iron out the differences amongst workers and the constraints within which they work.

Alienation from the capitalists (whose interests are directly opposed to those of workers)—in this case the owners and managers of software firms—has myriad sources and diverse manifestations. A number of companies keep strict attendance records and monitor the comings and goings of employees through electronic card swiping machines and surveillance by security personnel at the entrance. Furthermore, most firms use surveillance cameras installed in different parts of the workplace. Specific spatial strategies are deployed at times to attempt to increase the work day and the amount of time spent at the workplace, for example by providing services such as retail outlets and health clubs on the premises (which at least some of the larger software firms do).[8]

Gendering Software Work/Workspaces and Revisiting Alienation

As explained above, software work results in various forms of alienation reminiscent of industrial capitalism. However, in the post-industrial context and under post-Fordist regimes of accumulation, alienation is not just a result of exploitation of workers by capitalists but is tied in nuanced ways to the embodied experience of workers as gendered beings.

In India, software work is constructed as an ideal profession for women, and middle class educated women appear to have found new opportunities in these high-tech workplaces. But, despite the popular rhetoric about the increasing numbers of women in software firms, in reality the picture is far more complicated. The NASSCOM estimates, which are also the figures that the government purveys, are that in 2004 about 30 per cent of software workers were women.[9] Interviews with HR managers of software firms however reveal that the figure is closer to 16–20 per cent, but this too should not be taken at face value. Close scrutiny of the internal division of labour within software firms reveals that this statistic only pertains to lower level programming jobs. There are far fewer women in middle management and still fewer in top management. I return to this point in the section on flexibility because the predominance of women in entry level programming positions is intrinsically tied to gendered notions of flexibility.[10]

The rapid and targeted growth of the Indian software industry since 1998, and the remarkable changes to urban lifestyle and landscape it has fostered, are responsible for its tremendous visibility nationally and globally. This is despite the fact that the industry is highly concentrated regionally and unevenly distributed in India, and employs only 0.21 per cent of the non-agricultural workforce and 0.08 per cent of the aggregate workforce. Nevertheless, this industry has taken on enormous proportions symbolically: it has generated a discourse about India emerging as a possible high-tech super-power, a notion that seems to have gained a lot of currency in the mainstream media, government policies and especially amongst the growing urban middle classes. So what attracts middle class women and men to this industry? Irrespective of the numbers, software work has attained a degree of social status in contemporary urban India, at least amongst the educated middle classes, who see it as an avenue for upward social mobility.

The industry is also a symbol of modernity as it advertises 'global exposure'. An additional lure is the tax-free income that can be earned by a software professional working abroad. The industry also pays higher wages than other sectors, and is intricately tied to new spaces of consumption and a hyper-modern urban lifestyle. Moreover, the Indian state and the corporate sector very much depend on these middle class professionals and have been making consistent efforts to attract them to this industry—from special fiscal and monetary concessions such as tax breaks for 'India's Sunrise Industry', to deploying the media for recruitment campaigns, encouraging new computer training institutes and introducing new degree programmes (such as the MCA and PGSM)[11] in existing institutes of higher education. In effect, the Indian state has been propagating the image of 'new' India as a 'knowledge economy' and the software and IT sector as the key sector that will bring about economic growth, securing a robust future for India and ensuring its position as a serious contender in the global economy.

Part of the rhetoric and image building in selling this industry is the idea that it is ideal for women. For the IT industry, women have become symbols of progressive social change. But it is important to keep in mind that not all women are part of this discourse and neither are all part of a progressive change: it is the educated middle classes who are the backbone of this industry and who remain the main harbingers of a modern progressive and tech savvy India. Nevertheless, the workforce comprising English-speaking, middle class professional women and men has become a significant selling

point both for the industry and the state. The head of the HR department of one of the largest Indian software company emphasised in
an interview that:

> ... it is important to bring to the notice of our foreign clients
> that we have women in the company ... they often participate
> in making presentations on client visits. That way the clients get
> an idea what we are like.... We have the best and the brightest
> working with us ... we are very modern not like other industries
> where you will not find such a large presence of women...

But, why is software work considered to be ideal for women? This
is an important question that not only influences women's role in the
division of labour but also impacts gender relations of work within
software firms. The gendering of software work depends on defining
work as flexible, safe, meritocratic, non-physical/strenuous labour—a
cushy desk job. Thus, everything from its seemingly disembodied
functioning via digital media, private security at the premises, air-
conditioned offices and relatively higher remuneration present it as an
attractive package for women. Some of the specific issues that have
gendered software work are elaborated to argue that this gendering
has led to new forms of alienation that resonate with classical Marxist
understandings but in effect are also tied to the experiences of women
and men as gendered beings.[12]

Flexibility

The production process, organisational structure, and HR policy
imperatives in the Indian software industry reflect practices of both
internal and external flexibility (Storper and Scott 1990). The piece-
meal project based work, emphasis on teamwork, and broad and often
ambiguously defined job categories/roles reflect some of the practices
of internal flexibility, whereas the high rates of employee turnover
and use of vendors, temporary/contract workers and subcontracting
firms, reflect external flexibility.

The president of a Bangalore-based software company remarked
about the organisational structure of her firm: 'We have marketing,
technical, content and contact centre teams. Within the technical
team there are skill areas like Java and .NET. We keep it as flexible
as possible because in our engagement with the customer we may

need to pull different people from different teams and put them in groups.' In the software industry flexibility is popularly equated with 'flexi-timing', i.e., flexible working hours. Senior managers often point out the benefits of not having a nine to five job, especially for women burdened with other socially defined domestic roles: 'If I want to I can take an hour's break or come in late or leave a little early sometimes. We have flexi hours; nobody is behind my back breathing down my neck trying to see what I am doing'. Yet delivery deadlines are critical in this industry, there is tremendous pressure to perform and no scope of slacking. Moreover, flexibility does not in effect challenge the gendered social constructions that account for women's dual burden of managing home and work, which also impacts gender relations in the high-tech workplace. This point will be revisited shortly.

The gender division of labour, characterised by a greater proportion of women in entry-level programming, software engineering, quality control and human resource positions, is tied to gendered notions of flexibility. This notion of flexibility is often valourised by women in this field. Kaushalya, the CEO of a small software firm, remarked, 'Women can really succeed in this field because they have the ability to switch on and off…. When I am home I switch off office and when I am at work I switch off home'. However, such notions often aid in perpetuating gender stereotypes. Women are often seen as good 'managers'. They are adept at handling multiple domestic chores and family dynamics, which renders them well suited to 'multitasking' and 'managing' in the workplace. Women have also been traditionally considered more 'flexible' because their secondary status in the formal labour market (and normalised domestic roles) armours them with very little bargaining power at work.

Rajni, one of only four women vice-presidents in one of the largest Indian software firms, remarked: 'Women are there at the lower level, working as developers, and doing some basic designing. It has picked up now—10–15 per cent maximum. In the engineering line this is maximum at the entry level. As they grow into project managers etc. there are much fewer women. In this company there are only four of us as VPs and maybe about 150–200 men VPs. … it's a male dominated industry.'

Gendering of flexibility, however, holds true for both men and women, but in different ways. Younger men, mostly single and fresh out of engineering colleges, are similarly gendered; they too are considered to be flexible and most importantly, without family constraints and thus available for longer hours of work. This is especially true of those young graduates who have moved to Bangalore recently for their first job, and have no family and few friends outside of work. Many interviewees revealed that loneliness and boredom often compelled them to stay late at work.[13]

The privileges of flexibility do not accrue equally to everyone. Many of the junior software engineers, while recognising some of the benefits of flexi-timing, pointed to the fact that most of the benefits went to the CEOs, upper level management and the company. For them it merely translates into deliberately undefined job roles and responsibilities and often long working hours: 'You are at the company's beck and call at all times', as one of the informants remarked.

Furthermore, flexibility is valued as a behavioural competency, i.e., skill, qualification or expertise for software professionals, as revealed by the HR competency and role chart of one of my sample software firms. As a software engineer remarked, 'You have to be a fast learner (as technology and projects keep moving) in this industry. After one year or so you can ask to move to a different project, but sometimes it just happens; you are moved to a different project and you have to learn there and cope with it'. Interestingly, at entry level (for job category 'software engineer') the competency is defined simply as 'flexibility' without much clarification as to what it entails, which leaves room for 'multi-tasking' or allocation to multiple projects. For a project lead/manager, the competency is specifically defined as 'ability to demonstrate flexibility to meet organisation goals/plans'.

Meritocracy, Work Culture and Social Construction of Skills

The software industry conveys an appearance of a purely 'meritocratic' and performance-driven culture, but this is imbued with overt and covert forms of gender- and class-based alienation. Popular journals are replete with stories about the 'high tech lift to middle class Indian women' (Yee 2000), emphasising that this industry is ideal for women because it does not involve physical or manual labour but 'intellectual labour'. This has resulted in a social construction of skill sets that has 'gendered' software work. As one female software engineer observed, 'This is a desk job but requires a lot of brain power; you don't need to keep labourers in line. If you are in a mechanical shop the people under you are men who are doing physical work and you have to keep them in line. A female in that position does not really work too well. So, this is a better option. Many girls I think have chosen this industry for that.'

The sentiments reflected above also point to a distinctive self-identification with a separate social class that has redefined or brought into question traditional notions of 'labour'. IT workers in general and software professionals in particular take pride in working for the global market. In fact, through working for global multinationals they attempt to 'become' global themselves. Being global is a marker of modernity tied to perceptions of upward social mobility and new cultures of consumption in urban India.

The increased participation of women in this industry has to a certain extent demystified the notion of gendered science and technology. Women's analytical capabilities are not questioned as much as their commitment to the work and the company, given that the normalised social role of a woman in the domestic sphere remains intact. This is what results in gendered forms of alienation, which impacts women and men's professional experience but is neither limited to nor just derived from the workplace. As Kaushalya explains:

If you look at it, there are a lot of dropouts, because if you go to colleges, women shine in engineering colleges. There are more than 50 per cent in computer science. They enter the job market but pressures of marriage and children take their toll. So, you find [their] numbers declining. It is not even half, although at entry level, I feel the number is huge. The key thing is that in this industry the support systems are not in place. When people move out, and if they are from small towns, their ability to handle these are difficult. If you are married how do you manage the home and work, kids, etc. There is no adequate infrastructure or support system. ...There are a lot of women in the middle management level who are quite competent. So, I don't think that competence has ever been doubted in this industry. It is really the social issues; it is the society which is not able to grapple with it. So, the individuals who find their own solution are able to march ahead; there are others who are unable to do so or strike a balance.

So, some women have done immensely well for themselves, many of them having had consistent support on the home front from husbands, parents or in-laws and domestic help. For some, the industry has provided opportunities such as foreign trips, the acquisition of new skill sets or technical specialisations, and individual growth. Rajni, a VP in a large Indian firm, emphasised that '… this company taught me to speak my mind … I was a very reserved person. In college you know girls generally don't speak up … so along with technical skills I acquired confidence in myself'.

In their everyday interactions in the workplace, however, women as a group (junior software engineers and higher level managers) still face challenges that question both their technical skill and their authority because of their gender. This is clearly reflected in the following accounts:

> Once in a while my word will be doubted even if I am a module lead; one guy wanted to clarify a technical point and despite my telling him the right answer he went ahead to check with a male colleague.

> In my team I have often led people who were senior to me … once I had some trouble with this older guy who didn't want to report to me … now I don't know whether it was because of my age or gender … they often tend to overlap … sometimes, I feel maybe if I was a man I would have had a different experience.

Despite limited representation of women in senior management, the image of the generic empowered working woman is used as a symbol of modernity to attract MNCs to India. The head of HR (a 45-year-old man) of a large Indian software company explained:

> In India because of traditional expectations of women's role in the family, there are women who drop out of work after a certain stage to adhere to this. The gender structure is like a triangle or sometimes a rectangle. In our male dominated society, women naturally exit before reaching the top due to household/family responsibilities. However, we are realising the value of women leading teams; when a client observes a woman making a team presentation it says a lot about the organisation, it is a revelation.

While gender plays an important role in defining workplace relationships, it often gets mediated through social class. This has various manifestations, such as influencing mentoring networks. Very few companies have real and functioning systems of mentoring in the workplace although many do have some policies in place for entry-level engineers. In case of difficulties—technical or otherwise—employees predominantly resort to informal networks within and outside the workplace. These are closely aligned along social networks consisting mainly of college classmates or peer groups. There is an underlying class dynamics within these reflected in the kind of educational opportunities to which one has had access, i.e., whether one is a graduate of IIT/IIM/REC[14] which have large alumni organisations or is an alumnus of an American university or has attended a small engineering college with fewer networks. Often well-connected people find it much easier to cope with workplace stress and strain and are not as alienated as those who do not have access to such networks.

At times, despite working in teams, intra-group affinities get aligned on the basis of common language, regional background, educational institutions and prior company affinities. As Kamesh argues:

> While overtly there may be no biases and teams have people from all over the place and different backgrounds, once in a while it is easy to see that all the IIT and IIM people like to hang together. We REC types are not like that. Sometimes if the project manager and a couple of team members are from the same community I wonder if that matters when the appraisal time comes. I can't be definite but once in a while at least I feel information sharing ... little things about the project ... telephone conversations with clients, don't get to everyone in the team.

Safe and Secure Work Environment

There are also aspects of gendered alienation related to particular workplaces. While on the one hand large software companies, secure within their campus environment with private security, have been criticised for giving rise to 'gated communities', women workers find such campuses safer than travelling elsewhere and working on client sites. Namita, a 26-year-old software engineer, shared her experience of working for a government telecom project, to which she had to travel each day:

> The place is 13 km from home and late at night with five deserted buildings there, where do I run to? It is uncomfortable working in such places. In our company too I have worked nightshifts and late nights, but have never felt this way, maybe because my team members or people I work with are different. But I feel this mostly because it is a secure office and everybody is accountable, and you have the receptionist there, the security guards are there, who are all employees or at least accountable to the company.

Women particularly expressed concern over working late nights at client sites.

> In Karnataka in most of the government offices the ladies toilet is on the odd floor and gents on even floor. And our office was on the even floor—somehow we always end up with a second floor office. If I work after 5 pm, all the lights are switched off and I have to sort of grope my way through and go to the toilet. And only if I become close to the people there I can approach a male and ask somebody to walk with me ... but you can't really do that always ... [embarrassed laugh]. If I know that I have to go home at 7 pm I try to go once at 5 pm and keep tight after that. You know these things matter but you can't really discuss with anybody.

These accounts belie the hegemonic images of software work as purely non-physical, cushy desk jobs and workplaces as disembodied spaces. While there are some who do most of their work in air-conditioned offices—which itself involves the very bodily act of sitting in one place coding and programming all day—there are others who travel long distances to visit client sites or even abroad for onsite work.

Cultural Capital and Surveillance

As a service industry with software professionals physically working in diverse transnational spaces, hosting foreign clients on site visits to India or interacting with customers over the digital media, training people 'culturally' (sometimes referred to as 'etiquette training') has become a significant requirement. With the changes in the structure of the software industry and greater emphasis on consulting and closer client-vendor connections, there is a rising demand and increasing value attached to appearance. The CEO of a small software firm remarked:

> As more and more people are brought in the labour pool we can see more of a mix of background—people from rural, semi-urban background are coming in. This can be challenging as these people may not have lived in metros like Bangalore—their ability to cope, challenges they face—their lifestyles, the way they dress, speak, everything. People who are coming in require more help because their exposure is lower. So, the role of the HR department, especially the seniors and mentors, needs to be strengthened in those areas. They provide 'soft skills' training, mentor and coach them.

So, apart from technical skills emphasis is given to good grooming, right attitude, impeccable manners, communication skills and understanding of the business. This is one of the reasons why graduates from IITs and IIMs are much more in demand and coveted as ideal workers—for their technical training as well as these other 'behavioural/soft skills'. Thus the social characteristics of employees have become a key aspect of their employability: class, language skills and appearance—the entire set of characteristics that might be captured in Bourdieu's (1984) notion of 'cultural capital'—have become key in the division of labour in the new information/service economy (du Gay 1996; Leidner 1993).

HR policies on dress code are part of this image-making exercise, reiterating the importance of appearance in this service industry:

> We have a dress code in office—formals Monday to Thursday and casuals on Friday. But it varies from branch to branch. In some offices 'formals' means you have to come in tie and prim and proper salwar kameez and no short kurtas. Bangalore is quite relaxed.... Usually salwar kameez, and sometimes, western formal. When you are at a client's place you really have to be prim and proper—anything wrong means your lead or somebody will say something.

While cultural training and dress code are not overt forms of sur-veillance, in Foucauldian terms they could be seen as subtle ways in which workers are disciplined to make them ideal for the software service industry.

Mobility and Individualisation

Despite the various forms of alienation, and differences and inequalities in workplace experiences, the software export industry has a higher scale of pay in comparison with many other traditional industries in the country. As multinationals continue to flock to Bangalore to set up their offshore development units, the pay scales are competitively pushed up and attrition rates increase as software engineers vie with one another to secure ever higher rates of income by moving from Indian firms to MNCs. As Sujata, a 40-year-old VP in an Indian software firm explained, most commonly it is young people with less than five years experience that jump ship:

> Most of these software engineers, all that they are interested in is money and their resume for the day. Only when they move beyond one to five years do they get a larger perspective, but in the initial period they don't care. That is the reason for high levels of attrition. I think it's peer pressure for them. There is a huge generation gap between what we used to think when we joined work and what people have in mind these days. Everybody wants to become the CEO in six years and wants to make good money. Money was never the most important parameter for us. Nobody could woo us away from an organisation just because they offer 50 per cent more. There is no emotional bonding. We were very emotional people. ... So we end up losing people between one and five years who haven't emotionally bonded with us and also those who have a very short-term view of things. So, they are not looking at a career, not looking ahead 20–25 years. They all think that in the next five years they will make so much money that they will retire in the sixth year. But, they could be right to be sceptical of the industry and what will happen to it down the line, but I think its also an age gap in the way we think.

Peer pressure is also reflected in the consumption practices of software professionals and contributes to setting these 'knowledge professionals' apart from the larger society, despite differences amongst them. Sujata reflects again:

There is a lot of peer pressure, taking on different dimensions. There is this overall feeling that IT guys are so rich. These fellows are under great pressure—I don't think they will get married unless they acquire a car and a house. Earlier it was quite an achievement for people in their forties to acquire houses, then you saw people in their thirties ... and now these people in their twenties acquire houses. It has created some kind of complex in the society for those who are part of the crowd are okay, and those who are not feel envious—both the IT and BPO sectors are pretty affluent. There are contradictions there—people often pass snide remarks about IT people as if all of them are equally rich ... Yes, some are jet setters and travel onsite, but not everyone.

Conclusion

In this chapter, I have attempted to show the manner in which the spatial reorganisation of software production and India's role in the export of software services has redefined work in Bangalore. Software work has attracted large sections of the educated middle class with its high remuneration, the lure of global exposure and social status associated with this 'sunrise industry' in India. Many have succeeded in making their mark in the industry. However, the organisational practices, corporate policies and everyday interactions in the high-tech workplace re/produce gender-based inequalities often mediated through class and age. While some of these inequalities arise from the social construction of skills and gender- and class-based stereotypes about work, this discussion illustrates how organisational practices and policies recreate these inequalities and provide parameters within which identities of the 'knowledge professionals' are negotiated and re/produced. Career narratives of software workers, interviews with HR personnel and entrepreneurs, and ethnographic accounts of the work process reveal the embodied nature of software work and the various modes of alienation in the high-tech workplace that accrue from the work experiences of men and women as gendered beings. The atomisation and fragmentation of work under flexible production systems alienate the worker from the work as well as from one another. This is one of the factors that seems to discourage and limit any form of collective bargaining for grievances in this industry. The process of alliance building is further made difficult because this is still a rather new industry in India, and policies and processes are constantly in flux. Moreover, software professionals often identify themselves as 'intellectual/knowledge workers', disassociating themselves from traditional 'labour'. Their high pay supposedly compensates for the long hours of work, which because of the nature of the industry, is almost always justified as inevitable. Somesh, a 29-year-old engineering graduate working for an Indian company and earning 300,000 rupees a year, remarks candidly: 'Honestly speaking it is the money that matters. We wouldn't be earning one-fourth of what the software industry offered us if we were to work in another industry ... so when we were in our final year we were thinking of going for IT. I do not particularly care for the sector.'

Notes

1. There is some debate about when the liberalisation process began. Contrary to popular belief, economic reform in India was a gradual process and not merely the result of pressure from international institutions (Jenkins 2004). Some scholars have argued that while 1991 was the landmark year when official policies were implemented by the Narasimha Rao government in the aftermath of financial crises, some sectors of the economy—including software and computer services—were already partially liberalised by the mid-1980s under the auspices of Rajiv Gandhi (Heeks 1996). In fact, several scholars have increasingly embraced the concept of 'liberalisation by stealth' or 'hesitant liberalisation' of the Indian economy (Jenkins 2004).

2. There is considerable debate around the identity of the 'new' Indian middle classes. Generally, they are associated with economic liberalisation, new consumption patterns, and their attendant cultural, social and symbolic weight. Some have preferred to call them the 'New Rich' (Pinches 1999; Robison and Goodman 1996), i.e., 'the section of the middle classes that has increasingly been serving as the symbol of the benefits of liberalisation in comparative contexts' (Fernandes 2000: 88). There are actually various layers of the middle class (differentiated by caste, religion, income and social/cultural capital), ranging from low level and less skilled clerical workers to upper level managerial personnel, but it is a small segment of these urban upwardly mobile workers who seem to be associated with

the discursive construction of India's new middle classes. According to Salim Lakha, the new middle class comprises the '… rich farmers, labour elite, small business entrepreneurs, professionals, overseas workers in the Gulf region, and the salaried from diverse backgrounds. Needless to say, the high status global consumer goods that are popularly seen as the distinguishing markers of the middle class cannot be afforded by all the groups included above…' (Lakha 1999: 264). Others have argued that in the contemporary context of liberalised India '… the new middle class has become a sign of the promise of a new national model of development, one with a global outlook that will allow India to catch up with larger processes of economic globalisation' (Fernandes 2000: 91)

3. See article by Chen Mae Yee in the *Wall Street Journal*, November 1, 2000.

4. Infosys advertisement that appeared in several editions (February to August 2004) of the Indian national daily *Deccan Herald*.

5. The term 'new economy' refers particularly to the post-Fordist proliferation of service sector jobs that are dependent on the new informational and communication technologies in the global North. In recent years, the term has also been used to refer to the new export-led IT service sector and associated changes in the global South.

6. Neoliberalism is the governing ideology of free markets and attendant processes of deregulation, liberalisation and privatisation adopted in some form or another by most states in contemporary global economy. The roots of neoliberalism can be traced to the Chicago economists Hayek and Friedman, but it was institutionalised and operationalised in the 1980s through the economic policies of Reagan and Thatcher. Some scholars differentiate between 1980s neoliberalism characterised by the deregulation and dismantling of the Keynsian welfare state, and a reconfigured 1990s neoliberalism that is characterised by a proactive state-led institutional and regulatory reform regime (Peck and Tickell 2002).

7. Here the 'bureaucratic mentality' refers to both the hierarchical structures of colonial institutions, and the social prestige associated with managerial and administrative jobs. This mentality arguably continues to flourish in postcolonial institutions such as the civil service and large public sector establishments, but particularly in the context of governance via screenings, quotas and permits. It is thus intrinsically tied to the post-Independence economic policies of import substitution or the 'permit raj'. While India has embarked on a process of liberalisation since the mid-1980s, many still critique older Indian companies such as TCS (Tata Consultancy Services) for continuing to harbour a 'bureaucratic mentality' in its workplaces. In addition, despite the argument that economic reforms and jobs in the new service economy have given rise to the 'new Indian middle class' (Fernandes 2000), the social prestige associated with the traditional title of 'manager' or managerial positions continues to hold sway (although the composition of bureaucracy and civil service in contemporary India has undergone changes; Lakha 1999).

8. These facilities, however, are not just overt forms of control of workers by capitalists; rather, they are simultaneously symbols of modernity that help garner the consent of workers in subtle ways.

9. These figures are according to the *NASSCOM Strategic Review*, 2004. Estimates of the size and composition of the workforce vary even among NASSCOM sources: another source from around the same time (2003) mentions the proportion of women in the workforce as around 21 per cent (NASSCOM 2003). In fact, there is little reliable data on many aspects of the IT industry.

10. This could also be related to the relative newness of this industry and the increase in the number of women entering the high-tech workplace in recent years. However there is also a process of higher attrition among women in the upper ranks of the corporate ladder, which is related to gendered social norms about women's domestic responsibilities.

11. MCA refers to Masters in Computer Application, a degree that has been recently introduced in the Indian colleges. PGSM is Post Graduate Diploma in Software Management, a course that has been introduced by the Indian Institute of Management Bangalore, especially for software professionals and managers.

12. This is not to say that other subjectivities or identities such as class, caste, age or regional differences are irrelevant; in fact, gendered experience is always mediated through these other axes of difference.

13. In addition to this, some informants, who cannot afford or do not have internet service at home, have emphasised that unlimited access to internet at their workplace is another attraction to stay late at work; as many of them spend time on the internet to allay loneliness and boredom.

14. IIT refers to Indian Institute of Technology and IIM to Indian Institute of Management. Both these institutions (located in different cities) are renowned as nationally and internationally the most prestigious and highly accredited institutions of higher education in India. The annual tuitions in both institutions are relatively high, thus restricting entry mainly to the middle class. But even for people of limited means these institutions are perceived as a good investment due to their prestige and the prospect of getting recruited by well-known companies at very high salaries upon graduation. REC refers to Regional Engineering Colleges, which are also among the more prestigious institutions, but unlike the IITs and IIMs they are regarded as second-tier institutions.

References

Benner, C. 2002. *Work in the New Economy: Flexible Labour Markets in Silicon Valley.* Oxford: Blackwell Press.

Bourdieu, Pierre. 1984. *Distinction: A Social Critique of the Judgement of Taste.* Trans. Richard Nice. Cambridge: Harvard University Press.

du Gay, Peter. 1996. *Consumption and Identity at Work.* London: Sage Publications.

Duncan, N. (ed.). 1996. *Body Space: Destabilising Geographies of Gender and Sexuality.* London and New York: Routledge.

Fernandes, L. 2000. Restructuring the New Middle Class in Liberalising India. *Comparative Studies of South Asia, Africa and the Middle East* 20(1): 88–104.

Hanson, S. and G.Pratt. 1995. *Gender, Work and Space.* London: Routledge.

Heeks, R. 1996. *India's Software Industry: State Policy, Liberalisation and Industrial Development.* California: Sage Publications.

Jenkins, Rob (co-editor Sunil Khilnani). 2004. *The Politics of India's Next Generation of Economic Reforms.* Special Issue, *India Review* 3(2).

Lakha, S. 1999. The State, Globalisation and Middle Class Identity. In *Culture and Privilege in Capitalist Asia,* Michael Pinches (ed.), pp. 251–71. London and New York: Routledge.

Leidner, R. 1993. *Fast Food, Fast Talk: Service Work and the Routinisation of Everyday Life*. Berkeley and L.A.: University of California Press.

McDowell, L. 1997. *Capital Culture: Gender at Work in the City*. Oxford: Blackwell Publishers.

———. 2001. Men, Management and Multiple Masculinities in Organisations. *Geoforum* 32(2): 181–98.

Marchand, M.H. and A.S. Runyan (eds). 2000. *Gender and Global Restructuring: Sightings, Sites and Resistance*. London and New York: Routledge.

Marx, K. 1964. *Early Writings*. Trans. and ed. T.B. Bottomore. New York: McGraw Hill Book Company.

Massey, D. 1996. Masculinity, Dualisms and High Technology. In *Bodyspace: Destabilising Geographies of Gender and Sexuality*, N. Duncan (ed.), 109–26. New York: Routledge.

Nash, J. and P. Fernadez-Kelly (eds). 1983. *Women, Men, and the International Division of Labour*. Albany: State University of New York.

NASSCOM (The National Association of Software and Services Companies). 2003. Press release. www.nasscom.org.

Pearson, R. 1991. New Technology and the Internationalisation of Office Work: Prospects and Conditions for Women's Employment in LDCs. *Gender Analysis in Development Discussion Paper No. 5*, School of Development Studies, University of East Anglia, UK.

———. 1993. Gender and New Technology in the Caribbean: New Work for Women? In *Women and Change in the Caribbean*, J. H. Momsen (ed.), pp. 287–95. Kingston: Ian Randle.

———. 1995. Gender Perspectives on Health and Safety in Information Processing: Learning from International Experience. In *Europe and Developing Countries in the Globalised Information Economy*, Swasti Mitter and Maria Ines Bastos (eds), pp. 278–302. London and New York: Routledge and UNU Press.

Peck, J. and Tickel, A. 2002. Neoliberalising Space. *Antipode* 34 (3): 380–404.

Pinches, M. (ed.). 1999. *Culture and Privilege in Capitalist Asia*. New York: Routledge.

Pollert, A. 1988. The 'Flexible Firm': Fixation or Fact? *Work, Employment and Society* 2(3): 281–316.

Pringle, R. 1988. *Secretaries Talk*. London: Verso.

Robison, R. and D. Goodman (eds). 1996. *The New Rich in Asia: Mobile Phones, McDonalds and Middle-Class Revolution*. New York: Routledge.

Standing, G. 1999. *Global Labour Flexibility: Seeking Distributive Justice*. London: McMillan Press.

Storper, M. and A.J. Scott. 1990. Work Organisation and Local Labour Markets in an Era of Flexible Production. *International Labor Review* 129(5): 573–91.

Webster, J. 1996. *Shaping Women's Work: Gender, Employment and Information Technology*. London and New York: Orient Longman.

Yee, Chen May. 2000. High-tech Lift for India's Women. *Wall Street Journal* (1 November): B1.

3

Betwixt and Between? Exploring Mobilities in a Global Workplace in India*

Marisa D'Mello and *Sundeep Sahay*

The intensification of linkages between international or global and local or national levels suggests that globalisation can be conceptualised as a process of flows (Castells 1996; Urry 2000, 2001), moving along global 'scapes' (Appadurai 1996)[1]—including the various systems of transportation of people. To understand these forms of flows and mobilities, Urry (2000) called for a sociology of mobilities, for thinking 'beyond society,' urging sociological analysis to recast its subject material by focusing on 'mixtures' or forms of heterogeneously composed networks, commodity chains, fluid social spaces and global institutional forms. In this chapter, we contribute to the development of Urry's agenda of developing a sociology of mobilities through an empirically informed analysis of a global software development workplace and its workers.

A common understanding of mobility is the movement of a body between locations in geographical space. Mobility is inherent in processes of globalisation, whether it concerns the global movement of money or people, the spread of terrorist activities or the movement of information in service-oriented work. In the contemporary reflexive world, economies are increasingly made up of signs—information, symbols, images, aspirations, desire—and of space, where both signs

---

* Some of the theoretical ideas presented in this chapter have been further developed in another paper titled '"I am kind of a nomad where I have to go places and places..." Understanding Mobility, Place and Identity in Global Software Work from India', *Information and Organisation* 17: 162–92, 2007. The empirical base for the paper is the same as in this chapter.

and social subjects—refugees, financiers, tourists and citizens—are mobile over ever greater distances (Lash and Urry 1996). An analysis of these mobilities, Lash and Urry argue, contributes to an understanding of changes in social relations, from the organisation of work to the formation of new forms of citizenship.

The context of global software work (GSW) undertaken by global software organisations (GSOs) is fundamentally about mobility, which is often taken for granted. In GSW, knowledge systems such as programming languages, software development, project management methodologies, and specialised domain knowledge are applied to software development and maintenance activities at diverse geographical locations (Sahay et al. 2003). GSOs undertake such work across national boundaries through arrangements such as alliances, outsourcing or subsidiaries, using information and communication technologies (ICTs) to coordinate tasks at various stages of the software lifecycle. Such work is intangible, heterogeneous and mobile, in contrast to traditional service or manufacturing activities. GSW metaphorically represents 'models-of' and 'models-for' globalisation, implying that they are made possible by globalisation processes and also help to shape them (Sahay et al. 2003).

An analysis of mobilities inherent in the technoscape[2] of GSW is appropriate for a variety of reasons. Such work is inherently distributed, where some parts of a software project or product are developed in one location and some in others—typically different countries. The coordination of these activities involves the movement of pieces of code, developers, methodologies, technologies and documentation of different types across multiple places. These movements are fraught with tensions because they involve the interaction of different and sometimes conflicting people, firms, technologies, and practices across time, space, place and cultural conditions. This mobility, we will argue, occurs at least three interconnected levels of the work, the organisation and the individual, and is best understood and engaged with in particular, situated contexts. This chapter thus focuses on the following key question: What is the nature of mobilities that characterise people and organisations engaged in GSW?

This question was addressed through an in-depth case study conducted between 2002 and 2004, drawing primarily upon semi-structured, in-depth interviews of 50 IT (information technology) employees at different levels in a GSO in Mumbai, India. In addition to employees at various levels in this firm, further interviews were also carried out with other consultants and opinion leaders of the industry. Participant observation and analysis of secondary data related to company policies and other publicity material have supplemented interview data.

Place, Space and Mobility

The theoretical basis developed for our analysis rests on the concepts of place, space, and mobility and their inter-relationships. Place and space have been described as the two central and contrasting contours in the time–space configuration of modernity (Giddens 1990). The concept of place helps to understand how social meanings and the existential significance in this particular context are related to places—physical, social and electronic. Place has been related to a person's sense of boundedness and particularity, a sense of belonging, situatedness and emotional attachment, where tradition holds sway (Giddens 1990; Harvey 1989; Tuan 1977). Space, on the other hand, is typically associated with an abstract and infinite expanse through which people and ideas freely move, offering possibilities for newness and growth through a logic of replication and standardisation (Casey 1997; Schultze and Boland 2000).

Proponents of globalisation believe that place is no longer relevant and that social transactions including work related transactions can be carried out in spaces (rather than places). Harvey (1989) has argued that because of globalisation, novel technologies of transportation and communication increasingly 'compress' time and space, whereby many characteristics of place are abstracted or eliminated while space is increasingly unified. Giddens's (1990) notion of 'disembedding' refers to a key mechanism of globalisation in which space is separated from place and social practices are 'disembedded' from local contexts and rearticulated across indefinite spans of global spaces (and time). Similarly, Castells (1996) puts forth the notion of 'placeless space' to emphasise the assumption that organisations make about the increasing irrelevance of the 'local'. Castells (1996) argues that in contemporary capitalism, while organisations may be located in spaces, their components, people and processes are fundamentally place-dependent. In this way, he argues for a dialectical relation between the 'net and the self', metaphorically representing space and place, respectively.

Emphasising the social, Massey (1998) views space as constructed out of multiple social relations. Contained within a particular place or stretched beyond a specific locality, she argues, these nets of social relations are inherently dynamic, constructed, laid down, decayed and renewed. Given these features, she argues that places are more like processes in that they cannot be fixed to bounded areas with some long internalised history. Rather, places are a construction of a particular assemblage of social relations interacting or meeting at a particular location, '...imagined as articulated moments in networks of social relations and understandings...' (Massey 1998: 154). Further, places are seen to retain their uniqueness through a peculiar mix of wider and local social relations given the geographical differentiation of locations and heterogeneous influences of globalisation.

Theorists have also pointed to the role of ICTs in shaping these ongoing, changing space–place influences. ICTs are seen to paradoxically build relationships between places and locales through processes of time and space compression (e.g., Harvey 1989), as well as contribute to undermining a stable and unitary conception of place, sometimes resulting in fragmentation, disorientation and a sense of placelessness (Friedland and Boden 1997; Giddens 1990). ICTs in general, and mobile communication technologies such as mobile phones and Personal Digital Assistants (PDAs), are seen as influencing spatial, temporal, and contextual experiences and creating fluid interactions in work environments (Kakihara and Sørenson 2002). ICTs enable organisations, work relations, and workers to be mobile. In this scenario, work is assumed to be liberated from fixed places, as evident in practices of virtual teams/organisations and distributed work arrangements across space, time, and place boundaries of organisations and nation-states (Lipnack and Stamps 1997; Jarvenpaa and Leidner 1999; Dahles and Stobbe 2004). Further, independent workers symbolically depicted as 'e-lancers' (Malone and Laubacher 1998) or 'self programmable workers' (Castells 2001) who, unconstrained by organisational boundaries or traditional employment contracts, are seen to seek 'boundaryless careers' (Arthur and Rousseau 1996).

In the conduct of GSW, Sahay et al. (2003) argue that places—both physical and social—are emphasised at the levels of the individual, the organisation and also inter-organisational relationships. This emphasis stems from various reasons, including the individual's 'compulsions for proximity' (Friedland and Boden 1997) and an organisation's need to project an image of its local rootedness to place and simultaneously project its global capabilities to operate in space while working in parallel with partners from different countries. Sahay et al. (2003) further argue that these organisations' simultaneous needs for place and space are in constant dialectical tension and are being constantly redefined by various forms of mobilities. In particular, the notion of mobility helps to analyse how such movement redefines meanings and the significance of places to individuals with implications for understanding the context of GSW.

To summarise, the mobilities necessitated by globalisation processes in GSW imply changed notions of place and space relations. Theorists point to how ICTs shape these place–space influences in work, workplaces and workers. In the next section, we describe the empirical context of this study and analyse and discuss the various kinds of mobilities that were noted.

The Indian IT Industry

A myriad of interconnected technological, geographical, demographic, and socio-cultural shifts and movements characterise the Indian IT industry. Policies of the Indian government—specifically the liberalisation reforms after 1991—shifted the Nehruvian icons of a modernising India built on dams, steel, and power plants and the rhetoric of poverty reduction, to an 'export orientation' in science and technology arenas (Heeks 1996). IT became a major 'cause' that the Indian government committed to endorse, as a global industry, given the considerable knowledge base as well as the large pool of skilled, English-speaking professionals in the country. The market was opened to foreign firms and simultaneously the government augmented its export promotion policies in various ways such as creating software technology parks (STPs) that provided for software companies to be located in tax-exempt, designated zones with guaranteed access to high-speed satellite links and reliable electricity (D'Costa 2004). These reforms also resulted in a sharp increase in IT education institutes and skill-oriented training centres in India, resulting in large numbers of young people from big cities as well as small towns entering this field. Simultaneously, the Indian consumer market opened up to foreign, 'global' companies and brands, introducing new forms of entertainment and 'lifestyle' products—including technologies such as mobile phones that support mobilities.

From the late 1980s and early 1990s the IT sector has been the fastest growing industry in the country, and its contribution to India's GDP has nearly tripled from 1.2 per cent in 1998 to 3.5 per cent in 2004 (NASSCOM 2005). While in the early years almost 75 per cent of the export-related work was carried out at the client's location overseas and 25 per cent was done in India, today these figures are reversed (Heeks 1996; Sahay et al. 2003). Over time, most large IT players have transcended the software coding and maintenance barriers and moved up the 'value chain' into higher-end IT consulting and product development realms.[3] These shifts in the distribution of onsite–offshore work and in the nature of work place new demands on firms in managing mobilities. These are discussed in the following section in the context of a particular firm.

Mobilities in a Global Software Organisation

IN-Sync is a mid-size software applications outsourcing company, established in 1980 and headquartered in Mumbai. It offers business solutions in insurance, financial services and government as well as application management outsourcing services. In two decades IN-Sync grew from three individuals to over 2,300 professionals worldwide. In 2004, its annual revenue was US $120 million. Initially catering to only domestic customers, IN-Sync has since aggressively moved into the export market and now has offices in US, UK, Germany, Austria, Japan, Singapore and Malaysia, besides several offices in Mumbai. Over the years, IN-Sync has restructured itself several times—revised its vision and mission, merged functions, and shut down units and opened new ones—to respond to ongoing market changes. One constant feature of the company has been the leadership of its founder directors, and the inculcation of place-based values of family and being Indian while simultaneously emphasising its global competitiveness.

The empirical material collected during the research process revealed multiple, interrelated socio-spatial trajectories that converged within this GSO. Several kinds of mobilities were seen to cut across the levels of individual, work and the organisation. We have categorised these as geographical, existential and social mobilities. We use the term *geographical mobility* to refer to physical shifts of various sorts across space and place. *Social mobility* includes moves across a network of social relations such as from a caste to a class hierarchy, shifts up and down the corporate hierarchy, and moves across groups such as work teams and onsite social spaces. By *existential mobility* we mean shifting internal processes related to the IT worker such as fears and hopes, insecurities and successes, experienced primarily in relation to career trajectories and work contexts. These various mobilities are analysed below in terms of statements of 'from' and 'towards' movement. Each set of mobilities is seen as situated on the nodes of global–local flows of GSOs, intersecting, mutually shaping and sometimes colliding—in tension with each other. Rather than being separate categories, the examples from the empirical material illustrate these intersections.

City Travels and Travails

IT workers were seen to inhabit different places and spaces (physical, emotional and social) during the course of their workdays and home lives. For example, Mumbai—the economic and financial capital of India—is 'home' to around 60 per cent of IN-Sync employees who are also Maharashtrians. A busy metropolis of more than 15 million people, Mumbai was the hub for software activities in India until the mid-1980s, attracting IT job seekers from all over the country. In the city's urban landscape, renaissance-styled skyscrapers stand cheek by jowl with sprawling slums. Celebrated as 'a metaphor of Indian modernity' (Patel 1995), city planners and state agencies have desired to transform Mumbai into a global city like Singapore or Hong Kong (D'Monte 2002). Its peninsular geography has limited its expansion, creating a shortage of commercial, residential, public and private space and also making travel difficult.

Several employees at IN-Sync from outside the city spoke of Mumbai as a 'happening' place, referring to the various social and cultural events in the city. They also spoke of how 'clubbing', partying and seeking new entertainment options was increasing in their peer group. Several employees talked about how stressful it was to juggle family and work, coupled with the pressure of commuting in Mumbai. Pursuing hobbies is also adversely impacted. For example, a project manager in his mid-30s, with a one-year-old child, said:

> I feel torn ... I am not adept at balancing these. People outside Bombay are luckier as they don't spend time and energy in traveling ... Presently, I don't have any projects so I don't get calls at home ... I have started taking some meditation classes once a week. But as software professionals we are very bad at managing our time. If someone can do a good job of it he is an exception. Work takes priority.

IN-Sync employees often leave home around 8 am and return around 9 pm, including on Saturdays. With deadlines to meet, these timings are stretched and Sundays too are often spent at the office. The staff spend hours commuting on poorly maintained and polluted roads in humid weather. In stark contrast, the office locations in Software Technology Parks (STPs) have a calm and relaxing ambience with wide roads, lush greenery and perhaps even a lake.

The physical layout of the STP has common cafeterias located strategically, crowded with people from various IT companies during lunch hours, indicating a place functioning as a node in the network of flows. Serving 'Jain pizzas', 'Chinese chopsuey', as well as 'American burgers', conversations and face-to-face interactions provide the conduits for informational and social flows. Here, apart from job possibilities, 'inside' stories about companies and teams circulate freely and are used strategically to make career moves. These cafeterias as well as canteens within individual organisations can be seen as places that encapsulate and circulate local informational and social flows, which often create global mobilities in terms of staff finding global employment opportunities.

The Workplace

The physical (or corporeal) experience of the journey to the office is juxtaposed with the experience within the workplace. The IT office spaces in Mumbai are typically centrally air-conditioned and aesthetically designed, housed in large buildings. Granite and marble are generously used in IN-Sync and are well maintained. Security 'guards' with pin striped uniforms stand at the office entrance to sign in visitors, ensure employees display their identity cards, and assist in reception and other administrative tasks. In the elevators, an American accented voice announces the floor. On each floor, self-service cafeteria facilities supply (free) tea and coffee. Office buildings also house training rooms, a library, and meeting rooms equipped with phones, computers and white boards or projector screens. Conference rooms are equipped with state-of-the-art videoconference facilities.

Employee seating is open in order to maximise use of space, reduce hierarchy and increase opportunities for social exchange. IT employees, particularly at developer levels, rarely decorate their workstations with pictures or photographs and minimally use their storage space. Managers may sit next to developers and other team members but they have wider workstations, more phones on the table and often more corporate material adorning their softboards. The head of the unit sits in a spacious cabin with a semi-transparent glass door. From the windows there are views of the road outside the secured complex, dotted with shanties, piles of uncleared garbage, large cement pipes, children running around and sleeping stray dogs with misty mountains in the distance.

The company tries to create a 'home-like' environment in the office through various spatial and social arrangements. For example, the family metaphor is often invoked by the CEO of the company in his address to employees. Employees express religious sentiments through screensavers of deities, tiny idols placed on the monitor or hard disk, or pictures pinned on the soft board in the workstation. New offices are inaugurated with a traditional *puja*[4] ceremony. Prayers and religious mails are freely circulated among some employees. Religious festivals such as Holi, Diwali, Christmas and Id are celebrated by decorating the office, distributing sweets, wearing specified dress codes and exchanging greetings. Events such as an annual company-sponsored picnic at an outdoor location for employees and their families, monthly meetings and celebration of the company's anniversary are organised. Employees and their families mingle and participate enthusiastically at these events as they 'mix business with pleasure'. In these ways the organisation strives to create an existential sense of home at work, providing employees with a sense of rootedness in what we might call 'placed' locality and socio-historical continuity, for ultimate business benefit.

Shifting Socially

Socially, IT workers constitute an expanding section of the professional, Indian middle class in 'new economy' jobs such as IT and the service sector. Today young professionals from big cities as well as small towns aspire to work in private companies or multinationals. Liberalisation reforms have enabled many middle class Indians to satisfy their aspirations for consumption without overseas travel or connections. IT people especially can easily consume goods earlier deemed as luxuries but which now are indicators of social and geographical mobility: households appliances, packaged foods, branded and 'imported' goods, as well as vehicles and apartments. In these ways, movements and shifts range from literal spatial movements to aspirations of social and professional mobility, increased affluence and consumption, as well as shifts towards more meritocratic and professional organisational structures.

An HR (Human Resource) manager noted that IT professionals were more affluent than people working in the manufacturing industry and they occupied a place of pride in their families as they travel overseas frequently. Several IT employees echoed this view, suggesting the pride and shifting social status engendered by this industry. Purchase of a vehicle—two-wheeler or car (enabled through low-interest loans and high salaries)—was referred to as promising mobility, comfort and status. A 23-year-old developer proudly stated that while his retired father could never afford a vehicle in his entire career, he could own a motorbike early in life. While the purchase of a flat (an expensive decision in Mumbai city) was certainly an objective, for most IT workers at IN-Sync this was quite unlike their parents who typically would have purchased a flat after retirement. Commenting on these aspects, a project manager said:

> Despite higher salaries, IT people are not really satisfied. The urge to earn more is unsatiated. Twenty years back one would feel grateful to the God if one could have one's own flat in Mumbai at the time of retirement. Now, at the age of 35, unless you have a fancy car and a nice house, you have not arrived.

Another shift in attitudes was towards dress. In the early years of the industry, IT people were referred to as 'geeks' or 'nerds' and dressing for work reflected this image. This has dramatically changed today as indicated by an informant in his early twenties: 'Image and branding oneself is part of the work scene today'. Another also emphatically stated, 'Appearances are an important part of the job scene today and IT work is very international. Dressing up smartly does not mean anymore that we are flighty or not serious software engineers. That era is gone'. IT companies now stage in-house fashion shows—earlier unheard of or labelled as frivolous.

For the IT person, economic affluence, a higher standard of living and increased consumption choices are coupled with an ever-present array of job opportunities dotting the landscape of software outsourcing work, which is on the rise globally. Attributing a consumerist mindset to the 'nomadic' and 'opportunistic' nature of the Indian IT professional in response to the large number of 'tempting' job opportunities available, an IT industry opinion leader said: 'There is the consumerist 'have it now' mentality of the US... And so there is a feeling 'why do I have to wait for anything?' Whether it is the next job, the higher position, a house to live in, a car, whatever. It is this instant I need-it-now mentality which has now pervaded the youth. They were in their teens and their college days when this started and now they are in the workforce.

Emphasising this, a quality manager at IN-Sync noted:

> People come to the software industry because of the money involved and travels abroad. For that he is willing to sacrifice things like staying away from the family, going to remote corners, staying in different places.... This is a place where if you are successful you can just rise to any limit.... You see the success immediately. You don't have to wait.

Many IT workers admire icons of success in the Indian IT industry, particularly N.R. Narayana Murthy, the co-founder and former Chairman of Infosys Technologies, whose public image emphasises that, hailing from a lower middle class background, he has created immense wealth not only for himself but for others too, in a 'respectable' and professional manner. They say that they drew inspiration from people like him to 'make the leap' socially and professionally.

From Caste to Class

This industry has defied traditional ascriptions of caste and emphasised shifting across classes. In Mumbai, the influence of the traditional caste system, where one's place is ascribed and determined at birth and by kinship, is increasingly eroded by forces of secularisation, urbanism and consumerism. The IT industry was described by one of the CEOs at IN-Sync as an 'aspirational' space for engineers '...who are drawn from the lower middle class and the middle, middle class, the solid doing community rather than the Kshatriya[5] caste'. On the one hand, the transnational context of GSW coupled with the social and physical geography of Mumbai were seen as neutralising or transforming the caste system in India into one based on merit and skill. While kinship still operated at the entry level where qualified relatives could be recommended, this was diluted or altogether mitigated along the work trajectory of software projects. At IN-Sync it was anathema to speak of caste in public. A project manager emphatically stated: 'You end up reading the caste and religion from a resume and beyond that it is just a data point among others, of no consequence. See, in this industry I am in desperate need of a good person. And it just doesn't matter if he is Hindu or Muslim or male or female'. While this new system holds out a promise for individuals to carve new social spaces for themselves, the fact remains that caste is still inferred indirectly, from Hindu surnames. This may tacitly reinforce existing negative attitudes or beliefs about individuals and groups.

In India, sanskritisation[6] was traditionally the means for groups to move up the caste hierarchy. Today, individual agency, acquired knowledge, and competence are seen as the means for individuals to move up skill-based, meritocratic hierarchies typical of the private sector and especially so in GSW. This is contrasted with the pre-liberalisation days of licences and quotas, when people would ply their caste-related network ties to secure employment or business licences. In selecting a spouse for marriage, however, many inform-ants expressed a preference for the traditional 'arranged' marriage, as opposed to 'falling in love', where caste, kinship and religion were implicitly factored in. This suggests that in a globalising workplace, some sets of relations are mobilised while others are deeply em-bedded, remaining untouched, forming almost an 'enclave' where local continuities, deeply grounded in place, thrive. So while IT workers seek newness, growth, and the pursuit of an almost bound-aryless career in a volatile and transnational industry, and GSOs in-creasingly operate with a 'placeless logic', redefining their internal and external boundaries, individual employees remain 'historically and biographically place-dependent' (Sahay et al. 2003: 39), creating or reinforcing their own boundaries.

Juggling the Personal and the Professional

A concern frequently expressed by interviewees was juggling profes-sional priorities with family demands. A project manager observed:

> There is a thin line between professional and personal life. In personal life I sing, I deal with my family. When I come here I am a business person. This keeps pushing that line. The area oc-cupied by family and others keeps reducing. I measure my own importance based on my value on the other side. As an Indian male I am supposed to the one earning bread and butter....

Echoing a similar view, another senior manager in his mid-forties said:

> The IT person stops enjoying his life compared to the others, because of the extended working hours and odd timings. Sometimes you start at 8.00 and then finish at 10–11 pm five days a week. And anytime you can be called.... Also you don't develop any hobbies. You see, life IS beyond the office. That realisation comes to you only at age forty. Till such time you will run, busy climbing things … it is an early retirement job.

An article circulated at IN-Sync entitled 'Stress Kills 6 IT Geeks' (Srinivas 2005), reported the results of a study showing that the rate of suicides, divorces, heart ailments, high blood pressure, diabetes and mental depression were highest in the software industry. The article cited lack of routine, constant deadlines, working on weekends, lack of physical exercise and new food habits such as the 'pizza culture', as factors causing stress in this group. A manager commented on the article as follows:

> When some incident takes place, people are stunned and shocked but life flows on. I think the community is still young and these incidents are isolated. Many people think it is a matter of individual choice and how much risk they take. Besides, I think the need to earn more and more and pursue new lifestyles is what is driving people mad. Where do you have time to think about health and peace of mind?

Marriage alters how IT people straddle their work–home spaces. A recently married male project leader said, 'Before marriage, I would come to the office on Saturday or Sunday and work late. Now I can't do that … So I make it a point to leave at 7:30 pm nowadays. Before, only when I was tired I would leave. Now I have to think that she is waiting for me.' A 26-year-old female developer, when asked how she balances her work and family demands in a joint family, reported: 'After marriage, I have to be more focused because I have to go earlier to do household work. Yes, that mentality has automatically come. But still I never compromised on work. When I come to the office I can't think of my family. There are different places and so definitely they have to be separate. They intersect in terms of money ... you need money to buy things.'

Managing Social Networks

Social life, for IT people, is closely intertwined with work demands. A female senior manager with two teenage children expressed this view:

> Because of inevitable long hours at work, IT people build up strong social networks within the company. Outside of office, apart from family members, there is little time and energy to socialise. This phenomenon, along with overseas travel, impacts family relationships. International travel or long stays abroad are common now. On the one hand, my family can be with me overseas for short vacations which is great. However, my family seems to have found other support systems in my absence, and sometimes I wonder about my place in the home!

This response suggests how one's personal and work life is intricately intertwined, creating dilemmas which have to be dealt with every day. Further, notions of career growth and the shifting demands of the global marketplace in terms of technologies, skills, and work influence subjective experiences and existential feelings among IT workers. When mobility signifies growth, it simultaneously encompasses a range of instability, and change for both the organisation and the individual.

Careers and Professions

The 'growth imperative' was a common thread running through responses of employees at all levels. For developers, shifting jobs and technologies was a definite sign of growth. A 23-year-old developer, who has been in the company for 16 months, said:

> People just want to move. One is technology. If the person does not have work for a month or so he starts looking for another job. You get frustrated, not enhancing skills. What is my value in the market after three years? Software people get frustrated

very fast. It is different from manufacturing.... So you see people are just moving. ...The more skills you have the more valuable you are in software ... even within the same company.

Reinforcing this view, a project manager, while unhappy that two of his team members had quit for better opportunities, said with a hint of pride in his voice, 'I believe that I have grown because I have moved organisations. This is my ninth organisation. My smallest stint is one day, the longest is five years.'

A few module leaders expressed career growth in terms of moving up the projects chain into project management. A solution architect spoke of assignments becoming bigger, more complex or time critical and shortening the learning curve for himself. Yet another spoke of the 'challenges of influencing business growth and profitability by technology' while some took pride in being a 'techie' worker rather than a project manager.

While career growth conjured up different meanings for individuals, in an attempt to decrease the high salary cost-to-company and improve productivity, IN-Sync had fine-tuned and made its performance monitoring and competency assessment systems more stringent, which also reflects the 'flexible' and dynamic market conditions. From a paternalistic notion of 'taking care' of employees' careers, the notion of 'employability'[7] replaced the rhetoric of 'employment security'. Individuals are 'responsible' for their own careers while the company supported rather than actively enabled their aspirations. This shift propelled individuals to actively chart their career paths and training inputs and seek support from the company in the form of training programmes or sponsored certifications. Employees as well as recruitment agents use the term 'value addition' and 'deliverables' to refer to tangible contributions they can make or that can be made to them via a programme, job, role or their team members.

Informants noted that today while there were many jobs and many careers, none of them are for life, unlike in the previous generation. As one developer said, 'In the IT industry, secured employment is extinct'. Expressing his anxiety about the pervasive sense of uncertainty, Arvind, a project leader said,

In IT today, there is no job security as such unless you as an employee are performing and performing and performing. In spite of this you can be shown the door as we saw in the company located a floor below in our building. It is very insulting. You can literally feel the insecurity. The question mark is always there, like the sword of Damocles.

IT workers expressed fears and concerns about sustaining on a long term their recently acquired more affluent lifestyle in an expensive city like Mumbai, given the tumultuous market conditions with inherent risks. The volatile nature of the industry, the increasingly temporary and 'flexible' nature of employment contracts, the demise of job security, the intense work schedules, the stringent performance measures and surveillance systems in IT companies, and the introduction of 'demotion' policies (for the first time), question and also disrupt the seemingly smooth trajectory of an upwardly mobile, secured position for the worker, both socially as well as within the organisation. Besides the resultant disturbing, existential feelings, these changes also adversely affect how the IT worker is perceived by his or her social group within the organisation as well as by family and friends. Even if the reason for a downward shift is attributed to market factors rather than individual performance, employees spoke of 'losing face' in their various social groups and experience a loss of place or favourable social position in their extended family relations. In these ways, the uneven social trajectory of the IT worker is closely intertwined with the inherent mobility as well as the risks of the industry.

So IT professionals experience a significantly higher level of freedom and choices in their work compared to other professions in India. Thus, they have the option to exercise more discretion in the type of work they want to do and where they want to be. Yet, this wide array of choices is also accompanied by increased anxiety, stress, and an uneasy sense of precariousness and uncertainty about one's future in a fluid and mobile labour market. The fear of obsolescence often fuels the imperative of growth in which workers are in a constant 'learning mode', either reskilling themselves or shortening their learning curve, to enable a 'permanently marketable' state of being. In this way, GSW can be seen as a crucible for capitalist work regimes in which labour is a disposable commodity and workers are in a constant state of preparation and alertness to increase their market value as they move or are moved around places and spaces. The conscious and intentional rhetoric of 'deliverables' and 'value addition' are ingrained, used in daily work conversations and also in their personal lives.

Given that technologies and skills change very rapidly, the sense of security or worth secured as a result of a plum job, a 'hot' platform or a prestigious project is short-lived, resulting in an itinerant state of existence that we refer to as 'permanent transience'.

Moreover, while technical skills (commonly referred to as 'hard' skills) are basic to GSW, 'soft skills' (Gilleard and Gilleard 2002; D'Mello 2005), such as knowledge of foreign languages, cultural curiosity, managing diversity and interpersonal communication, are becoming increasingly important. An interviewee observed:

> Earlier if the IT professional knew COBOL or any specific technology, they could survive. If they were technically brilliant they could shine. Today softer skills like socialising, learning ability, and cultural adaptation to the country are required ... Nowadays adapting to a culture is not an issue as you watch a lot of TV.... Youngsters nowadays are more tuned to the culture than 15–20 years back.

Changes in Lifecycle of the IT Person

While diverse mobilities are fraught with multiplicities and ambiguities, they also intersect and mutually constitute one another. This is reflected in what was described as 'the lifecycle of the IT person' by the Head of HR, who said:

> I see two or three layers of IT people. The first layer is those who have just come out of school, bursting with energy and excitement, full of self-confidence and creative ideas, willing to work all hours and have fun at work even when they are slogging. They go out for movies in gangs, trekking, like an extension of college. Then they move to the Module Leader [ML] level and suddenly there is a change in their personality.... They start thinking about getting married or having a baby or buying a car or house and so on. They are also suddenly expected to look after other youngsters who are out of college, and most organisations do not provide them any tools or training or any idea of how to handle others. So as ML, the pressure increases and all the fun and joy comes down .... And then he goes up to the PM [Project Manager] or PL [Project Lead] level and it

steadily gets worse.... The tensions and stress increase ... By then they have kids who are going to school. So there is additional expenditure and there is worry about how will I make more money? Will it be enough? So those things, which they did not have to worry about, get aggravated....

So as the IT person moves across his/her typical professional 'life-cycle', stepping across various physical places and social spaces, the accompanying existential states of feeling, values, and attitudes is described as dramatically shifting from passion and enthusiasm to pessimism and resignation. The climb up the corporate hierarchy is coupled with even more responsibilities, challenges, enhanced visibility in the market, social status, and affluence, going hand in hand with higher levels of stress and pressures to perform. While the global nature of GSW and the 'glamour' of frequent overseas travel give an 'international' flavour to the image and position of the IT person in his/her social group, it also works as a double bind, intensifying the sense of personal as well as professional insecurity as well as disrupting family life. The increasingly porous boundary between personal and professional spheres that is an outcome of this work can have fatal personal consequences (such as high stress levels), which often go unnoticed or labelled as insignificant by a relatively youthful workforce, caught in frenzied mobilities of all sorts.

Moving across Borders

The geographical mobility of workers across borders, such as for onsite work, has financial, social and existential implications. Employees reported social pressure to travel overseas when they joined an IT company. A developer said:

> When an IT person meets someone else from another industry, people ask is, '*onsite kya gaya hai tub* [have you gone onsite]'? In India, an IT company is equated with you going onsite as soon as possible. So if you have not gone outside there is some serious problem with you. If not, then '*kabh jaa raha hai onsite* [when are you going onsite]'?

Earlier, the potential to save money was a major factor behind the desire to travel abroad. Now, given their high salaries and annual increments, employees are more choosy about the kind of onsite assignments they prefer as well as the duration of stay. However, the act of going overseas was widely seen as a critical *rite de passage* for IT workers and many said they are not comfortable unless the 'ghost of going abroad was exorcised'.

Onsite postings come with a set of uncertainities and tensions that are inherent in GSW and are inextricably linked with the mobility of the individual. On one hand, an overseas posting provides an enhanced social status, increased possibilities for saving money, and a chance to experience a different set of cultural and social relations both within and outside the customer location. On the other hand, often the duration of the onsite posting is ambiguous and this uncertainty affects family life, such as interruption of children's schooling or the spouse's career as well as housing decisions. This puts stress on traditional structures of support. For example, rental accommodation is expensive and hard to find in Mumbai, often making it difficult for ageing parents to live with their children as traditionally happens in India. Low cost domestic help for household tasks and child care, while available, is seen as unreliable and untrustworthy, placing the burden of these tasks primarily on women household members.

Longer overseas posting, particularly for a period of a year or more, creates a different set of challenges. Several informants mentioned that while they enjoyed professional relations at the customer site, it was difficult to make friends socially as such relations come with a set of nonverbal codes or tacit social norms and rules, not easily transferable from one social context to another. For example, rules relating to 'small talk' or what is understood as 'personal' in one context as opposed to another, differ across geographical places. Not knowing these rules immediately makes it difficult for those who are posted onsite, particularly those who are travelling overseas for the first time, to easily fit in or relate informally to local people. While some IT professionals may eventually choose to become residents in another country (typically, the UK and US) and 'enjoy' a stable family life, this stability comes with its own set of destabilising forces such as the weather, the limited or complete absence of family or social networks, unfamiliar schooling systems and the experience of better living conditions. Often this destabilisation is dealt with in ways that suggest a reinforcement of a common history of place-based rules related to region or even religion. These include subscription to Indian TV channels such as Zee TV, conscious consumption of goods and food from 'home', and potlucks and social gatherings[8] with people from one's region and/or country. These activities were reported to satisfy a sense of belonging through deeper, place-based roots and ties while also pursuing professional goals. Project team members would often share the same house and socialise with each other, not venturing to join local interest groups. Spouses (mainly wives) of employees who came to live onsite would make friends with one another, since they were generally unable to work due to their visa status.

Informants expressed concerns and fears about the divergent norms of a foreign culture, particularly in the US and Europe. Responding to a question on family relocation back and forth across physical and social borders, a 33-year-old project leader with a two-year-old child said:

I found it is very easy at 25–30 years to integrate into society there [UK]. But I have found problems with kids growing up there. No matter what, they are in a dilemma of being pulled in two directions. Even in India you do grow up in two regions where culture is different and kids do manage to come out okay. I get the feeling that in the UK the cultures diverge too far. On the one hand one may say I will adopt the country's culture, which creates one set of problems. And there is another set of people who become ultraconservative and everyone for example learns Indian music and dance. Very few have a balance going around.

Sometimes employees requested to return earlier than the stipulated period of posting, while others consciously focused on what changes they wanted to adopt. A senior manager with two children said: 'Having lived abroad and travelled quite a bit my standard of living has changed because of earnings. Value system has not changed. Certain amount of quality, finished professionalism has improved…. Values in terms of relationships, family … nowhere that is changed'.

Some differences were seen in how men and women experienced their onsite stint. A female module leader was the only woman in a UK location, in a team of 35 males, where she often felt alone and marginalised. She wanted to return home early from her assignment because her house was once burgled and she felt unsafe. Her request to return home was not immediately granted as a replacement was hard to find at short notice. When she asked her manager what he would have done if his daughter were in her place, he said that he would have got his daughter married before sending her alone onsite—a response that shocked and angered her. In this way, frequent relocation across physical and social borders is not an easy transition. Sometimes (as illustrated in the above example) a place-based chauvanistic response is transposed, with limited consideration or concern for the new context or the worker involved. The circuit of mobilities of the IT person is in continuous tension, with some immobilities in the form of norms and values making it an uneven course.

Living overseas also creates another lens through which practices in the home country are viewed. A module leader who had recently returned from a year-long posting in the UK, said:

> After being abroad we become generally more intolerant of sloppiness. We say, how long do I have to stand in this queue? The positive part is that the more the intolerance, the more the service provider is going to improve. If you look at the whole country, as a proportion IT people are a small number. But IT opens up the path, and now we have BPO [Business Process Outsourcing].... Look at the way the banks deal with you now compared to what it was even ten years ago, there is a big difference. Rather than asking you to do 30 forms in triplicate, they now fill the forms themselves ... No more of a *chalta hai*[9] mentality.

The growth of high end offshore work in India is contributing to what some analysts call 'reverse brain drain', in which qualified expatriates who had earlier migrated to the US in search of greener IT pastures are returning to India to work. By doing so, they seek to combine a comfortable lifestyle with a sense of belonging and comfort that their children will be exposed to 'Indian family values'. However, this return, often based on a nostalgic yearning for the past, turns out to be problematic as people find that 'things have changed'. They are more intolerant of dirt and sloppiness, comparing the present 'here' with their more affluent, efficient and 'clean' life experienced 'there', abroad. Also, they note with concern the increasing Western influences on their children as a result of globalisation, comparing their own upbringing with that of the 'new generation'.

In summary, place and space are socially constructed configurations in the time-space continuum, holding diverse meanings. GSOs are sites that are both embedded in as well as embed globalisation processes in the form of multiple mobilities related to GSW. Various mobilities within and between geographical or physical, social, career-related and existential realms illustrate processes of 'to and fro' movement across places and spaces that is constant, intense, unpredictable and ever-present. These intersecting mobilities are directly influenced by local particularities such as class and position in the section of Indian society occupied by this group of workers. Individuals and GSOs cope with the influences of mobilities by trying to recreate what they have left behind, whether it is creating their home in the office or vice versa, or their homeland in the foreign country and vice versa. Such movements can be contrasted with earlier mobilities such as migration and the formation of diasporas, where the process was more one way and predictable. While this state of 'to and froing' is not unproblematic, it refutes the argument that place is a fixed and bounded area, providing a sense of rootedness and an unproblematic identity in a globalising world. Also, the nature of 'permanent transience' noted among IT workers includes place-based identifications as opposed to the fragmentation, disorientation, and sense of placelessness associated with ICT-mediated changes that have significantly reconfigured space–place relations (e.g., Giddens 1990; Friedland and Boden 1994; Harvey 1989).

Conclusion

More often than not, mobility is an uneven and unpredictable process in which the hope of going in some upward direction is counterbalanced by the risks of the profession, market, industry, as well as norms of social relations and the individual's conditioning and beliefs. We conceptualise these trajectories in terms of Massey's (1998) notion of 'nets of social relations' that are encased within worldwide GSW networks. These nets of social relations are inherently dynamic and changing, subject to diverse and sometimes contradictory temporal-spatial as well as cultural pressures and flows. Simultaneously, they are also local places where people assemble and continuously shift within social and professional networks across time and space. In this way, we can conceptualise GSW and

GSOs as increasingly locked into complex and co-evolving cycles of continuous interaction with, as well as reacting to, the global. Reflecting the inherent tensions between stasis and mobility, space and place, these cycles and relations are seen to forge the everyday lifeworlds of IT workers, resulting in an itinerant state of existence that we refer to as 'permanent transience'.

This work contributes to Urry's (2000) call for a sociology of mobilities by providing a detailed description of multiple mobilities and their intersections in the context of GSW. Resonating with Urry (2001), we can say that a distinctive feature of this industry is that IT workers 'dwell' within mobilities, and this contributes to the networked pattern of economic and social life in the GSO. It also reinforces the notion of the relation between the net and the self, as proposed by Castells (1996). This dialectical relation creates an experience of being 'betwixt and between' places and spaces, encased within globalisation flows along the 'technoscapes' (Appadurai 1996) of GSW. This state of being necessarily implicates, transforms and also produces new kinds of workers, identities, and networks of economic and social relations. We suggest that identities of the multiple interconnected levels of the worker, the firm, the industry and the market can be situated within a set of mobilities, rather than as confined to a single place, such as a specific geographical location. Rather than viewing global workspaces as locales that necessarily transcend place-based moorings, this chapter suggests that place cannot serve as an inert setting but must be viewed as a key axis in further conceptualising global workspaces and individual workers' identities and how they mutually constitute as well as construct each other.

Notes

1. Appadurai (1996) proposed five interrelated 'scapes' conceptualised as fluid, flowing and amorphous, as an alternative spatial rendering of the traditional global order. These include flows of people, technologies, money, images and information, and the spread of ideas such as democracy and freedom.
2. Appadurai uses this term to refer to the '... global configuration, also ever fluid, of technology and the fact that technology, both high and low, both mechanical and informational, now moves at high speed across various kinds of previously impervious boundaries' (1996: 34).
3. www.nasscom.org.
4. A Hindu religious ritual.

5. The second highest stratum in the traditional *varna* order, traditionally the warrior and ruling caste.
6. This term was introduced by Srinivas (1996) to refer to mobility processes of groups within the caste system. When a local, endogamous unit of the caste system acquired political power or became wealthy, it moved up the caste system by sanskritising itself, i.e., by imitating the customs rituals and lifestyle of a higher caste. Over time, noble origins could be claimed.
7. Kanter (1995) has described this concept in her book, *World Class: Thriving Locally in the Global Economy.*
8. A popular game at such gatherings is *antakshari,* a musical game based on songs from Hindi films. This game is immensely popular in India and is also played at company events or social gatherings at IN-Sync.
9. Easy going, let it be attitude.

References

Appadurai, A. 1990. Disjuncture and Difference in the Global Cultural Economy. *Theory, Culture and Society* 7(2&3): 295–310.

———. 1996. *Modernity at Large: Cultural Dimensions of Globalisation.* Minneapolis: University of Minnesota Press.

Arthur, M.B. and D.M. Rousseau. 1996. Introduction. In M.B. Arthur and D.M. Rousseau (eds), *The Boundaryless Career: A New Employment Principle for a New Organisational Era,* pp. 3–20. New York: Oxford University Press.

Casey, E.S. 1997. *The Fate of Place: A Philosophical History.* California: University of California Press.

Castells, M. 1996. *The Rise of the Network Society.* Oxford and Malden, Massachusetts: Blackwell Publishing.

———. 2001. *The Internet Galaxy.* Oxford: Blackwell Publishing.

D'Costa, A.P. 2004. The Indian Software Industry in the Global Division of Labour. In A.P. D'Costa and E. Sridharan (eds), *India in the Global Software Industry,* pp. 1–26. New York: Macmillan Palgrave.

D'Mello, M. 2005. 'Thinking Local, Acting Global': Issues of Identity and Related Tensions in Global Software Organisations in India. *Electronic Journal for Information Systems in Developing Countries* (EJISDC) 22(2): 1–20.

D'Monte, D. 2002. *Ripping the Fabric: The Decline of Mumbai and its Mills.* New Delhi: Oxford University Press.

Dahles, H. and L. Stobbe. 2004. Managing Cohesion in Transnational Organisations: An Introduction. *Culture and Organisation* 10(4): 267–72.

Friedland, R. and D. Boden. 1997. NowHere: An Introduction to Space, Time and Modernity. In R. Friedland and D. Boden (eds), *NowHere Space, Time and Modernity,* pp. 1–60. London: University of California Press.

Giddens, A. 1990. *The Consequences of Modernity.* Cambridge: Polity Press.

Gilleard, J. and J.D. Gilleard. 2002. Developing Cross-Cultural Communication Skills. *Journal of Professional Issues in Engineering Education and Practice,* (October) 128(4): 187–200.

Harvey, D. 1989. *The Condition of Postmodernity: An Enquiry into the Origins of Cultural Change.* Cambridge, Massachusetts: Blackwell Publishing.

Heeks, R. 1996. *India's Software Industry: State Policy, Liberalisation and Industrial Development*. New Delhi: Sage Publications.

Jarvenpaa, S.L. and D.E. Leidner. 1999. Communication and Trust in Global Virtual Teams. *Organisation Science*, 10(6): 791–815.

Kakihara, M. and C. Sørenson. 2002. 'Post-modern Professionals' Work and Mobile Technology. *IRIS* 25, Copenhagen Business School, Denmark.

Kanter, R.M. 1995. *World Class: Thriving Locally in the Global Economy*. New York: Simon & Schuster.

Lash, S. and U. Urry. 1996. *Economies of Signs and Space*. London: Sage Publications.

Lipnack, J. and J. Stamps. 1997. *Virtual Teams: Reaching Across Space, Time and Organisations with Technology*. New York: John Wiley and Sons.

Malone, T.W. and R.J. Laubacher. 1998. The Dawn of the e-lance Economy. *Harvard Business Review* 76(5): 145–53.

Massey, D. 1998. *Space, Place and Gender*. Cambridge, UK: Polity Press.

National Association of Software and Services Companies (NASSCOM) 2005. *Strategic Review: The IT Industry in India*. New Delhi: NASSCOM.

Patel, S. 1995. Bombay's Urban Predicament. In S. Patel and A. Thorner (eds), *Bombay: Metaphor for Modern India*, pp. xi–xxxiii. Bombay: Oxford University Press.

Sahay, S., B. Nicholson and S. Krishna. 2003. *Global IT Outsourcing: Software Development Across Borders*. Cambridge: Cambridge University Press.

Schultze, U. and R.J. Boland, Jr. 2000. Place, Space and Knowledge Work: A Study of Out-sourced Computer Systems Administrators. *Accounting Management and Information Technologies*, 10: 187–219.

Srinivas, M.N. 1996. *Caste: Its Twentieth Century Avatar*. New Delhi: Viking.

Srinivas, S. 2005. Stress Kills 6 IT Geeks (India). *The Asian Age*, Chennai.

Tuan, Y.F. 1977. *Space and Place: The Perspective of Experience*. Minneapolis: University of Minnesota Press.

Urry, J. 2000. Mobile Sociology. *British Journal of Sociology*, 51(1): 185–203.

———. 2001. *Sociology Beyond Societies: Mobilities for the Twenty-First Century*. London: Routledge.

4

Management of Culture and Managing through Culture in the Indian Software Outsourcing Industry

Carol Upadhya

The rise of the software and information technology (IT) enabled services industry in India is emblematic of the latest phase in the development of global capitalism, in which services and 'knowledge' work are increasingly relocated from the post-industrial economies to low-cost locations in the developing world. The development of enclaves of high-tech offshore production and services (as well as low-end services such as call centres) in industrialising countries such as India raises new questions about globalisation, labour and cultural identity. First, the outsourcing of IT services across national borders, and the organisation of software development projects through multicultural, multi-sited 'virtual teams', have foregrounded the question of culture and cultural difference in the corporate workplace. Second, key sites of global capitalism such as Bangalore's IT industry have produced culturally marked categories of globalised technical workers who are linked into the global economy in novel, technology-mediated ways. The emergence of the figure of the Indian software engineer in the global cultural economy is the outcome of several processes, both discursive and practical. These include theories and techniques of 'cross-cultural' or 'global' management that have been developed to manage multinational workforces; the specific conditions and modes of organisation that govern outsourced offshore work, such as the 'virtual team'; and the transnational work experiences of both Indian software engineers and their Western counterparts, which have produced standardised narratives about cultural difference that in turn structure interactions in the workplace and shape the subjectivities of workers.

This chapter draws on interviews and observations carried out in Bangalore and Europe to explore the discursive construction of the Indian software engineer as a new type of global technical worker and the deployment of this discourse as a mechanism of control over work and workers. The ethnographic material illustrates the ways in which global capital subjects Indian software engineers to an array of conflicting cultural discourses and techniques that invoke 'culture' to mould them into competent global professionals, while simultaneously marking them as different and invoking this difference as a strategy of control.[1] I also argue that such discursive strategies, although integral to the management of the contemporary global workplace and linked to structures of power, are never totalising, and that the very nature of the culturalist management ideology leaves scope for play, critique and resistance by its subjects—Indian software engineers.

Culture, Labour and Management in the Global Economy

With the advent of the post-industrial 'informational' economy (Castells 1996), processes of economic and cultural globalisation are becoming ever more interdependent. As capital seeks new sites of investment and new markets, it invokes, plays upon, appropriates, and transforms pre-existing cultural tropes and images, creating and recreating new forms of cultural difference and social identities. According to Ong, the emerging 'cultural logics' of globalisation involve the '... reciprocal construction of practice, gender, ethnicity, race, class, and nation in processes of capital accumulation' (1999: 5). This process is, of course, not new: the history of global capitalism is replete with examples of the appropriation and generation of ethnic, racial and gender identities in the creation of specific categories of workers, for instance the emergence of new feminised workforces in Southeast Asia and Latin America in the 1970s as a result of export-oriented industrialisation (Mills 2003; Ong 1991). In earlier periods as well, culturally marked labour forces were created to service the plantations and mines of colonial economies, such as tribal 'coolies' in India (Ghosh 1999; Prakash 1990). Most of the recent literature on the segmentation of the labour force by gender, ethnicity and race is concerned with industrial workers in the 'global assembly line', such as women in the global garment factories of Mexico or Indonesia, while much less attention has been paid to the emergence and cultural marking of professional, technical and managerial global workers.[2] Yet the processes that create gendered, ethnicised and racial hierarchies within the global labour market are similar in both cases. Nurses from Kerala working in the US, transnational Chinese businessmen (Ong 1999), and Indian IT professionals are examples of professional, entrepreneurial, and technical groups that are culturally defined and slotted into specific niches in the global economy.

This is not to argue that the workforce is 'segmented' by capital in a straightforward or mechanical way. The deployment or creation of cultural identities in the service of capital is a dialectical process in which pre-existing cultural communities, gendered identities or racially marked groups are transformed into labour forces that perform particular roles in the production process, which in turn marks these social identities with the stamp of capital. For instance, the type of work that is performed or the working conditions have implications for the reconstitution or reinforcement of masculinities or femininities (Mills 2003). The intersections between capital and cultural identity become ever more complex as globalisation gathers pace and both 'cultures' and identities get increasingly commoditised, becoming the subject of capital itself (du Gay and Pryke 2002).

In the case of Indian software engineers, the threatening but also comical (as in the Dilbert comic strip) image of the Indian techie is stock-in-trade for anti-outsourcing ideologues. Such ethnicised images circulate within the global cultural economy and can be invoked by different actors for their own ends. For many Indians, the figure of the Indian techie represents the success of the IT industry, which has finally thrust India onto the world stage, and is cited as evidence of Indians' greater intelligence and skill in technology fields, while to some Americans it only represents cheap labour out to steal their jobs. Thus, there is a complex ideological dimension to the construction of new global workforces, which encompasses hegemonic discourses that emanate from politicians, corporates and the global media as well as contestations by the subjects of these discourses—or what Ong (1991) terms 'cultural struggles'—that produce counter-narratives and alternative images. As Freeman observes, '… states, transnational corporations, and local groups of social and economic actors both challenge and support each other as they face new sets of circumstances and contexts for enacting power and identities' (2000: 30). In this section, two currents in contemporary management ideology that pervade the global corporate world and produce culturally segmented workforces, as well as new kinds of working subjects, are examined.

Global Management

While there are substantial bodies of literature in sociology and anthropology on globalisation and labour (e.g., Kelly 1983; Nash and Kelly 1983), cultural processes in the formation of new workforces under capitalism and cultural forms of resistance (Ong 1987), and on globalisation and identity formation in general (Appadurai 1997; Featherstone 1990; Friedman 1994), one facet of these processes that has been less well studied is the role of transnational management ideologies and practices. The increasing integration of the global economy through networks of production and services and the activities of transnational corporations has brought companies, workers, managers and customers located in different 'geographies' into close interaction. Those who work in globalised workplaces, whether they are employed in multinational enterprises in their own countries, travel to other sites for work or are engaged in 'virtual migration' (Aneesh 2006; Freeman 2000), are forced to grapple with questions of cultural difference. For multinational and internationally networked companies as well, globalisation has foregrounded the question of culture as they do business across borders and with people from various cultural backgrounds, attempt to create new markets for their products, or establish subsidiaries in offshore locations to take advantage of cheaper wage rates. For this reason, the management of cultural difference has become a key problem for international management theory, which has generated a distinct discourse and set of techniques for 'cross-cultural' or 'global' management. These theories and practices are a major source for the production of cultural difference in the corporate world and perhaps beyond it as well.

The bible of international cultural management is Geert Hofstede's *Culture's Consequences: International Differences in Work-Related Values* (1980a), which engendered this new area of training and practice and stimulated a large body of research based on his 'cultural values' framework (Kirkman et al. 2001).[3] In this literature, national cultures are categorised according to various 'pattern variable' schemes that are based primarily on Parsonian modernisation theories as well as an older tradition of anthropology, such as the work of Ruth Benedict, on 'national cultures'. This analysis is then used to develop strategies for more effective intercultural communication and cooperation. Hofstede's original schema is based on four basic 'dimensions of culture': individualism–collectivism, power distance, uncertainty avoidance and masculinity–femininity.[4] This framework has been widely used by Western multinational companies to achieve a 'fit' between the organisational culture (usually American or European) and the dominant cultural values of employees of subsidiaries located in other countries by highlighting and negotiating cultural differences (Kirkman et al. 2001: 13).

Software companies in India, both Indian and multinational, utilise these theories of cross-cultural management to develop training programmes and techniques to aid in the integration of their 'virtual teams'. Offshore software projects are usually carried out across national borders using sophisticated computer and telecommunications technologies. The problems in coordination that arise from the geographical dispersion of work are addressed in part through strategies aimed at promoting better cross-cultural communication and collaboration. But while these management strategies apparently embrace the idea of multiculturalism, they also valorise a singular model of 'global corporate culture' into which Indian software engineers are expected to fit.

'New Age' Management and the 'Entrepreneurial Employee'

With the increasing integration of the global economy, diverse management styles (American, German, Japanese) have tended to merge together into a single dominant model—an ideal type 'global' corporate culture that every company, worker and manager must work towards in order to compete in the global market. Most IT companies operating in India—both Indian and multinational—follow, or attempt to follow, this model. The 'new model' corporation—or what was referred to by an HR manager we interviewed as 'new age management'—was developed primarily in the US and embodies

American cultural values such as egalitarianism, teamwork and individual initiative. The preferred structure of the modern corporation has shifted from the earlier hierarchical, bureaucratic and centralised model with direct systems of control, towards more open, 'flat', flexible, networked organisational structures that are designed to 'empower' rather than regulate employees. By minimising hierarchy, bureaucracy, and formal procedures, the 'new workplace' is supposed to give more autonomy to workers and encourage individual initiative and creativity, thereby stimulating greater productivity as well as employee satisfaction (Gephart 2002).

The 'new workplace' is considered to be typical of the post-industrial 'information economy' and is exemplified by Silicon Valley's informal, individualistic work culture. In the rapidly changing software industry, maximum scope for autonomy and creativity is given to programmers in order to promote product innovation. The new model corporation thus produces and requires a new kind of individualised working subject, the 'entrepreneurial' worker (Beck 2000).[5] Rather than being controlled and directed by the management, employees are managed primarily through indirect and subjective 'cultural' techniques (Kunda 1992). Self-management by workers is a defining feature of the new work systems, whose key words are 'autonomy', 'empowerment' and 'self-motivation'. Work is driven by the ethic of individualisation in which workers (especially professionals and technical labour) focus on completing individual deliverables and on doing high visibility work to achieve personal goals (Perlow 1997: 34, quoted in Gephart 2002: 335).

In addition, the culture and organisation of large corporations around the world is increasingly based on a hegemonic model of 'global best practices' that they must follow if they want to succeed in the global marketplace. Because Indian software companies position themselves as 'global', they also tend to follow these practices and to replicate the global corporate model described above. Thus, there are two rather contradictory cultural processes at work in the practice and ideology of global management—one that recognises, draws upon, generates, and validates cultural difference, and another that attempts to erase difference by imposing a single ideal of corporate and business practice.[6]

Ong suggests that to understand the multifarious effects of the expansion of global capitalism into developing countries such as India, we must pay attention to the '… regulatory effects of particular cultural institutions, projects, regimes, and markets that shape people's motivations, desires, and struggles and make them particular kinds of subjects in the world …' (1999: 5–6). Below, the management regime that operates within the Indian software outsourcing industry to produce a 'particular kind of subject'—the global Indian IT professional—is explored. This regime invokes and utilises ideas about Indian culture and cultural difference in the management of Indian software workers, even as it attempts to mould them into competent, self-directed global professionals who are able to function effectively in the new corporate workplace. In particular, several sites for the discursive production of the 'Indian techie', and some of the ways in which cultural typing is employed in management ideology and practice, are examined.[7]

Enculturing the Global Software Professional

Most outsourced software projects are carried out by teams composed primarily of Indian software development engineers located in India ('offshore'), who interface with customers, colleagues and managers located at the client site ('onsite') or one of their company's other offices located in the US or Western Europe. This means that many software engineers employed by companies located in Bangalore, Hyderabad or Mumbai work as part of 'virtual teams' whose members are distributed in different locations. Outsourced service work has two dimensions—much of it is carried out 'offshore', with work being performed remotely (or 'virtually') through sophisticated information and communication technologies (Aneesh 2006), but it also requires physical mobility as Indian software engineers are sent to their client's offices to work 'onsite' or to other locations of the parent company. Offshore and onsite work are both essential components of most outsourced IT projects, and the common element is that both kinds of work entail the close interaction of Indian IT professionals with their clients, colleagues and managers in other countries—both 'virtually' or remotely and face-to-face. The management of such multi-sited projects and multicultural virtual teams presents a specific set of issues to both client companies and Indian service providers—issues that are usually framed in terms of cultural difference and are sought to be resolved in part through the management of culture.

Effective communication across locations and among culturally diverse employees is increasingly regarded as key to the success of software outsourcing projects, as well as a major weakness of the Indian IT industry. At some point in their careers, most Indian software engineers must interact and collaborate with foreign customers or colleagues, either in person or remotely, through conference calls, emails and other electronic media. This interaction and communication is considered to be crucial to the management of software projects and constitutes a major site of slippage. Most managers interviewed said that they frequently receive complaints from customers and parent companies about the 'poor communication skills' of their engineers. The problem that they identify is not so much unfamiliarity with English as lack of the appropriate social skills and communication styles needed to interact effectively with foreign customers and colleagues. To address this problem, the Human Resource (HR) departments of most Indian software companies organise frequent 'soft skills' training programmes for engineers—especially communication and 'inter-cultural' skills. These programmes are aimed at moulding the personalities of software engineers and inculcating the behaviour patterns, social skills, and cultural styles that are required to interact with foreign (mainly Western) colleagues and clients, and which are deemed to be appropriate to the global workplace. Apart from communication skills (business communication, presentation skills, how to write emails and conduct conference calls, etc.) and 'cultural sensitivity' training, a range of soft skills training is offered by many companies, such as time management, team-building, and management or leadership skills, all of which feed (in various ways) into the production of the self-managed, individualised worker. This paper focuses primarily on cultural and communication skills programmes, and on how cultural difference is both erased and constructed through them.

In the early days of the software industry in India, cultural training programmes were often designed on an ad hoc basis by outsourcing companies or 'bodyshoppers'[8] to acculturate engineers to the countries where they were sent for onsite jobs. They focused on imparting advice on social etiquette, table manners, local food habits, appropriate dress and so on. Gradually, cultural training became more organised and professionalised and a category of professional cross-cultural trainers emerged (across the world and not only in India) to cater to this demand. Today, most of the major Indian software companies as well as multinationals provide at least minimal training in the culture (i.e., 'customs and manners') of the countries to which engineers are being sent, especially when they are going there for the first time. Trainers explain the niceties of social manners in the target country, such as what kind of suit to wear for what occasion or how to make small talk with the boss's wife, or they tell trainees not to waste time in the office in idle chat or to ask their co-workers personal questions. An employee of an MNC posted temporarily in Germany described his company's 'cultural sensitivity' training in this way:

> These inter-cultural and etiquette training sessions are more for fresh recruits, like those who have recently graduated or never been abroad before, or with very little work experience. It's more for those technical guys, who have to meet and interact with whites for the first time. We even have personal grooming sessions and we tell them not to use hair oils but gels, use deos and don't put too much talcum powder, because it all shows and looks bad ... things like that. We tell them not to wear white socks ... guys shouldn't wear white socks for formal occasions, since it gives a sporty look. Here it's more like Mondays are for formals and Fridays are for casuals and on other days smart casuals ... Of course it's all unwritten and we don't really follow it. There's no one around telling us what to wear and what to do anyway!

Although this kind of coaching in etiquette continues, cultural training has now become more sophisticated and broader in scope, and trainers incorporate psychological and anthropological theories in order to explain cultural differences and to teach engineers how to change their behaviour. Such training is aimed not only at engineers going abroad but also at improving communication within multi-cultural virtual teams. In fact, cultural sensitivity and communication skills training are often combined in the same programme, because communication problems in multi-sited projects are usually attributed to the cultural gap between Indian software engineers and people at the client site or head office. As the manager in charge of soft skills training in an Indian software major said:

> Four years ago, we got this feedback from the clients. They said our engineers have very good technical skills, but when sitting across a table, there is hardly anything to talk about. When we got this feedback, we realised that our techies do not understand

the clients' interest areas. There was a clear frequency mismatch. Hence we had to start cross-cultural sensitivity programmes.

Clients had reported that the techies who come for onsite projects do not socialise with their local colleagues, so the company wanted to mould its engineers into 'good business professionals' by teaching them about other cultures and inculcating them with social skills. The programme that was designed to address this problem includes modules on general communication skills, corporate etiquette (how to write emails and use the phone) and basic manners (don't stand too close to a lady in the elevator). Participants are acquainted with norms of behaviour in foreign countries, such as differences between American and Indian notions of sociability and distance. Appropriate and inappropriate behaviour in the corporate setting is also discussed, including repeated warnings about behaviour towards women that might be construed as sexual harassment.

'Cultural Sensitivity' Training

Having observed several 'cultural sensitivity' and inter-cultural communication programmes offered by software companies in Bangalore, we found that they all tend to draw on the standard cross-cultural management theories discussed above and to follow a similar pattern. While Hofstede-type theories of global cultural management are intended to promote better inter-cultural communication and collaboration, in Indian software companies this training appears to be oriented more to fit Indian techies into the dominant culture of the global workplace. To illustrate this, a communication skills programme that was offered by one of the top soft skills consultants in Bangalore for employees of the overseas software development centre of an American IT major is described in detail.[9] This five-day workshop covered a range of topics; only a few of the salient paints are discussed here.

The trainer, a young Irish woman,[10] first explained to the participants the concept of culture, citing common definitions revolving around 'shared values', 'ways of behaving', and so on. She then asked participants to describe the features of different cultures (Indian, American, etc.) and to describe their own cultures. She used the variety of answers that were given to make the point that identity is context-dependent and flexible (whether I identify myself as Indian, Tamil, South Indian, Iyer, etc., depends on the context and to whom

I am speaking). She then gave the participants a small lecture on ethnocentrism, saying that cultures are 'neither good nor bad, just different'.[11] These preliminaries were apparently aimed at preparing the participants to relativise their own cultures and to accept certain aspects of Western or 'global corporate' culture.

Drawing on the standard typology of national cultures found in the cross-cultural management literature (based primarily on Hofstede's framework), the trainer outlined the differences between two of the 'mainstream cultures':

(1) Pluralistic—the 'WASP' cultures (Australian, Canadian, American), characterised by:

- individualism
- personal achievement
- orientation to career
- materialism
- change as progress
- lifestyle diversity

(2) Extended family cultures—(Latin American, African, Middle Eastern, Indian) characterised by:

- social structure built around the family
- importance of where you are from
- authoritarian power structure
- family as source of social identity
- business carried out within a network
- minimal social change
- sharp gender differences
- tradition-bound
- religious

She then argued that corporate cultures around the world are merging into a common 'global corporate culture' model and suggested that we need to accept this global culture because it is now the dominant one. This dominant global corporate culture is based on the 'pluralistic' or 'WASP' type, which contrasts with the 'extended family culture' of India—a juxtaposition that clearly reflects the hoary social science dichotomy between the traditional and the modern.

Having neatly catalogued the differences between Indian and global corporate culture, the trainer's next task was to convince her audience that they can adapt their behaviour and communication style to the culture of the global workplace without giving up their 'own culture'. She repeatedly drew a distinction between 'behavioural changes' and changes in 'core values', to drive home the point that you can change superficial behaviour patterns in order to fit into the global workplace without losing your own identity. She asked the participants to accept the notion that 'I can behave differently during my eight hours at work in order to help my career, without changing myself fundamentally'.

What are these behavioural changes that are required? At work, she said, you have to be assertive and direct, especially when inter-acting with the Americans in your team. To illustrate these differences in communication and behavioural style, she outlined two different personality types marked by distinctive behaviour patterns:

(1) 'Linear active':

- plans ahead methodically
- likes privacy
- punctual
- dominated by timetables
- sticks to plans
- completes action chains
- separates social and professional life

(2) 'Multi-active' type:

- inquisitive
- multi-tasking
- works any hours
- timetable unpredictable
- completes human transactions
- changes plans and juggles facts
- people oriented
- pulls strings
- interweaves the social and professional

According to the trainer, the first type is typical of behaviour in the corporate world and is linked to the 'WASP' or 'pluralistic' culture, while the second is more typical of India. She then had the following discussion with the participants:

> Trainer: If the corporate world expects and behaves in the linear active mode, while you belong to the multiactive type, then what needs to be done?
> Participant: I need to change myself.
> Trainer: Are you comfortable with that?
> Participant: It will help me in my career.

But a woman participant argued with the trainer, saying that she could choose her own style of working (such as 'multiactive') and 'still produce results':

> Participant: Why don't others adopt the multiactive style [i.e., why should we adopt their style]?
> Trainer: We have to be realistic—who dominates in the corporate world? It's the US, and the American system is what has come to characterise the corporate world all over, so we have no choice but to follow that style.

This training programme was clearly aimed at getting Indian software engineers to understand American or global corporate culture so that they can behave appropriately in that context, but also to make the process non-threatening and acceptable by convincing them that adapting their behaviour to these cultures does not entail giving up their own 'culture' or values. As another cultural trainer argued, 'It's not about changing culture, it's not a one-way process. Instead of a tug-of-war, we are trying to create a third culture' (i.e., the culture of the global workplace). But note that this 'global culture' embodies modernist values and expects its employees to transform themselves into modern, individualised and self-directed subjects.

One effect of these cultural training programmes is that the world gets divided into distinct culturally-defined workforces and locales that must be integrated into a functioning network. Indians, Americans, Germans and other nationalities are catalogued according to a list of typical cultural and personality traits. Ironically, this process of cultural classification is critiqued by trainers when they give their lessons on the evils of ethnocentrism and ethnic prejudices. In one training session, for instance, the trainer pointed out that most people have preconceived ideas, or stereotypes, about what others are like. He asked the participants to list the characteristics that they associate with American culture and Americans. Their list included:

- Easy-going
- Casual in dress
- Punctual
- Professional
- Orderly
- Organised
- Rich
- Specific/to the point
- Social
- Forthright
- Good communicators

He then asked them to list how they think Americans see them (Indians):

- Conservative/traditional
- Hard working
- 24/7
- IST ('Indian Standard Time', a joke about Indians always being late)
- Intelligent
- Bad communicators
- Family values
- Varied culture
- Poor
- Not forthright
- Hospitable

Not surprisingly, many of the characteristics the participants listed were the negative ones that are commonly attributed to Indian software engineers in the industry (poor communicators, no sense of time), but they also included other traits that are associated with the image of the Indian techie that circulates in the global economy—'sloggers' who are willing to work round the clock (this stereotype is discussed in the following section). The trainer used this exercise to argue that it is important to 'break such stereotypes' if we want to create more 'cultural awareness' and better inter-cultural communication. Yet, the creation, reproduction, and deployment of stereotypes is precisely what much of this sort of training does, and the cultural images that were voiced by the participants were much the same as those that are retailed by trainers.

Thus, there are two processes happening simultaneously in these culture and communication programmes. On the one hand, cultural difference is validated and trainees are told that 'no culture is good or bad, cultures are just different', while on the other hand they are told that they must learn to adapt to the now-dominant 'global corporate culture' (which is based on the Anglo-Saxon 'pluralistic' culture) because, implicitly, their own culture is not suitable to that context.

Producing the 'Empowered' Worker

Another key area of soft skills training for software engineers is personality development and assertiveness training, using standard psychological theories such as Transactional Analysis (TA) and Myers Briggs Type Indicator (MBTI™). These programmes have been introduced in response to feedback often given by customers to HR managers that Indian engineers are too passive and have a 'feudal' mindset. Frequent comments include: they 'always say yes' even when they cannot complete the work given; they require 'micro-management' and constantly want positive reinforcement from managers, and they do not 'take ownership' of their work. These programmes attempt to teach software engineers to be self-directed and to take independent decisions. Because one of the reasons for poor communication skills is supposed to be lack of assertiveness (which in turn is considered to be a cultural characteristic of Indian engineers), some soft skills training consultants include modules on assertiveness training in their communication skills workshops.

The demand for psychology-based training is linked to the fact that most software companies have adopted the 'new age' management style discussed above. Most of the CEOs and HR (Human Resource) managers that we interviewed, as well as many employees, described their companies as having more 'open' work cultures and 'flatter' and more flexible structures, compared to the rigid, authoritarian and hierarchical cultures of 'traditional' Indian companies (especially the once dominant public sector companies). Of course, these statements reflect the official position and not necessarily the reality, but what is significant here is that Indian software companies have self-consciously adopted the contemporary international management ideology that stresses employee 'empowerment' and self-management. This explains why managers and foreign clients often complain that Indian engineers are too passive and subservient, needing continual direction and feedback, and why these companies attempt to mould their engineers into proactive and self-motivated workers. But in the context of the Indian software services industry, this demand appears to be more ideological than real, for while managers and customers voice their desire for autonomous and creative engineers, the industry's actual requirement is for a malleable, flexible and passive workforce. Moreover, although managers pay lip service to employee autonomy and empowerment, many companies in fact have imposed rigid top-down systems of organisational control that appear to contradict the dominant management ideology (Upadhya and Vasavi 2006: Chap. 6).

The deployment of this battery of psychological, behavioural, and cultural theories and techniques in the contemporary workplace is discussed in detail in Sathaye's article (chapter 5 in this volume). Here, the connections between this kind of training and the production of a new kind of working subject in the context of the software outsourcing industry is highlighted. From a critical perspective, soft skills training can be understood as an organisational practice aimed at ideological control over the workforce; rather than empowering employees, it is associated with 'domination, disempowerment, and undemocratic practices' (Ogbor 2001). Corporate training programmes, especially of the 'soft skills' variety, require trainees to acknowledge a lack in themselves, which they are encouraged to remedy by transforming themselves into the management-approved personality type. Employees are expected to learn and display modes of behaviour and attitudes deemed appropriate to the corporate workplace, and assimilationist themes such as 'organisational fit' and 'team play' are highlighted. Through training in interpersonal and communication skills, self-appraisal systems, and so on, '… employees are provided with the skills that enable them to regulate themselves in the absence of managerial gaze—an "internalised panopticon" [Boje 1993], where employees turn the disciplinary gaze on themselves through the assimilation of cultural values and norms' (Ogbor 2001).[12] In particular, the new knowledge-intensive 'high tech' workplaces depend on the deployment of diverse 'technologies of the self' as a means of domination (Deetz 1998). In the case of Indian software companies, employees are expected to adapt themselves to the culture of the global workplace by transforming their personalities and interactional styles. But this process is built upon the delineation and juxtaposition of objectified images of 'Indian' and 'Western/global' work culture.

This leads us to ask: What are the regulatory effects of the extensive cultural psychological training to which IT workers are subjected? Is there a more subtle logic operating behind the 'culturalisation' of management? Should cultural/psychological profiling be understood as a mechanism of control over labour or as a method through which particular kinds of worker–subjects are produced? To answer these questions, in the following section the narratives of software engineers and managers about cultural difference, and the role that this discourse of difference plays in the management of outsourced software projects and onsite engineers, are examined.

Controlling Labour through Culture

The construction of national–cultural differences through cross-cultural management theory and cultural training programmes is echoed in the narratives of Indian software engineers and their managers, both Indian and Western.[13] For instance, cultural profiles similar to those imparted by cultural trainers are invoked by managers and clients of software companies to explain why Indian software engineers are not behaving or performing as expected. The discourse of culture emerges most sharply in 'onsite' situations, where Indian software engineers tend to explain and negotiate the conflicts and problems they experience in terms of cultural difference. This section explores the ways in which the discursive construction of cultural difference identified in the narratives of both Europeans and Indians involved in outsourced software projects operates as a regulatory practice in controlling transnational software labour, in the process producing culturally marked working subjects.

Discursive Constructions of Cultural Difference

On closer investigation, the often-repeated claim that Indian software engineers lack appropriate social and communication skills points to a much wider discourse about cultural difference that structures relationships in the context of outsourced software projects. Interviews with Indian software engineers and managers in India and Europe revealed that typical notions about differences in work culture are retailed by both sides. The differences that are often cited include:[14]

- Indian work culture is hierarchical and feudal, as opposed to the more egalitarian culture in Europe. For instance, Indians tend to treat their managers with deference and find it difficult to say no to them, whereas European managers treat their subordinates as equals and employees are more assertive. As the Dutch owner of a small software company said: 'The Indians always said yes for everything, even if you asked them to do something impossible'.
- Europeans are good at organisation, planning, and time management, in contrast to the inefficiency of Indians. These traits are associated with the greater 'professionalism' of Westerners in general, and the longer working hours kept by Indian employees is often explained or justified by reference to their lack of 'professionalism' and poor organisation.
- Europeans value their leisure and private family time and maintain a good work-life balance; one consequence of this is that they strictly adhere to office hours, unlike Indian engineers.[15]

This discursive construction of Indian-European differences in work culture is central to the way in which both European and Indian managers handle outsourced projects and Indian software engineers. For instance, managers often invoke these cultural differences to account for differences in working habits and communication problems, and they develop management strategies to overcome what they define as 'inter-cultural' problems within their organisations. The major strategy employed is to induce behavioural changes in employees through the kind of soft skills and cultural sensitivity training programmes described above. For example, Andrea,[16] the anthropologist who is in charge of 'Indo-German team integration' for a major German company, organises workshops such as 'Getting to Know Germany', inter-cultural training for Indian techies in Germany, as well as a cultural sensitisation programme for German engineers who work with Indians.[17] She enumerated the 'intercultural difficulties' faced by the company as:

- 'power distance' or hierarchical mindset of Indians;
- 'task orientation' of Germans versus 'personal/relationship orientation' of Indians; and
- implicit communication style of Indians versus explicit style of Germans.

According to Andrea, the objective of these training programmes is not to mould Indian engineers to suit the German work atmosphere but rather to 'sensitise' both Indian and German employees to cultural differences. However, she conceded that in practice more changes are expected from the Indians than from their German counterparts. For instance, Indians are perceived as needing constant supervision and guidance ('micro-management')—a characteristic that clashes with German work culture—and training interventions are designed to make Indian techies more 'proactive' and independent. She stated:

I think it is necessary for Indians to learn to work independently (without any hand-holding or constant supervision). But generally we want to sensitise both the parties. In terms of work style, more adjustment is expected from the Indian side. We are just facilitators. There are some standardised procedures that we help them to follow.

Although Western companies expect Indian engineers to be proactive and self-managing, there are certain aspects of 'Indian work culture' that are seen as positive and are consciously sought to be retained. One of these is Indians engineers' alleged propensity for 'slogging'.

The 'Slogger' and the 'Time Slave'

A strategy that is now employed by Indian companies operating in Europe is to hire local people (in our study, German or Dutch) for 'customer facing roles'.[18] However, employing both Indians and Europeans in their European offices gives rise to a new set of problems, because it means having to negotiate between two different 'work cultures'. As a solution, the (Indian) head of an Indian software major's office in Germany said that they retain a 'strong Indian component' in the work culture of their local operations because most of the engineers are Indian, but they also integrate a 'German component' into it because their people 'should know how to handle German clients well'. When asked to define the elements of Indian work culture that they are trying to retain, he answered, 'ability to deliver at any cost'. To the researcher's query whether this simply means working long hours, he agreed: 'Of course there are many ways to do it. But the bottom line is there is a strong motivation to deliver goods at any cost. There is more willingness to do it [among Indians].'

Similarly, many respondents attributed the long working hours that are typical of the Indian IT industry to 'Indian work culture' and/or to inefficiency and poor organisational skills. Indeed, time is one of the major issues about which many software engineers and managers spoke: their narratives highlight the lack of time to do the things they want to do, the need for better time management, the pressure on time created by project deadlines, and especially the long working hours put in by Indians compared to Europeans. In part this focus on time is because long working hours are in fact typical of the Indian software industry, and managing time is one of the major problems faced by most managers and software engineers.[19] This pattern of overwork, referred to by one informant as 'time slavery', is justified by some managers in terms of the individual motivation and aspirations of employees, reflecting the individualised work ethic that is promoted by IT companies. This hinges on the self-motivation of 'entrepreneurial' employees who accept individual responsibility for completing work assigned, even if it means working very long hours.[20]

The difference in working hours and management of time was a key theme in informants' narratives about Western and Indian work culture. When asked to talk about these differences, Indian software engineers most often mentioned working hours, and this difference was often explained or justified in terms of Indian inefficiency and poor time management, in contrast to the greater efficiency and pro-ductivity of Europeans. It was also linked to the greater value placed on 'work-life balance' by Europeans, in contrast to Indians who are said to be willing to work '24/7'. It is significant that the difference in working hours, like so much management-speak, is cloaked in the garb of 'Indian culture'.[21] While many respondents complained about their extended working hours, for many it is a source of pride and a positive attribute of Indian work culture. A top manager of a large services company commented that long hours are 'part of our [Indian] psyche'.

The cultural justification for long hours masks the fact that it is largely the organisation of outsourced projects, the status of the employees, and the work culture of the Indian IT industry itself that account for the difference in working hours, rather than some abstract difference in 'work culture'. Of course, cultures of work are constructed within particular social and economic contexts: just as labour struggles within the industrial system of Europe gave rise to fixed working hours and extensive labour regulation, the specifics of transnational service work in the global informational economy produce 'flexible' labour regimes and extended and 'flexible' working hours. As relatively new players in the global IT industry, Indian companies and software engineers are under pressure to prove their individual and collective capability by working harder than their competitors.[22]

'Willingness to deliver at any cost' is a central element of the image of the Indian software worker that is circulating in the global economy. This produces resentment on the part of European and American co-workers who believe that it is the Indian techie's propensity to 'slog' for long hours at lower cost that poses the main threat to their jobs. This image is partially linked to anti-outsourcing rhetoric, but it should be noted that the Indian reputation for being 'sloggers' emerged before the backlash against outsourcing. It is also an image that enables and justifies the exploitation of onsite techies. Indian engineers working abroad are under pressure to work harder than locals in order to gain recognition. Remarks one engineer: 'We being Indians just have to work hard and can't take it easy or rest like the local people.'

The cultural marking of Indian techies as 'sloggers' may operate in practice as a justification for over-work. An engineer interviewed in the Netherlands said that he had left his previous company because they had expected him to learn new technical skills 'hands on', without any training. He remarked:

> I was in a hotel in Germany for one month, and each night I would be up till 3.00 a.m. reading manuals and learning stuff. Of course I could manage it, but it was hell. These people [the management] think, 'Oh Indians are sloggers after all, so they can learn things at short notice or as they start working'. I got fed up with that sort of mentality and that's one of the reasons I left.

This remark points to another key component of the Indian software worker's global image—his/her 'flexibility', which includes the ability to work on various technologies and platforms and to learn and adapt quickly to new work environments. Indian software services companies train their people to be 'generic programmers' so that they are able to work on all kinds of projects, a strategy that reinforces the Indian techie's reputation in the global software labour market for versatility, adaptability, and hard work (Upadhya and Vasavi 2006: 47–48). Indeed, apart from lower cost, this is one of the main selling points of Indian services companies.

Ideology in Practice

Managers of multi-sited or outsourced projects tend to attribute most problems and conflicts that arise to cultural differences, a strategy that effectively deflects attention away from organisational issues, deeper structural conditions, or contestations over power that could account for these conflicts. The following comment by an Indian manager suggests that it is not so much a propensity for disorganisation and poor planning on the part of Indian engineers, as demands from management, that account for long working hours: 'In Germany, everything is about planning. If something comes up at the last minute, they come and request us and make it sound like a favour. But in India, they think we can be asked to do anything any time.'

Although the idea that Indian software engineers work longer and harder than Europeans because they are inefficient, badly organised, and careless by nature appears to have been internalised by many of them, their narratives also reveal that the pressure to work often comes from above—whether they are in India or onsite in Europe. The economic (rather than cultural) roots of the Indian habit of 'slogging' were pointed to by several critical informants, as in the following remark: 'Mostly those who work on support [systems maintenance] go abroad and slog. They have to work both on Indian and American standard times. This means they have to work any time and be prepared to show up any time. They are forced to work overtime.'

Similarly, the frequent characterisation of Indian workers as having a 'feudal' or 'hierarchical' mindset ignores the structural context in which they work. Most Indian techies are in the position of contractors who have to cater to the client's needs and demands, and so can hardly afford to 'argue with the boss' as European employees are wont to do.

Also, onsite engineers must negotiate between the demands of their Indian employers and those of the European customers. The following comment by a Dutch manager points to structural factors that may also explain the alleged 'hierarchical' mindset of Indian engineers. He said that the engineers who came to work in his company on contract were not given a choice of assignment by their company (an Indian software services major), and could not leave until the job was done:

> Some adapted well, and others felt homesick throughout. But even those who were homesick and wanted to go back would stay on. They felt it was their duty to stay and do their work since their boss told them to. Basically the Indians do exactly what the boss says. Here we are spoiled—we can refuse work and argue with the boss. But the Indians are probably happy to have a job and so don't want to risk it.

In addition, the notion that Indian software engineers are not proactive and are too respectful of authority is linked to the 'process-driven' nature of management in large software companies. Andrea noted: 'It is much easier to introduce standardised procedures like CMM[23] among Indians because they find it easy to follow exactly what they are told. This tradition is not found in Germany.' This suggests that the same qualities that are derided by European and American managers (need for micro-management, willingness to 'follow directions') may be considered necessary and desirable for software engineers working in CMM Level 5 software services companies. What are labelled as Indian cultural characteristics, then, are largely produced by the nature of the work and the way in which software projects are organised.

More broadly, problems in managing outsourced projects or virtual teams may arise simply from the struggles over time, deadlines, and allotment of work that take place within any software development team.[24] A very similar situation has been described in the case of Irish programmers working in virtual teams for US clients (O Riain 2000), which suggests that there is nothing specifically 'Indian' about the cultural characteristics attributed to Indian engineers. As O Riain's study shows, there is a continual process of negotiation over these issues between engineers and managers, and among engineers within a team. When the team is a virtual or multi-sited one and is managed by a 'remote' manager (who is physically separated from most of the team members), these problems are exacerbated because the engineers have more leeway to strategise about the amount and kind of work they accept. In this struggle, rather than confronting the manager directly they may use indirect tactics to buy time or to avoid certain tasks, such as repeatedly asking for instructions or not completing work unless reminded. What are labelled as 'communication problems' may in fact be subtle forms of resistance that are linked to the 'politics of time' that characterises the contemporary workplace (O Riain 2000: 178). In the context of the Indian outsourcing industry, such behaviours may be interpreted by managers as 'cultural' in origin and understood as Indian personality traits. In such situations, the posited cultural difference between the multinational parent company and its Indian software centre, or between the foreign client and the Indian service provider, provides an acceptable explanation for problems. Rather than exploring the structural realities of the organisation of work in software outsourcing projects, managers attempt to resolve these problems by inducing behavioural and attitudinal changes in their employees through soft skills training and other such strategies.

The following remark by Andrea reveals how this discourse works in practice: 'Germans notice that there is more hierarchy among Indians. Indians expect more guidance from their superiors. There is also a bit of power distance—sometimes Indians keep information to themselves.' It is significant that she illustrated the point about 'power distance' and hierarchy with a comment about 'keeping information to themselves'. This points not only to the structural relationship between Indians and Germans (which is less egalitarian than managers of that company claimed), but also to a subtle strategy of resistance by Indian engineers that may stand in for overt assertiveness—withholding information from managers or other engineers. From other interviews as well, it appears that refusing to part with crucial information, or parcelling out information only to certain people, is a common strategy employed by software engineers as well as managers in negotiating their positions within their organisations.[25] It is also a tactic that is increasingly resorted to by European engineers whose projects are being moved to India. For instance, in one company we were told that German engineers dragged their feet on handing over key elements of a technology to the Indian engineers who had come to Germany on a 'transfer of technology' assignment. Thus, control over information and 'knowledge management' (itself an important management area in software companies) can be seen as key sites and strategies of struggle within software outsourcing projects, in which decisions to share or withhold knowledge are interpreted as stemming from Indian cultural traits.

The discussion in this section suggests that Indian software engineers are subjected to different and often contradictory demands and discourses: that they should be more 'dynamic' and proactive at work but still should be willing to follow directions and finish their work without reference to time; or that they should be more assertive and direct in their communication style but also compliant and service-oriented towards customers. The contradictions in these management discourses leave space for play, as software engineers may appropriate narratives of cultural difference in devising strategies to pursue their own ends.

Contradictions and Counter-narratives

As in any complex social process that is imbued with relations of power, questions about consent or resistance to the 'dominant ideology' (in this case, the management discourse about culture and cultural difference) must be foregrounded. While many of the software engineers we interviewed appear to have internalised the cultural stereotypes described above, several informants voiced subtle or overt counter-narratives that reject or critique the dominant discourse. In this section these alternative narratives and critical voices are highlighted in order to point to the complexities of the ideological operation of this discourse and to suggest that it, like any discourse, is not completely hegemonic.

Many of the Indian software engineers we interviewed were highly conscious of the cultural stereotypes about them that are held by their European colleagues, and have even internalised them. Some have attempted to overcome what they see as their own deficiencies by adapting to European work culture as well as to the larger society. These adjustments often take the form of personal emotional and behavioural restructuring, which most see as a positive step in their own personality development rather than a negative movement entailing loss of identity or culture. For instance, many informants mentioned that they have become more 'professional', 'organised', and time conscious as a result of working in Europe. However, informants also criticised some aspects of Western work culture. For instance, not all ascribed a positive value to the European habit of working limited hours and going on long vacations, and several were shocked by the fact that people in Holland easily take leave even when there is a project deadline approaching, which is 'unheard of in India'.

In cultural training programmes too, trainees do not necessarily accept what they are taught. Indeed, many are very critical of soft skills training—they may find it irrelevant, a waste of time, or even offensive, and few engineers reported that they found such training useful or insightful. During one workshop we observed, several participants repeatedly argued with the trainer about her characterisation of the Indian culture: while she attempted to elicit certain responses from them (for instance, about the authority structure of the Indian family), participants repeatedly challenged her generalisations with counter-examples. These exchanges suggest that trainees are not passive recipients of this potted cultural knowledge or are being mindlessly moulded into global workers. Similarly, as noted above, not everyone buys into the 'cultural' explanation for differences in working habits. An informant said: 'They [Germans] also want to achieve, like Indians, but their working hours are limited by labour laws; if they are made to work longer the union will take it up. It's not just a cultural thing—law frames culture.'

Just as the discourse of culture is reworked to suit the context and is deployed in diverse ways by managements, software engineers too may turn the discourse to their own advantage and use it to engage in 'cultural struggle' in the workplace (Ong 1991). Ailon-Souday and Kunda argue in their study of a globalising high-tech corporation in Israel that national identity is not a fixed attribute but a '... symbolic resource that is actively mobilised by members for the social goals of resistance' (2003: 1074). As in the Indian software industry, '... within corporations undergoing globalisation, organisational and national identities are constituted through relations of mutual inclusion rather than mutual exclusion and ... undergo transformations in the process' (Ailen-Souday and Kunda 2003: 1092). As this chapter shows, far from erasing or submerging national/cultural identities—as some theorists of the network society have suggested (Castells 1996; Poster 2002)—globalised workplaces invoke and deploy these identities in multifarious ways, in the process reinforcing and objectifying them. But the reification of culture also provides a weapon for workers in their struggle against managements or one another. The authors of the Israel study found that employees 'symbolically recruit' Israeli national identity in their struggle to maintain separateness from their American merger partners. Like Indian software engineers, Israeli workers were told in cross-cultural workshops that they should submerge their Israeli cultural identity during global interactions and act more 'American' to avoid misunderstandings (Ailon-Souday and Kunda 2003: 1083), but instead they employed an essentialist notion of national identity for their own ends (2003: 1089). Ailon-Souday and Kunda thus argue that Israeli national identity plays '… a central role as a widely utilised, flexible, and powerful symbolic resource that is used in the constitution of difference through subordination' (2003: 1084).

Similarly, Indian IT workers in their narratives sometimes invert the usual cultural hierarchy, for instance in coffee room talk in which they frequently refer to Western colleagues as 'dumb' ('stupid *goras*').[26] An Indian manager interviewed in Europe maintained that Europeans need to learn how to work with Indians, just as Indians are forced to learn how to work with Europeans:

> I've tried to teach my team here [European employees] how they can better communicate with Indians—how to ask questions and get answers, how to understand the kind of answers that are given. These people with their white skin think they are on top of the world, but I have learnt to change their attitude. They scare Indians by asking, 'Can you finish on such and such a day?' The poor guy thinks it's rude to say no or just can't say no. Instead, I've taught them to ask open-ended questions like, when do you think you can finish this and this? Most importantly I've told them that if the Indians need more time, then just give them that time, don't try and force them to do something that's not possible. It's still very frustrating to deal with the mentality of these white people. Divide and rule is what they did years ago and they still practice it here! Earlier I would get bogged down by the whites, but now I have fairly good relations with them.

This narrative points to the complex negotiations of power that may take place in multicultural work teams, in which hegemonic discourses (such as about India and the West) may be invoked as well as inverted and deployed by subordinates in hierarchical situations for their own subversive ends. Thus, while cultural training programmes and management discourses promote a highly essentialised notion of culture that feeds into the rigidification of national identities and their utilisation as a mechanism of control, such identities may also be used in workers' strategies of resistance.

The Cultural Logics of Software Outsourcing

This study of software outsourcing projects and Indian software engineers illustrates the multiple and complex ways in which the discourse of culture operates within the global economy. Just as cultural representations of 'Chineseness' in discourses about the triumph of 'Chinese capitalism' are part of the new 'cultural logics' of global capitalism (Ong 1999), the deployment of narratives of cultural difference in the Indian software industry is linked to new modes of control over mobile and virtual workforces. The remote management of software engineers from Europe or the US in the context of outsourced projects and virtual teams, and the integration of onsite Indian engineers into local workplaces, present a new set of 'inter-cultural' problems that are addressed in contradictory ways. On the one hand, Indian software engineers are expected to fit themselves socially and psychologically into the dominant global work culture, while on the other hand they are classified by multicultural management discourse as 'different' (and deficient) in specific ways. This cultural typing has both positive and negative aspects: they are considered to be passive and 'hierarchical', inefficient and disorganised, yet are hard workers ('sloggers') who are technically competent and good at following directions. They are said to lack the social skills and cultural disposition needed to function in the global workplace, so they are subjected to training programmes to outfit them with the skills needed to work effectively in multicultural teams, but they are enjoined to retain the 'positive' aspects of Indian culture such as working long hours and with great dedication in the service of customers.

As Ong (1999) has argued, cultural discourses often intersect with the new global economy in contradictory ways: Indian software engineers as a cultural-economic category have come to occupy a prominent place in the social imaginary of global capitalism, exemplifying the new global technical labour force that is threatening to steal American (and European) jobs, but which also provides an important means of cost-cutting for corporations located in those countries. While they position themselves within the Indian middle class as upwardly mobile professionals, when they work abroad they are labelled as 'cheap Indians' or 'sloggers'. Recent attempts by the Indian software industry to sell itself on its quality, efficient cross-border organisation (the 'global delivery model') and customer orientation cannot easily erase the essential cultural features that have been assigned to Indian software workers and the Indian IT industry in general: low costs based on lower wages and long hours, combined with technical competence in low-end routine IT work.[27]

On the surface, there appears to be a contradiction between the substantialised categories of cultural identity that are purveyed by global management theories and the increasing hegemony of a singular model of 'global corporate culture', based on an ideology of individualism and worker autonomy. That is, contemporary management theory celebrates cultural diversity through ideas such as the 'multicultural workplace' and cross-cultural management techniques even as it promotes the idea of a uniform global corporate culture as a way of handling the conflicts that appear to arise from diversity. This contradiction is only apparent, however, because global industries deploy 'culture' in multiple ways for diverse ends, producing conflicting meanings and effects. This raises the question, left mostly unexplored in this chapter, of how these myriad meanings and practices of 'culture' in the workplace inflect the subjectivities of IT workers.

Notes

1. This chapter is based on a sociological study of the Indian IT/ITES (information technology and IT-enabled services) workforce in India and abroad that was carried out by A.R. Vasavi and me along with a research team at the National Institute of Advanced Studies, Bangalore. The research project was funded by the Indo–Dutch Programme on Alternatives in Development (IDPAD), The Netherlands and was carried out in collaboration with Peter van der Veer. Fieldwork for the study was conducted for 18 months, between January 2004 and June 2005, in Bangalore and in three European countries. Research methods included formal and informal interviews with a large number of software engineers, BPO employees, managers of IT and ITES companies, their family members, and with many others connected

with the industry, as well as observations of training programmes, company events, meetings, and formal and informal interactions at workplaces and elsewhere. For a comprehensive report on the study's findings, see Upadhya and Vasavi (2006), available on the NIAS website, www.iisc.ernet.in/nias. For comments and suggestions on the earlier draft, I thank A.R. Vasavi, Sonali Sathaye, Supriya Roy-Chowdhury, and the participants in the International Conference on 'New Global Workforces and Virtual Workplaces' at which this paper was first presented. I am especially grateful to Madhava Prasad for his insightful comments that made me substantially rethink the argument. I hope that I have neither appropriated his argument for my own ends nor misrepresented it.

2. Freeman (2000) is one of the very few ethnographic studies of workers in an off-shore 'high tech' (rather, informatics) service industry.

3. Other key texts of cross-cultural management are Hampden-Turner and Trompenaars (1993, 1997).

4. 'Individualism–collectivism' and 'power distance' are the variables most often used to differentiate Indian–Western cultural differences. Individualism is defined as '… a loosely knit social framework in which people are supposed to take care of themselves and their immediate families only', while collectivism '… is characterised by a tight social framework in which people … expect their in-group to look after them, and in exchange for that they feel they owe absolute loyalty to it'. Power distance is defined as '… the extent to which a society accepts the fact that power in institutions and organisations is distributed unequally' (Hofstede 1980b: 45, quoted in Kirkman et al. 2001: 3).

5. On the 'new workplace' and the emergence of new forms of organisational control in the West, see for example Thompson and Warhurst (1998) and McKinlay and Starkey (1998). On the individualisation of work and employment relations in post-industrial US and Europe and their implications for workers, see Benner (2002), Carnoy (2000), and Beck (2000). The process of individualisation is linked to the flexibilisation of labour in the new economy; see Castells (1996) and Harvey (1989).

6. It should be stressed that the deployment of culture as a management strategy is not unique to the software outsourcing business. Rather, 'culture' in various forms has become central to management theory in general and to capitalism itself, over the last twenty years or so (du Gay and Pryke 2002; Ray and Sayer 1999; Vasavi 1996). For instance, most modern corporations consciously 'engineer' distinct 'corporate cultures', a strategy that is linked to the shift in the theory and practice of corporate management away from direct forms of control towards more flexible organisational structures coupled with indirect or 'normative' forms of control (Kunda 1992; Ezzy 2001). The Indian software industry (at least the large service companies and the multinationals operating in India) has self-consciously replicated these strategies, so that employees are expected to accept and conform to the company's culture and identify closely with the company itself. Although this is an important type of cultural management in the software industry, issues related to the production and inculcation of corporate cultures are not addressed in this article.

7. This article draws on interviews and observations in two types of software company in Bangalore—large Indian software services companies that get contracts with customers located abroad for various kinds of software services, and overseas software development centres (ODCs) of multinationals, which are usually wholly-owned subsidiaries of their parent companies. Both types of company are concerned

with the management of cultural difference, but the problems they face are somewhat different due to the nature of their work and the type of outsourcing. The discussion also draws on interviews with Indian and European software engineers and managers in Europe.

8. 'Bodyshopping' refers to the system of contract labour in which consultants hire software engineers in India and send them to client sites abroad. This system was common in the early days of the industry but declined with the rise of more organised labour contracting through the software services companies. For an account of bodyshopping, see Xiang (2002, 2007).

9. Examples of communication skills and cultural training are shown in the NIAS–IDPAD film 'Fun @ Sun: Making of a Global Workplace' (NIAS 2006).

10. One outcome of the demand for soft skills training by IT companies is a burgeoning ancillary industry of consultants who specialise in providing such training programmes for corporates, which outsource much of this work—although some companies have large in-house training departments. Significantly, several of the most successful soft skills training consultants in Bangalore are expatriates (Europeans or Americans). This field has also given an opportunity to a number of young Westerners to work in places like Bangalore for a year or two as providers of cultural knowledge about their own countries as well as (ironically) about India.

11. In another cultural training programme run by the same company, the trainer ran through the same set of lessons about culture and ethnocentricism, and went on to argue that cultural differences matter only when they affect business relationships and the way we work with others:

> When you are confronted with a cultural difference, you need to ask yourself, 'What? So What? Now What?' What's the difference? Does it affect the way I build relationships? If not (like differences in food), it doesn't matter, it's just a difference. If yes, then I have to do something about it, maybe I need to adjust myself a bit.

12. Critical organisation theory draws primarily on the work of Foucault, pointing to the emergence of new forms of 'panoptical' disciplinary power in the modern corporation through the normalisation of certain practices, rules, and routines as well as normative systems of control. See, for example, McKinlay and Starkey (1998).

13. This section draws on an IDPAD Working Paper based on the European phase of the IDPAD research project (Upadhya 2006).

14. Most of the narratives cited refer to Germany and the Netherlands, where we conducted fieldwork, although a similar discourse is found with regard to India and the West in general among software engineers in India.

15. Meijering and van Hoven (2003) found that the same differences were articulated by their informants in their study of Indian IT professionals in Germany.

16. A pseudonym.

17. The objective of this workshop is to make the German engineers aware of 'Indian work culture' and to induce them to change their working style, for instance by giving a more 'personal touch' to management.

18. The diversification of the workforce employed by Indian software companies is a recent development, as the large service providers have transformed themselves into transnational corporations with offices in many countries.

19. This is true of the global software industry in general. As O Riain (2000) notes, when projects are executed by geographically dispersed teams, the main instrument that is used to control the use of time is the project deadline, which governs the rhythm of the projects and creates up and down cycles of work pressure (see Shih 2004). But project deadlines also become the focus of struggles within teams and between developers and their managers, especially when engineers are pressured to complete additional work within the deadline. 'The politics of the contemporary workplace is increasingly the politics of time' (O Riain 2000: 178).

20. This is the case in the 'new economy' generally, in which speed to market is crucial, organisational success is contingent on working long hours, and workers view spending the largest part of their waking hours at the workplace as necessary for career success (Gephart 2002; Hayes 1989; Shih 2004). The issue of working hours in the IT industry, and their ideological justification, is discussed at greater length in Upadhya (2006) and Upadhya and Vasavi (2006).

21. It is striking that the same discourse was voiced by Israeli employees of a high-tech company to explain their much longer working hours compared to Americans— that Israelis are 'crazy when it comes to work' (Ailon-Souday and Kunda 2003: 1084).

22. This discussion points to a major disjuncture between the public image that software companies attempt to retail—the 'global' quality of their work and working conditions—and the fact that their competitiveness is still based primarily on the labour cost differential, which in turn is based not just on the difference in salaries but also on the long working hours put in by Indian engineers.

23. CMM refers to the international quality certification that has been achieved by many Indian software services companies (the highest level is CMM Level 5). In order to signal quality to potential international customers, the Indian industry has gone in heavily for such quality certifications. The main feature of CMM type models is that they are extremely 'process oriented': they prescribe rationalised and systematic processes for the organisation of workflows at every stage of the software cycle and for management practices, as well as systems of detailed monitoring, measuring, reporting and evaluation of work completed. Quality processes are supposed to reduce the incidence of errors in software ('bugs') that are caused by the individualistic nature of programming. Most programmers dislike having to follow 'process' because it removes the scope for creativity and innovation. The informant is referring to the frequently noted attribute of Indian software engineers—that they are 'good at following directions' (and less good at creative tasks).

24. The case studies of software outsourcing arrangements presented in Sahay et al. (2003) show that these issues are ubiquitous in cross-border collaborations of this kind.

25. Of course, this would be true in almost any organisation, but in the software industry control over knowledge is particularly crucial because the successful execution of projects depends on the free flow of information. As O Riain (2000: 185) points out, information flow is always problematic in multi-sited projects, and in such contexts there is greatest scope for using control over information as a weapon in workplace struggles (see Sewell 2005).

26. *Gora* is a somewhat derogatory term for whites.

27. While successful Indian Silicon Valley entrepreneurs have created an alternative image of the Indian 'techie', these wealthy NRIs (Non-Resident Indians) find a place primarily within Indian middle class and diasporic imaginations rather than in the global narratives of the new capitalism.

References

Ailen-Souday, Galit and Gideon Kunda. 2003. The Local Selves of Global Workers: The Social Construction of National Identity in the Face of Organisational Globalisation. *Organisation Studies* 24(7): 1073–96.

Aneesh, A. 2006. *Virtual Migration: The Programming of Globalisation.* Durham: Duke University Press.

Appadurai, Arjun. 1997. *Modernity at Large: Cultural Dimensions of Globalisation.* New Delhi: Oxford University Press.

Beck, Ulrich. 2000. *The Brave New World of Work.* Cambridge: Polity Press.

Benner, Chris. 2002. *Work in the New Economy: Flexible Labour Markets in Silicon Valley.* Oxford: Blackwell Publishing.

Boje, D. 1993. Anti-Total Quality Management Debate. *Journal of Organisational Change Management* 6(4): 2–57.

Carnoy, Martin. 2000. *Work, Family and Community in the Information Age.* New York: Russell Sage.

Castells, Manuel. 1996. *The Information Age: Economy, Society and Culture.* Vol. 1 of *The Rise of the Network Society.* Oxford: Blackwell.

Deetz, S. 1998. Discursive Formations, Strategised Subordination and Self-Surveillance. In McKinlay and Starkey (eds), *Foucault, Management and Organisation Theory: From Panopticon to Technologies of Self,* pp. 151–72. London: Sage Publications.

du Gay, Paul and Michael Pryke. 2002. Cultural Economy: An Introduction. In Paul du Gay and Michael Pryke (eds), *Cultural Economy,* pp. 1–19. London: Sage Publications.

Ezzy, Douglas. 2001. A Simulacrum of Workplace Community: Individualism and Engineered Culture. *Sociology* 35(3): 631–50.

Featherstone, M. (ed.). 1990. *Global Culture: Nationalism, Globalisation and Modernity.* London: Sage Publications.

Freeman, Carla. 2000. *High Tech and High Heels in the Global Economy: Women, Work and Pink-Collar Identities in the Caribbean.* Durham: Duke University Press.

Friedman, Jonathan. 1994. *Cultural Identity and Global Process.* London: Sage Publications.

Gephart, Robert P. Jr. 2002. Introduction to the Brave New Workplace: Organisational Behaviour in the Electronic Age. *Journal of Organisational Behaviour* 23: 327–44.

Ghosh, Kaushik. 1999. A Market for Aboriginality: Primitivism and Race Classification in the Indentured Labour Market of Colonial India. In Gautam Bhadra, Gyan Prakash and Sussie Tharu (eds), *Subaltern Studies: Writings on South Asian History and Society,* Volume X, pp. 8–48. New Delhi: Oxford University Press.

Hampden-Turner, Charles and Fons Trompenaars. 1993. *The Seven Cultures of Capitalism*. London: Judy Piatkus.

———. 1997 *Riding the Waves of Culture: Understanding Diversity in Global Business*. New York: McGraw-Hill.

Harvey, David. 1989. *The Condition of Postmodernity; An Enquiry into the Origins of Cultural Change*. Oxford: Blackwell Publishing.

Hayes, Dennis. 1989. *Behind the Silicon Curtain: The Seductions of Work in a Lonely Era*. London: Free Association Books.

Hofstede, Geert. 1980a. *Culture's Consequences: International Differences in Work-Related Values*. Beverley Hills: Sage Publications.

———. 1980b. Motivation, Leadership, and Organisation: Do American Theories Apply Abroad?. *Organisational Dynamics* 9. Quoted in Kirkman et al. 2001.

Kelly, Patricia Maria Fernandez. 1983. *For We are Sold, I and My People: Women and Industry in Mexico's Frontier*. Albany: State University New York (SUNY) Press.

Kirkman, Bradley L., Kevin B. Lowe and Cristina B. Gibson. 2001. *Twenty Years of Culture's Consequences: A Review of the Empirical Research on Hofstede's Cultural Values Framework*. Centre for Effective Organisations, Marshall School of Business, University of Southern California.

Kunda, Gideon. 1992. *Engineering Culture: Control and Commitment in a High-Tech Corporation*. Philadelphia: Temple University Press.

McKinlay, A. and K. Starkey. 1998. *Foucault, Management and Organisation Theory: From Panopticon to Technologies of Self*. London: Sage Publications.

Meijering, Louise and Bettina van Hoven. 2003. Imagining Difference: The Experiences of 'Transnational' Indian IT Professionals in Germany. *Area* 35(2): 174–82.

Mills, Mary Beth. 2003. Gender and Inequality in the Global Labour Force. *Annual Review of Anthropology* 32: 41–62.

Nash, June and Patricia Maria Fernandez Kelly (eds). 1983. *Women, Men and the International Division of Labour*. Albany: SUNY Press.

National Institute of Advanced Studies (NIAS). 2006. Fun @ Sun: Making of a Global Workplace. In film series, *Coding Culture: Bangalore's Software Industry* by Gautam Sonti in collaboration with Carol Upadhya. Bangalore.

O Riain, Sean. 2000. 'Networking for a Living: Irish Software Developers in the Global Workplace. In *Global Ethnography: Forces, Connections, and Imaginations in a Post-modern World*, M. Burawoy, Joseph A. Blum, Sheba George, Zsuzsa Gille, Millie Thayer, Teresa Gowan, Lynne Haney, Maren Klawiter, Steve H. Lopez, Sean O' Riain, 175–202. Berkeley: University of California Press.

Ogbor, John O. 2001. Critical Theory and the Hegemony of Corporate Culture. *Journal of Organisational Change Management* 14(6): 590–608.

Ong, Aihwa. 1987. *Spirits of Resistance and Capitalist Discipline: Factory Women in Malaysia*. Albany: SUNY Press.

———. 1991. The Gender and Labour Politics of Postmodernity. *Annual Review of Anthropology* 20: 279–309.

———. 1999. *Flexible Citizenship: The Cultural Logics of Transnationality*. Durham: Duke University Press.

Perlow, Leslie. 1997. *Finding Time: How Corporations, Individuals and Families Can Benefit from New Work Practices*. New York: Cornell University Press.

Poster, Mark. 2002. Workers as Cyborgs: Labour and Networked Computers. *Journal of Labour Research* 23(3): 339–54.

Prakash, Gyan. 1990. *Bonded Histories: Genealogies of Labor Servitude in Colonial India*. Cambridge: Cambridge University Press.

Ray, L. and A. Sayer (eds). 1999. *Culture and Economy after the Cultural Turn*. London: Sage Publications.

Sahay, Sundeep, Brian Nicholson, and S. Krishna. 2003. *Global IT Outsourcing: Software Development across Borders*. Cambridge: Cambridge University Press.

Sewell, Graham. 2005. Nice Work? Rethinking Managerial Control in an Era of Knowledge Work. *Organisation* 12(5): 685–704.

Shih, Johanna. 2004. Project Time in Silicon Valley. *Qualitative Sociology* 27(2): 223–45.

Thompson, Paul and Chris Warhurst (eds). 1998. *Workplaces of the Future*. Hampshire: Macmillan.

Upadhya, Carol. 2006. The Global Indian Software Labour Force: IT Professionals in Europe. IDPAD Working Paper No. 1. The Hague: Indo-Dutch Programme on Alternatives in Development.

Upadhya, Carol and A.R. Vasavi. 2006. Work, Culture, and Sociality in the Indian IT Industry: A Sociological Study (Final Report submitted to IDPAD). Bangalore: National Institute of Advanced Studies.

Vasavi, A.R. 1996. Co-opting Culture: Managerialism in Age of Consumer Capitalism. *Economic and Political Weekly* 31(21): M-22–23.

Xiang, Biao. 2002. Global 'Body Shopping': A New International Labour System in the Information Technology Industry. Unpublished. D. Phil Dissertation, University of Oxford University.

———. 2007. *Global 'Body Shopping': An Indian Labour System in the Information Technology Industry*. Princeton: Princeton University Press.

5

The Scientific Imperative to be Positive: Self-reliance and Success in the Modern Workplace

Sonali Sathaye

Over the last twenty-five years, management schools and corporate offices across India and the world have put their faith in a variety of psychological training techniques in order to make employees more effective at their jobs (Salaman 1997; du Gay and Pryke 2002). While their content may differ, these trainings share a common directive: that of bringing employees' affective lives or at the least their affective behaviour into the ambit of their professional lives. Given the apparently universal and ubiquitous requirements for certain 'psychological propensities' (du Gay and Pryke 2002: 2), workers have had to be tutored in this 'emotional labour' (Hochschild 1983). Moreover, whereas earlier such work was perceived to be essential for those in the service industries—the hospitality business or sales departments, for example—today corporate employees, from civil engineers to university secretaries, are the recipients of a range of affective-behavioural training. Even the information technology (IT) industry, whose rise to prominence in the new 'knowledge economy' has been dependent upon relentless technological innovation, has made such trainings mandatory for employees. 'Soft skills' workshops designed to produce smoother relationships among colleagues, afford employees a sense of autonomy and creativity or resolve interpersonal conflict, have become an accepted part of the Human Resource (HR) portfolio at IT companies. All in all, psychological prescriptions and descriptions offered by experts in the field of psychology and management appear to have become as integral as technical training to the business of business.

Recent writing in the social sciences on work, more specifically on the changing nature of corporate work, tends to focus on the psyche of the employee as part of a 'cultural turn' in the economy (Lash and Urry 1994; du Gay and Pryke 2002). By that phrase, scholars refer to contemporary workers' concern with self-actualisation through work as well as the efforts to create a customised managerial culture on the part of corporations (Miller 2002; Heelas 2002; Hochschild 1983). To these academics writing primarily of experiences in the US or the UK, the 'cultural turn' is automatically allied with 'culture' because of its concern with producing a total ethos at the workplace, complete with values, emotions and rituals.

The term 'cultural turn' reproduces itself somewhat differently in India, where it might mean both the managerial culture that companies seek to engender as well as a broader notion of that word in which employees and management are thought of as drawing upon the values of a larger, national culture. And within Indian business, the IT industry's use of the word 'culture', in particular, exemplifies this approach. In the public imagination, both in India and abroad, the Indian IT Industry finds its centre of gravity in Bangalore. Visiting heads of state as well as Bill Gates come to speak with the heads of top IT firms about future technological collaborations, to launch new products and, at least in their rhetoric, endorse the cutting-edge nature of the IT industry in the city. Self-congratulatory pronouncements about India being brought into the 21st century on the shoulders of software engineers, startup companies and the information technology boom in general, run regularly in the media—some of it proclaimed by politicians and some by IT entrepreneurs. The Indian IT industry is heavy with the weight of its meaning in contemporary India, since it appears to bring together the twin virtues of a forward-thinking occupation with rationality and science, and a value-laden engagement with tradition and patriotism. In this rendition, 'culture' is very much about national culture.

Yet the meaning of 'culture' as corporate, managerial culture imparted through HR training programmes is not absent from the discussion. The IT industry is also in the media spotlight for the personal and the social difficulties faced by its participants, difficulties that involve, mainly, a serious lack of time for things other than work—especially family. These have necessitated talk about 'people problems' made familiar by earlier discussions of Western work environments, viz., the 'work-life' balance, high stress levels and high divorce rates. Moreover, for the resolution of these problems the industry turns to the same set of globally-established, standardised psychological techniques taught in the West. 'Indian values' are conspicuous by their absence in this version of self-help courses. Indeed, when Indian meanings, concepts or feelings do crop up in the course of sessions, employees are taught to re-learn those in favour of more 'universal'—typically American—understandings. The can-do interpretations of intangible phenomena taught in soft skills trainings run smoothly alongside current management techniques, which place a high premium on individuality.

The relationship between emotion and commerce manifested by soft skills programmes is intriguing. Popular notions of emotion and commerce pit the two against each other; emotion is understood as untutored, spontaneous and of the personal, and commerce is typically seen as profit-driven, the product of calculation and technique and belonging to the public realm. And yet corporations employ professionals to teach emotional work under the rubric of 'skills' and 'techniques' to their employees. Standardised tests are routinely used to determine a person's personality type, and definitions of self-confidence and assertiveness are taught which are assumed to be universally applicable and legible. Due to this expectation of intelligibility there is a high degree of uniformity in the psychological, 'soft skills' training accorded to workers across companies, professions, cultures and countries.

The attraction of such trainings is derived in large part from the assumption that they stem from 'science'—in this case, a popular science of psychology and human behaviour, made teachable and learnable by breaking it down into how-to packages, 10-point lists and practice sessions. Although the goal of this self-work remains professional, the trainings suggest that the route to that success has much in common with other kinds of psychological, more personal, success—smoother relationships, peace of mind, work-life balance, job satisfaction/fulfillment—and that all of these may be had through the pursuit of the techniques taught in corporate trainings.

The chapter begins with a description of some of the ways in which 'Indian culture' is invoked in IT-India. I follow that with an account of the key messages provided to employees in soft skills training programmes, paying particular attention to the techniques taught by the Myers-Briggs Type Indicator™ (MBTI ™) and Transactional Analysis (TA). Next I discuss employee responses to the trainings. The second half of the chapter explores the particular appeal that soft skills trainings hold for management professionals at this point in corporate history. In this context, the current managerial culture with its emphasis on self-actualisation, self-reliance and 'flat structures' is examined. The chapter ends with a discussion on the popularity of trainings as dependent on science and rationality and the deployment of these meanings in the contemporary IT business world in India.[1]

Indian Culture in a Space Warp

A single culture permeates across [be it in India or in California]. You almost feel you are in a space warp, you shouldn't feel like you are in Santa Clara or in Bangalore

—Vijay Anand, CEO, India Engineering Centre,
Sun Microsystems
(in film 'Fun @ Sun', NIAS 2006a)

Dr Chopra,[2] a professor at a premier management institute in Bangalore, laments the fact that 'we'—Indians—not only no longer know who we are but are instead turning to others to help us define ourselves. We are in the midst of a long interview one sunny May morning, chatting in his office in the leafy environs of the institute. He says this in the context of the professional classes' contact with the West in India's booming, globalised IT industry. He asks me if, in the course of my study on psychology and management, I am going to look at the question of identity. When I say I am not, at least not explicitly, he assures me it is a topic that bears close study, especially in these times. 'We have a very poor sense of Indian identity. ...the IT industry has a big exposure to abroad [*sic*], leading to a greater definition by outsiders of what "Indian" is.' In any case, things have changed so much in terms of values that 'Macaulay's vision', he says, 'has come true'.[3]

Whatever the truth of Dr Chopra's assertion that what qualifies as representatively 'Indian' today is determined by Western notions of 'Indianness', many in the IT industry speak easily of an entity called 'Indian culture'. Like Samuel Huntington who equates the success or failure of economic liberalisation with the values and principles of a country because 'culture matters' (2000), Indian culture and values are frequently cited as reasons for India's growth in the IT global market. Analysing national cultures in terms of 'value-based' variables to understand why some countries appear to successfully transition to global capitalism where others fail is a well-established, legitimate topic for research in the management industry. I attended a class for first-year students at the same institute as a senior professor lectured on the spiritual precepts taught in the *Bhagavad Gita* as a guide to business as well as to life. In that management class, while students discuss the corruption apparently inherent to Indian public life, there is still heated affirmation of the need to keep intact and alive 'Indian values' in business. It is, amongst other things, India's special 'USP [Unique Selling Proposition]'.

One of the primary pairs of categories in studies on 'cross-cultural management', as best evinced in the work of Geert Hofstede (1980), is that of 'collectivism' versus 'individualism'. Other national character traits—such as relationship with authority ('power distance'), work ethic and company loyalty—appear to flow out of this central node. It is something that management studies and psychologists agree on. When successful psychoanalyst (and anthropologist) Alan Roland treats corporate clients from Japan, India and the US, he explains their relationships with subordinates and superiors, with keeping deadlines and handling criticism, in terms of their national cultural characteristics (1996).[4] Dr Dinesh Bhugra from King's College, London, at an international conference on psychiatry in Bangalore in 2005 to celebrate 55 years of the National Institute of Mental Health and Neuro-Sciences (NIMHANS), also pitted these categories against one another. He argued that immigrants to the West from South Asia and Africa come from 'collectivist' cultures and have to learn to adapt and become 'individualist' themselves if they are to survive and not fall subject to schizophrenia and other mental illnesses.

Even Dr Chopra talks of the collectivist nature of Indians versus the individualist nature of Europeans and Americans. In the film 'Fun @ Sun',[5] the Indian manager of a top American IT company appears to confirm Alan Roland's observations on the relationships of Indians with their bosses. He compares Indian employees with their American counterparts in terms of their 'need to share'. In the US, he says, '… an effective manager gives [the employees] clear goals and lets them go. Over here, they need to share, to get that feedback…' Later in the film he adds, 'In India people are known for socialising at work, it's not just about doing some amazing innovation and getting recognition and going home it's about sharing, it's about having fun'.

IT companies, Indian or foreign-owned, translate the fact of difference along national cultural lines, a difference with its roots in fundamentally diverse ways of configuring social relationships. Yet, in practice, the value of the Indianness of India is an add-on. It is there because, in the words of Vijay Anand, it '… adds value to that base culture [of the American IT firm]'. Ultimately however, 'a single culture permeates across [be it in India or in California]… you almost feel you are in a space warp, you shouldn't feel like you are in Santa Clara or in Bangalore.… You should feel that you are in Sun' (NIAS 2006a).

Being Anywhere as Being Yourself: Some Weird and Wonderful Techniques

Practice and in time you will be able to be yourself naturally.

—Padma S., Trainer,
'Effective Inter-personal Communication'

At an all-day course on 'Effective Inter-personal Communication for Women Executives', held at a hotel in central Bangalore, the trainer Suhail asks a group of about sixty participants, 'Why is it important, this communication?' In response to the shouted-out answers, she says, 'Exactly! You cannot work alone in today's context. You need to mix with people. You need to be proactive, to take the initiative, you cannot just sit there and expect people to approach you'. The content as well as the format of this call-response routine is now familiar to me. I have heard it repeated in more or less identical fashion across various workshops in Bangalore. The basic lineaments of the messages do not vary, whether conducted by an Irish trainer at the posh Taj West End hotel for new managers at Sun Microsystems, or at a somewhat run-down hotel for a predominantly Kannada-speaking group of civil engineers, university secretaries and HR managers. Du Gay and Pryke, writing of the ubiquity of psychological training in today's corporations, say: 'Through sustained exposure to an often weird and wonderful range of interpersonal and communication management techniques—such as transaction analysis ... service workers have found themselves being trained in how to fashion their conduct—bodily comportment, aural and visual characteristics, and so forth—in order to produce certain meanings for customers...' (2002: 3). The workings of HR departments of corporations as well as the syllabi of management courses confirm that this is as true for India as for the UK.

Management courses teach their students the disciplines of Organisational Behaviour (OB) and Human Resource Development (HRD). Organisational behaviour operates at four distinct levels: the individual, the group, the organisation and 'inter-organisational relations,' according to Dr Chopra. He tells me that under 'individual' is '... where most of your psychology comes in—usually personality, motivation, perceptions, cognitive schema. That's also where we'll do something like the MBTI™. Transactional Analysis fits into the more interpersonal relationship-group dynamic area...' In this section some of the more prominent content common to soft skills trainings are outlined. I also write in some detail of the still-popular TA method for understanding human communication and of the MBTI™, which is widely used in categorising personality types.

On the whole, soft skills trainings hinge upon two interdependent imperatives. Trainers concentrate on teaching employees ways of successful self-presentation, but in order to be able to pitch these accurately, trainers also claim to teach them ways to identify their own and other people's personality types. The reading of personality types therefore occupies a central position in the standard repertoire of training content. The fundamental axes of classification appears to run along a neat grid of supposed binary opposites—between rationality and emotion, between body and mind, between spoken and unspoken communication, between self and society, between confidence and insecurity.

Although the precise labels may differ, personalities are typically divided into the 'aggressive', the 'passive' and finally, the most desirable, the 'assertive' type. Employees can be taught how to distinguish these from one another by matching them against sets of behavioural characteristics, verbal and non-verbal. The non-verbal behaviour for 'aggressive', according to one trainer, is for example 'narrow cold eyes, threatening gesture'. The 'passive' personality inspires 'pity, and eventually irritation' in those around them. To signal assertiveness verbally involves speaking in a 'lot of 'I' statements'; the assertive person is 'in touch with [her] feelings' and her attitude towards herself gives those around her 'a feeling of being respected'.

Keeping intact the phenomenon of category creation in order to describe and interact with people, some methods purport to go deeper. Two of these methods, the MBTI™ and TA, are especially popular in the Indian corporate environment. The former is based in Jungian psychology; the latter finds its origins in a Freudian approach. The Myers-Briggs Type Indicator, according to Sushma (who is one of the official representatives of the school in India), has a 'strong psychological base', taking off as it does from Jung's theory of 'archetypes'.[6] Briggs had no formal training in psychology, statistics or instrument creation but she just believed that 'if ordinary people had access to this then their life would be more far more effective'. 'Transactional Analysis,[7] says Lakshmi, was also designed for 'ordinary people' in order to make human relationships easier by exposing the bases upon which communication takes place. Padma, another TA trainer, says: 'TA is nothing but a tool to analyse, assess, and see how to make interpersonal communication more effective.'

The MBTI™ claims there are four grids—basic sets of dichotomies—along which all human personalities are divided. These are the Extrovert/Introvert (E or I), the Sensing/Intuitive (S or N), the Thinking/Feeling (T or F) and the Judging/Perceiving (J or P). Participants in a MBTI™ course are taught that introverts 'tend to energise by going into their inner worlds' (NIAS 2006a) while extroverts are 'very social, very outgoing'. They will be taught that there is a difference between a 'thinking' and 'feeling' person, in which one relies more on facts and arrives at decisions through logical deductions (as does the 'S' type person too) rather than intuition and gut-level feeling.

Transactional Analysis does not talk about universal basic personality-types. Instead it talks of four basic 'Life States'—made visible in the 'OK Corral'—and three basic 'Ego States' into which all human interaction, anywhere, may be divided. These are the Parent, Child and Adult ego states. At a TA seminar, participants will be taught to identify 'Parent' as 'authoritative', 'rule-bound', 'overbearing' and a Child as 'playful' or 'spontaneous'. In both of the TA courses I attended, trainers often translated interactions into their terminology by beginning with the phrase, 'oh, this is nothing but [Parent/Adult/Child] talking.'

Trainings emphasise the need for employees to be, at once, assertive, self-confident and open, and to craft their verbal and non-verbal ('body language') skills accordingly. Courses on effective communication, listening skills and conflict resolution offer a set of simple skills to smoothen the 'Disagreement Process' and ways to 'Say No'. Precise nuggets of information, presented as facts, are used to drive home the same point. For instance, I came across this fragment of information in at least five different 'listening-skills and communication' workshops offered by three trainers from different agencies: 'Communication is only 7 per cent verbal. The other 93 per cent is non-verbal'.[8] From such statements, the workshops draw near-identical implications: Given the miniscule impact words have on getting one's message across, one should work on cultivating body language, on tone and facial expressions, to do so. The work of this cultivation depends, according to trainers, on displaying one's trustworthiness, or, in the words of one trainer, one's 'believability'. Trainers teach various ways to display this, ranging from advising participants to look straight into the eyes of their interlocutor to advising against crossing their legs (for the men) at an important meeting.

Typically, trainings include some means of quantifying the self and/ or other people. With the help of faux-quantitative psychometric tests, participants plot their responses to situations so as to 'discover' their true states-of-being or personality-types. Participants are expected to read the results of these tests in ways that help them to cultivate a personal style that exudes authority and self-confidence. At the end of most soft skills programmes, participants are asked to make an 'action plan' in which they note down the 'skills' they have learnt and the goals they seek to achieve through the practice of those skills.

The quantification and categorisation which is essential to all trainings, regardless of the particular allegiance to a method or philosophy, is supposed to bring about greater clarity in understanding oneself and others, and hence less wastage of effort and time in the completion of tasks at work. In this scheme, definitions of 'effectiveness' attempt to weed out the regular push-and-pull unpredictability of human interactions as problems to be tackled deliberately. Trainers urge employees to work on their selves, at home and at work, in order for them to be successful in their professional lives. If one were to believe the workshops, the ideal employee is one who casts a continuously rational eye on her personal and professional relationships with a view to maximising efficiency.

Just Another Way of Categorising People: What Employees Think

It is just like the zodiac, isn't it? Nowadays we call this scientific, these therapies and all, but basically it is just another way of categorising people to make them easier to understand.

—Shiva, new manager/employee at an
MNC software development centre

Hochschild (1983), in her close ethnography of the training offered to stewardesses at Delta Airlines, writes of the 'deep acting' techniques that demand that these women (for they were all women) incarnate a constant, caring attentiveness not through mere facework (Goffman 1959) but by achieving an 'authentic' personalised feeling towards clients. For the stewardesses this required continual practice, a constant monitoring and masking of one's self and emotions, particularly towards rude or unruly passengers, in order to be good 'professionals'. Hochschild details the intimate cost of this understanding of professionalism when she writes of the ways in which it clouds and warps the self-understanding of these women, many of whom had to seek professional help (i.e., counselling and therapy) in order to unravel their 'professional' from their genuine feelings.

Unlike Hochschild's overwhelmed flight attendants, employees in IT industries do not seem to worry overmuch about the whys and wherefores of their professional emotional lives. Much to the chagrin of trainers, most cheerfully submit to the trainings, seeing in it 'a day-off eating different food and a respite from the office', in the words of Suhail. It is 'time-pass', something for which companies have to show the required 'man-hours' by the time their annual review comes up. A couple of young inductees, Ashish and Priya, said that they prefer to go to soft skills trainings when they were still new. When I press to know how it is that they settled on these particular trainings, they grin, look at each other and say, 'Well, basically, we were on the bench, we're new and we hadn't been assigned any work'. 'So, it's 'time-pass'? I ask. 'Exactly', they nod. And grin. A few employees from different companies also commented on how soft skills trainings are 'too simplistic', offering little in the way of actual new learning.

Still, employees are quick to intuit the benefits of such instruction, even when they do not know the theory behind it. Ignoring the 'playful, emotional, spontaneous' meaning of 'Child', Ashish and Priya both take it to mean themselves as new young employees in the company. Ashish says, 'See, as freshers, it was very nice because it gives us an insight into how to talk within the hierarchy of managers, our superiors…' Priya says, 'I liked the Parent, Adult, Child [concept]… it told us how you should talk… because, we being freshers, we relate to the Child mentality.' Also, they said, there was a video clip in their 'Communications Skills' workshop which was 'very informative…. It showed a relationship between a person going to a client—first, the person is not able to convince her [the client] to give him the project but later, with communication skills, he is successful'. Even though they might be 'theoretically' wrong in their understanding, Ashish and Priya liked what they learned from the training, viz., to stick to facts, the right tone to adopt when speaking to superiors and so on.

Shiva, the seasoned engineer and new manager at the Bangalore software development centre of an American multinational, is more sceptical about the reasons companies arrange soft skills trainings. Yet, in sum, he too appears to agree with Ashish and Priya's versions of trainings and therapy: 'A motivated employee is important because I can generate more wealth', he says, darkly. These trainings are useful, though, according to him, because they 'bring some semblance of order' to relationships otherwise distressed by 'greed and competition.' So there is a point to the creation of categories through which to understand human beings, but, he says, 'It is just like the zodiac, isn't it? Nowadays we call this scientific, these therapies and all, but basically it is just another way of categorising people to make them easier to understand.'

Why Now?

Soft skills make them a complete person. Also it helps us because onsite they present a better image [of the company].

—Ankush S., Manager, HR, in a software services company

Indian IT employees seem, overall, less than impressed by the benefits of soft skills trainings. And yet companies pour in money and trainers earn their livelihoods—sometimes very good ones, too—through the regular circulation of such programmes. My running refrain throughout the research has been—why have soft skills trainings become *de rigueur* for companies everywhere over the last 25 years? The answers from managers and trainers fall into two broad categories: that trainings are good for the employee and that they are good for the company. Both of these fuse together, however, in the larger picture: that what is good for the company is good for the employee. The answers serve to underline du Gay and Pryke's observation that the aim of psychological trainings

> … is to produce the sorts of meanings that can enable people to make what senior management consider to be the right and necessary contribution to the success of the organisation for which they work … managers are encouraged to view the most effective or 'excellent' organisations as those with the 'right' culture—that ensemble of norms and techniques of conduct that enables the self-actualising capacities of individuals to become aligned with the goals and objectives of the organisation for which they work (2002: 1).

Dr Chopra, perhaps because he is neither a manager nor a trainer, is unusual in baldly stating the place of such trainings in industry. 'The idea here based on psychological instruments such as the MBTI™, is to achieve a better person-organisation fit. There's a lot of research to suggest that the fit has a positive outcome—low turnover, high productivity, commitment, satisfaction, performance … you have to have a congruence over values, working styles'.

In answering my 'why soft skills now' question, most trainers and managers first turn seemingly naturally to larger societal considerations by way of explanation, more particularly to focus on the current breakdown of 'values' in India. One HR manager refers to a study conducted by psychologists at the National Institute of Mental Health and Neurological Sciences (NIMHANS), Bangalore and management professionals at the IIM-A (the Indian Institute of Management, Ahmedabad) to describe 'an increase in divorce and counselling, in stress', and an increase in materialism. Dr Chopra too cannot resist speculating along similar lines. He says, 'Maybe the social skills of people have deteriorated. Now we are bombarded with all this information on counselling and psychological health, see, but the thing is, there's also been an increase in conflict, family-conflict, etc. … an increase in divorce, nobody to turn to for help…. Also technology plays a big role. Earlier, you could easily compartmentalise your life, but now it is more difficult, what with cell phones, etc'. Lakshmi, at E-Now, observes:

> People are so emotionally-drained…. There was recently an article in *The Economic Times*—in fact, I couldn't believe it, initially, but—they [employees] have an 'office partner', they have this *in India*. So many people feel more comfortable with their manager or their subordinate. They need the emotional support [and they spend so many hours at the office, twelve, fourteen hour days]. But it's complicated, the family either ends in divorce, it's bad for the children…. But then, they need the emotional support. As a result of this, there are a lot of complications *vis-à-vis* societal values, social mores, so-called Indian traditional values…. It's a very common trend now, 'emotional partners'.

In this telling 'techies' and others like them—professional middle-class Indians—need these trainings in 'listening-skills' and relationships because they have lost touch with their feelings, their relationships and with them, their values—a fact exacerbated by the technology boom and longer working hours. However, I notice that managers' and trainers' exhortations of the benefits of soft skills trainings for employees' personal lives—social, pragmatic or, spiritual—usually end with an instrumentalist twist, usually a paean to the benefits that such instruction brings to company business. Typical is the response of a divisional head of HR of an Indian-owned MNC who explains, nodding his head for emphasis, 'See, these professionals are technically very sound but their accents, mannerisms … are very bad, you can call them robots, actually [or perhaps simply 'introverts'?]. Soft skills trainings make them a complete person.' And he then goes on to add, 'Also, it helps us because, on-site, they present a better image [of the company]'.

Even apparently fully developed counselling systems such as TA and the MBTI™, which claim an authoritative grasp of the fundamental mechanisms of self-knowledge and interaction, justify their deployment in similar terms. When I ask Lakshmi if the categories of TA correspond to the way one is in real life, she replies in the affirmative. Sushma, of the MBTI™, says, '[The test] helps me to explore myself and another person, over time.' But as Lakshmi goes on to say, 'If you don't have the soft skills, [if you are not] tinkering with your inner self, [working on] how to improve your quality of life outside work ... those are the things we aim to do as trainers... [Because] It's no longer enough for me to be a good techie. I cannot be a good leader without good people skills [with just technical know-how]. Operational skills are required, only then can I get things done. And in order to improve my people-skills I need to understand what kind of person *I* am...'.

Despite the promise of self-knowledge that TA and MBTI™ trainers formally hold out to participants at corporate trainings, in practice trainers do not appear to seek to set in motion long-term attitudinal or perspectival change in their clients. Instead, the emphasis is on demonstrating the usefulness of adopting a behavioural tactic in order that employees may get ahead in their positions, or that things get done. Trainers can be candid about the fact. When I ask the all-India representative of the MBTI™ about what is so essential to that test (as to all psychological tests), and ask about its use, Sushma says, 'One of the ways in which it is marketed is that it helps you to influence yourself or your subject, to present yourself better, in a way that captures the attention of the other person.' (She goes on to add, 'Though I don't do that myself, I present myself spontaneously...').

Lakshmi elaborates on the benefits of TA thus:

> Taking TA, if I'm always in Parent, then my team is not going to like me but if I'm in Adult, then I command respect and ensure that tasks are completed. See, if you tell a manager who's testing a new tool, I don't think it's going to work, then that's from your P state and the manager is not going to listen because he's also in his P state. But, also, if you just say, Ok, I'll do it, like a Child state then that way you get no respect. So, if you give him reasons, back it up, say, 'it's not going to work *because* [of so and so]', then the manager is going to have respect [for you]. The trainings serve to instruct employees—managers or subordinates—in ways to craft themselves in order to 'command respect and ensure that tasks are completed.

She adds, 'I don't want them to know the theory anyway, to be able to identify [states] is good.... One Fedex employee said that his primary Ego State was Child … He tried to control it by trying to 'up' his ES to the Adult State and it showed in his appraisal, his manager also noted it'.

At a training session run by a multinational, the trainer quotes from the August 1998 edition of *Fast Company.*[9] 'Establish a relationship with the best of the best so they know someone cares and they are not just a commodity.' A participant asks, 'That's a nice thought but what are the actual benefits?' The trainer responds: 'It's hard to quantify—it's a relation that's built after-hours, isn't it. And it's good for you too, not just for the company. Hang out with good people, some of it rubs off on to you too.' By way of further explanation, she uses a quote from Sun Microsystems co-founder Scott McNealy: 'One of the greatest things about hiring and retaining the smartest people is that they attract smart people'. Using a cost-benefit analysis according to which, to quote Suhail, 'to get something you need to give something', this advice culminates in the same projected result. Much like in Riesman's study (1961) of the capitalist 'company man' who submits his personal life to the higher good of the company, employees are expected to meld professional and personal selves, to ceaselessly husband personal responses to bosses, to clients, to their families, along pathways that maximise company profit.

Learning to be Oneself:
The Importance of Being Self-Reliant

Earlier [Indian] attitudes were more resigned … Now we have positive thinking. Earlier, [one would] just say, 'oh that's the way it is.' Now I have to do it because otherwise I don't have a job, don't have …a life.

—Suhail, Trainer, TA and 'Effective Communication'

The management style of the knowledge economy takes as given the fusion of company and individual worker interests. The new style advocates a 'flat structure', 'flexi-time' and attention to workers' need for 'self-actualisation' (Heelas 2002). In this, it is supposedly opposed to the older Fordist model of the clock-in and clock-out hierarchical culture of a manufacturing economy (Harvey 1990). In contemporary India, this new philosophy appears to have been taken on more intensely at work because it neatly links with a perceived need for transformation, not just in the work culture but more fundamentally in 'Indian culture' and Indian society itself. According to Rajesh Reddy, co-founder of July Systems and a successful young IT entrepreneur,[10] Silicon Valley (the IT capital of the world which is situated in California) best exemplifies the new culture. In its attention to workers' needs for self-improvement and satisfaction and the scope that it provides for innovation and creativity, Reddy claims, the culture of the Silicon Valley 'brings out the full potential of a human being'. By extension, adopting a culture which best suits the entrepreneurial IT industry involves a new understanding of 'full potential' and even, almost, of 'human being'.

Above I quote professionals lamenting the loss of Indian social relations and values. That complaint appears ambivalent in the light of professionals' simultaneous lauding of the change taking place in Indian attitudes. The major change appears to be the move towards an individualisation of life; in the new climate, one is encouraged to see the success or failure of all aspects of life, work, relationships, material circumstances and family as lying in direct proportion to the personal effort one has expended on it. 'Earlier our needs were limited but now [to fulfill our contemporary needs] we need to have a good frame of thinking, to achieve success', explains Padma, TA trainer, who regularly coaches IT employees on the need for self-confidence.

Several people—employees, trainers, managers, professors—all use one word to describe this change—'awareness'. Moreover, they all use it in exactly the same way that Lakshmi does. When I push Lakshmi past the answers of 'dealing with difference' and being 'emotionally drained', she says the reason these soft skills are more needed nowadays is because people are more 'aware'. When I ask her what this 'awareness' consists of, she responds: 'Primarily Indian society was a public sector society but now we're moving into the private sector and that means either you do or you're out. People understand that. They're much more aware than a decade back. They're much more aware and they want to bring in that change'. In another time and place, in interviews seprated by more than a year, Padma and Suhail, also TA trainers, echo Lakshmi almost verbatim. They also speak of the difference from earlier generations as one of an increase in 'awareness'—'people are more aware now'. People understand that 'either you do or you are out'. Today people understand—'much more than a decade ago'—that with the privatisation of the economy, individuals will have to become more 'self-motivated', in the parlauce of the day.

Whatever the claims to greater awareness and its implication of a self-generated drive to change old modes of thought and behaviour, it is observed that workers have to be tutored in the foundational attitudes and practices—at the very least the rhetoric—of this new culture. For a start they have to be instructed in some of its basic tenets of faith: to be communicative and assertive, to challenge authority, to be irreverent, to have fun. A frequently voiced complaint by managers and trainers across IT companies is that 'Indians do not [know] how to be communicative'. This prompts a beleaguered engineer from one of the top Indian IT companies to ask, 'They say Indians have poor communication skills but actually Indians are traditionally talkers—so...?' An HR manager helpfully explains: 'We can talk but not the way we should'. An IT entrepreneur clarifies this 'should' a little further: 'Not the gossipy-kind of talk, we don't argue with our bosses; that kind of communication is missing with us'.

In 'Fun @ Sun', an HR boss at Sun Microsystems tries to make clear the company slogan as articulated by their CEO, which is to 'go out there and have fun and kick some butt'. This entails the trainer explaining what it means to 'have fun' by telling them the story of engineers in California 'stealing' their boss' expensive luxury car and putting it in a pond so that the boss had to 'literally, get on a boat' and row to salvage it. The moral of the story, as one of the Sun founders explains in the training film that is screened at the workshop, is that at Sun 'you can be as weird, as different as you like ... it's just great fun, just good, clean fun'. In the film the camera pans over some twenty-odd deadpan faces, a few amongst them dutifully nodding.

Because people are still mired in the old ways of thinking, they have to be taught to re-think the ways in which they have been accustomed to thinking of themselves and their relationships.[11] At one TA training Lakshmi asks young IT professionals for their associations with the word 'parent'. They come up with 'mature, understanding, nurturing', and when she asks for associations for the word 'child', they say 'irresponsible, immature'. A somewhat nonplussed trainer attempts to steer the proceedings back to familiar theoretical ground by suggesting that "parent' is also 'authoritarian' and 'domineering', right? And a 'child' could also be 'playful' and 'creative', right?' Afterwards, when I ask her about the obvious discrepancy in meanings, Lakshmi first prevaricates. After a little pause, however, she breaks in with, 'Actually, it's true, It's true, I feel that our parents generally *are* predominantly in their Adult State. Like Yashoda telling Krishna don't do this *because*, otherwise ... and giving you a lot of reasons!' In this case, even the trainer, for her part, has to go through an extra step of translation, from her experiential, cultural framework into an objective language of 'humankind' in order for what she is teaching to be intelligible (to herself).

'So first, be yourself. Which is to say, cultivate yourself. Your own style. For example, if you see someone style's and like it, study it, so you can be spontaneous, be your own self. Be confident, make sure you shed your inhibitions, any fears, because there's really no need for them.' The CEO of Sun India urges employees to take charge of their lives and their jobs because: 'It's all within you and everything's possible, the opportunity is all yours ... A lot of people expect a lot of hand-holding [but] ... you can control your own destiny' (NIAS 2006a). Employees are constantly reminded that they have a 'choice' because it is their life to make of as they will. Any constraints that exist, any limitations they feel en route to realising their full potential, stem therefore from a lack of will or belief in themselves.[12] 'If I look at it as a constraint then it is; if I look at it as a challenge...' says Suhail, adding, 'It's just the way you look at it. It's all in the mind'.

Deep cross-cultural differences in notions of self, emotion, relationships and therefore of self-presentation have long been documented in anthropological literature (Wikan 1990; Grima 1992; Rosaldo 1980). More to the point in this case, these also form a staple of management literature, discussed above. Companies avowedly celebrate this difference, boasting of the fact of diversity within the workplace. Yet, when it comes to trainings, the content of a self frequently invoked—as in 'self-confident', 'self-actualised'—is treated as (self) evident. This is so despite the close relation that such a conception bears with a specific, historically produced American concern with the autonomous self. The ideal American self lies outside social and personal realities— realities which are seen as distinctly separate from and only an interference in, the truly effective functioning of such a self.[13] Thus the new 'knowledge-self', fashioned by the 'knowledge-economy', speaks in 'I' sentences, responds to the directives of its own will, is a team player and yet is entirely self-reliant.

The Science and Technology of Self-Reliance

Organisational Behaviour has emerged as a discipline, just like psychology was before... HR has all the science of professionalism; it has become a discipline in its own right [from starting out as a part of OB].

—Dr Chopra, Professor of OB at a
management institute in Bangalore

'Ma'am, I'm just wondering how do we get to there, by learning we get it [*sic*] or...?' asks one participant at an 'Effective Communication' programme. The trainer says, 'I agree some of what we are is what we call "personality" but also, we learn through lots of observation. There is always room for learning provided we have an open mind. Observe your boss [or anyone who] comes out a winner; observe him to see what he does right'.

Elsewhere, a trainer at once presents a problem and shows the audience the way out. 'If you are always aggressive in the long run, this leads to heart attacks, etc. If you are passive, you're on a downhill slide. You start believing you'll be down and you really are down.' The atmosphere in the room seems a little apprehensive, as if most people are aware that most of them—us—are hardly ever the ideal 'assertive' type. The trainer says, 'Don't worry, I'll show you tips, examples, so you can modify your behaviour accordingly, change'.

Trainers are able to confidently assert the universal attainability of being a 'winner'—and thereby place the onus of success on the individual—because they present success as the inevitable outcome of a series of pre-charted and standardised 'skills'. The confidence stems from an underlying belief in the universal truth of the remedies proffered. In our time only one institution can lay claim to such omniscient power, that of the natural sciences (Foucault 1990; Raina and Habib 2004). And this is precisely the canopy under which trainers and management professionals and academics attempt to find shelter for their work. Presented as the result of rigorous empirical observation and experimentation and standardised in the 'best practices' mode, trainings become the spaces where a science of human behaviour is brought into action. Below, I write of some of the specific trappings of science used by management experts and trainers. One trainer puts it best when she says, 'We collect all of this data and then it goes into a huge computer, a huge database. So far we don't have any material on India but, anyway, it's been found that results are pretty much the same the world over'.

Numbers and graphs are used as proof of the incontrovertible objectivity of psychological trainings and instruments. Although it is not clear how or why certain numbers have been decided upon, trainers insouciantly use standardised psychometric test 'results' to judge, predict and give advice on individual behaviour. The claim is that the tests reveal the 'true' nature of internal individual emotional processes. According to one trainer, a 'healthy graph' in one 'Interpersonal Communication Inventory' looks like an inverted 'U', rising and descending along a neat curvature, against an x–y axis on the whiteboard. She looks at it to say, 'You should be able to introspect and change for effective communication ... This gives you a picture, a true reflection of your own personality'.

Later, at the same training, we are handed out a thick set of questions from the TA handbook and are asked to 'draw our ego-gram'. The trainer cautions us, 'Don't leave anything unanswered because that will skew the scores.' At the end we are asked to compute our answers. 'The average for your age group', the trainer tells us, 'is 86. If there is anything below 72, there is cause for concern. If anything is above that, you are doing fine. But even with a score of 100, there are communication areas that you need to work on today ... make an action plan to improve your interpersonal communication'. An MBTI™ trainer notes that the 'ESTJ' personality-type has been found to be 'your classic corporate type'—based on the fact that when the test was administered to successful CEOs, the 'ESTJ' type was the most frequent outcome.

The deployment of specialised language, closely allied as it is with the generation of categories, is another important tool in the establishment of scientific authority (Foucault 1988, 1990; Rimke 2000). Dr Chopra says, 'It [the training] is very important because it helps you deal with different kinds of people. Previously, you might have dealt with it by your hunch or something, but this discipline kind of gives you a vocabulary to hang your insights [on] ... to make sense of your world.' As an example, he speaks of an Adam's Equity Theory to describe the fact of employees seeking more money and power, even though competition and comparison is wired into the very mechanism of capitalist income distribution: The 'basic premise of Adam's Equity Theory', according to Dr Chopra, 'is "I tend to compare my salary with other people [and] given skewed salaries, expectations are unrealistic, leading to stress". People expect to become CEOs and Project Managers very quickly and an organisation being a pyramid not everyone makes it and a lot of people are not psychologically fit'.

The language of soft skills trainings takes on a like revelatory cast in which everyday interactions are translated into objective phenomena. One trainer 'explains' a case of a linguistic misunderstanding between manager and clerk as '*actually* a difference in the "encoded" and "decoded" message'. Trainers also claim to diagnose the true underlying processes through their use of psychological categories—and thus to point the way forward to change. Lakshmi says, 'I feel that this client always was Parent, and he said to me, you need to tell me if it is Parent or Adult ... the reason the training is useful is because [the employees] can at least identify that this individual is in Parent, so I need to be Child ... that's when the manager is happy, when the employee is in Child'. Thus does the discipline of psychology appear in management curricula and employment trainings, including in ostensibly value-neutral (if vital) questions of compensation and commensurability, where it gives the sheen of professionalism through speaking a language of theory and science to matters more simply understood.

By laying claim to scientific methods of research—mainly through a re-coding of emotions in the language of socio- and psychobiology—soft skills trainings have succeeded in creating an apparently impregnable niche for themselves in today's office. It is a niche that seems here to stay, given the drive to individualise—which has meant, ironically, to standardise—the worker in and around the modern corporation. In such a situation, an industry that holds out the promise of turning out legions of uniformly motivated, dynamic, 'self-starters' becomes an obvious, imperative necessity.

Conclusion

There are sixteen ways of being normal. In other words, there are sixteen MBTI types.

—Vicki Nicholson, Trainer,
Myers-Briggs Type Indicator (NIAS 2006a)

The IT industry in Bangalore has been credited with bringing to India a positive work culture rooted in international notions of efficiency and productivity. Focusing on innovation and personal initiative, the new culture is seen to signal a shift away from parochial Indian red-tapism and bureaucracy ('babu-dom') to allow for greater freedom to the individual worker. Even as management professionals lament the loss of a certain 'Indian culture', they also laud Indian society's emergence into 'awareness'. The bracing quality of this 'awareness' forces individuals to recognise themselves alone as the font and architect of their success and, correspondingly, to fail to recognise structural or other barriers in the attainment of that success. Philosophically and practically, this ideology makes the profitability of a company the direct result of individual workers' attitudes (Kunda 1992). In this scenario, the emergence and continued strength of the soft skills training industry comes to be seen as a natural outgrowth. Managers and trainers urge the same instrumentalist messages: workers are encouraged to work on their personalities at work and at home in order that they may be most cost- and time-efficient, be positive and be rational.

But that is for the rhetoric. David Miller criticises the idea that an overarching 'economist' point-of-approach has meant that '… there are now more areas of cultural life, including symbolic systems … that can now be incorporated within a largely instrumentalist and economistic science' (2002: 174). I argue that there has been an attempt to bind and make reproducible inchoate emotions, to engineer the worker in loyalty and management culture. It is true—and ironic—that in fact there appears to be less 'science' and more irresistible cultural logic at work in the deciding upon and unleashing of management trainings. HR managers and academics agree that they do not demand that employees find meaning in their work, that they 'self-actualise'—the emphasis is to get through the day (or night), reach the latest deadline and not antagonise other team members in the process.

I contend that in the absence of any evaluative process, it is the allure of a supposedly quantifiable 'science' of human personality that makes psychological trainings ubiquitous in today's corporations, negating as it does all considerations of genuine cultural and personal difference and laying claim to universal psychological models for the achievement of corporate success. Diverse and specific histories have given rise to contemporary notions of professionalism and economic efficiency (Harvey 1990; Hochschild 1983). The multi-million dollar global soft skills industry ignores that history and turns instead to souped-up Darwinian notions of fitness and survival to justify the hyper-individualisation of present day work culture (Howell and Ingham 2001; Brown 2003).

Economic notions are no more value-free, however, than are notions of freedom or happiness (Weber 1958; Polanyi 1944; Riesman 1961; Sharma and Gupta 2006). Nor are notions of 'rationality' any more objective. Popular ideas of market-governed practicality are attached to ideas of profit, explained as the inevitabilities of brute, unmediated, scientific facts. To adopt the science of the human being proposed by soft skills trainings is to automatically agree with the definition of rationality as that which best furthers individual self-interest (albeit 'enlightened'). Yet, definitions of the self vary considerably across the globe, often to include society as well as the natural environment. This leaves little reason to accept the inevitability of a version of rationality that takes as its starting point definitions of self and economy based solely on utilitarian notions of the good life.

Notes

1. This article is part of a larger project examining the advent of the self-improvement industry in urban India, which I carried out as a Post Doctoral Fellow at the Centre for the Study of Culture and Society, Bangalore, between 2004 and 2006. I was also funded by the Indo–Dutch Programme on Alternatives in Development (IDPAD) for the portion of the research presented here, viz. the working of the soft skills industry in corporate India, specifically IT companies. This article is based almost entirely on ethnographic data gathered through participant-observations and interviews. My earliest field site was one of Bangalore's top management colleges, where I sat in on classes and interviewed professors. In addition, I attended trainings and interviewed personnel—managers, trainers and employees—in four software companies in Bangalore, besides attending trainings for more generalised corporate audiences. I also relied on material gathered by other colleagues on the NIAS–IDPAD project, especially Carol Upadhya Sahana Udupa and Gautam Sonti.

   I am very grateful to Carol Upadhya and A.R. Vasavi for their unstinting financial and intellectual support on this project. I appreciate the intentness and clarity of their thought. Moreover, their warmth and humour made the research and writing of this article a most enjoyable experience.
2. All the names used in this chapter are pseudonyms.
3. Prof. Chopra is referring to the famous 'Minute on Education' of 1835 by Lord Macaulay in which he argues forcefully for an English language education in India. In particular, he advocates the creation of 'interpreters' between the English and the 'millions whom [they] govern'. Such a class, he said, would be 'Indian in blood and colour, but English in tastes, in opinions, in morals and in intellect' (Bureau of Education 1965: 107–117).

4. For example, Japanese are hierarchical and loyal and have difficulty taking criticism, Indians look to their bosses to create nurturing, familial relationships that go outside the bonds of the professional, Americans believe in meritocracies and in talking about their feelings.

5. The film 'Fun @ Sun: Making of a Global Workplace' was made by Gautam Sonti in collaboration with Carol Upadhya and produced by the National Institute of Advanced Studies with support from the Indo–Dutch Programme on Alternatives in Development, the Netherlands. It is part of a series of three films entitled 'Coding Culture: Bangalore's Software Industry', which examines different aspects of the culture of the IT industry in Bangalore.

6. The Test, she says, is the work of a mother-daughter pair. In 1923, Briggs, the mother, first came across Jung's work in translation. Since then, there has been sixty years of research put into this questionnaire. Sushma says there have not been a lot of changes in the format.

7. Eric Berne, an American psychiatrist and psychologist originally trained in the psychoanalytic school developed Transactional Analysis. Berne's work, in particular the book *I'm OK, You're OK*, was popular all over the world—including India—in the 1970s and 1980s.

8. Apart from one set of trainers, no one offered to explain how or why these particular figures have been decided upon, but they are consistently cited in workshops throughout the city. One trainer said that this discovery (about the percentage of verbal to non-verbal in communication) was made by Alfred Mehrabian, an engineer trained in the natural sciences, who brought those same mathematical and scientific skills to the study of human interaction. Known for his pioneering work in non-verbal communication and his finely calibrated psychometric evaluations, Dr Mehrabian is currently Professor Emeritus of Psychology at the University of California, Los Angeles.

9. www.fastcompany.com.

10. As seen in the film 'July Boys' of the 'Coding Culture' series (NIAS 2006b).

11. For one thing, some of the language of these techniques is rooted in their cultures of origin. Transactional Analysis talks of the 'OK Corral', the name of a popular American TV programme. Also, one of its probing questions reads: 'I use expressions like "Boy", "Gosh", "Gee", "Wow".' No participant, however, asks for the meaning or translation.

12. See also Heidi Marie Rimke's (2000) article for a reiteration of this point in the context of self-help literature in the United States.

13. See de Tocqueville (1980), Bellah, et al. (1985), Appadurai (1990), Cohen (1998), Rimke (2000), Wikan (1990) and Kondo (1990).

References

Appadurai, A. 1990. Topographies of the Self: Praise and Emotion in Hindu India. In *Language and the Politics of Emotion,* L. Abu-Lughod and C. Lutz (eds), pp. 92–112. Cambridge: Cambridge University Press and Paris: Editions de la Maison des Sciences de l'Homme.

Bellah, R., Richard Madsen, William M. Sullivan, Ann Swidler and Steven M. Tipton. 1985. *Habits of the Heart: Individualism and Commitment in American Life.* California: University of California Press.

Bureau of Education. 1965[1920]. *Selections from Educational Records, Part I* (1781–1839). H. Sharp (ed.). Delhi: National Archives of India.

Brown, Megan. 2003. Survival at Work: Flexibility and Adaptability in American Corporate Culture. *Cultural Studies* 17(5): 713–33.

Cohen, L. 1998. *No Aging in India: Alzheimer's, the Bad Family and Other Modern Things.* Berkeley: University of California Press.

de Tocqueville, A. 1980 [1835]. *On Democracy, Revolution, And Society: Selected Writings.* J. Stone and S. Mennell, (eds). Chicago: University of Chicago Press.

du Gay, Paul and Michael Pryke. 2002. Cultural Economy: An Introduction. In *idem* (eds), *Cultural Economy*, pp. 1–19. London: Sage Publications.

Foucault, M. 1988. Technologies of the Self. In *Technologies of the Self,* L. Martin, H. Gutman and P. Hutton (eds), pp. 16–49. Amherst: University of Massachusetts Press.

———. 1990 [1978]. *History of Sexuality Volume I: An Introduction.* New York: Vintage Books Edition.

Goffman, E. 1959. *The Presentation of Self in Everyday Life.* New York: Doubleday.

Grima, B. 1992. *The Performance of Emotion Among Paxtun Women: 'The Misfortunes Which Have Befallen Me'.* Austin: University of Texas Press.

Harvey, David. 1990. *The Condition of Postmodernity.* Oxford: Blackwell Press.

Heelas, Paul. 2002. Work Ethics, Soft Capitalism and the 'Turn to Life'. In *Cultural Economy,* Paul du Gay and Michael Pryke (eds), pp. 78–96. London: Sage Publications.

Hochschild, A. 1983. *The Managed Heart: Commercialisation of Human Feeling.* Berkeley: University of California Press.

Hofstede, G. 1980. *Culture's Consequences: International Differences in Work-Related Values.* Beverly Hills: Sage Publications.

Howell, Jeremy and Alan Ingham. 2001. From Social Problem to Personal Issue: The Language of Lifestyle. *Cultural Studies* 15(2): 326–51.

Huntington, Samuel. 2000. *Culture Matters: How Values Shape Human Progress.* New York: Basic Books.

Kondo, D. 1990. *Crafting Selves: Power, Gender, and Discourses of Identity in a Japanese Workplace.* Chicago, London: University of Chicago Press.

Kunda, G. 1992. *Engineering Culture: Control and Commitment in a High-Tech Corporation.* Philadelphia: Temple University Press.

Lash, S. and J. Urry. 1994. *Economies of Signs and Space.* London: Sage Publications.

Miller, David. 2002. The Unintended Political Economy. In *Cultural Economy,* Paul du Gay and Michael Pryke (eds), pp. 166–84. London: Sage Publications.

National Institute of Advanced Studies (NIAS). 2006a. Fun @ Sun: Making of a Global Workplace. In film series, *Coding Culture: Bangalore's Software Industry,* by Gautam Sonti in collaboration with Carol Upadhya. Bangalore.

———. 2006b. July Boys: New Global Players. In Film series, *Coding Culture: Bangalore's Software Industry* by Gautam Sonti in collaboration with Carol Upadhya. Bangalore.

Polanyi, Karl. 1944. *The Great Transformation.* Boston: Beacon Press.

Raina, Dhruv and S. Irfan Habib. 2004. Copernicus, Columbus, Colonialism and the Role of Science in Nineteenth-century India. In *idem. Domesticating Modern Science: A Social History of Science and Culture in Colonial India*, pp. 60–82. New Delhi: Tulika Books.

Riesman, D. 1961. *The Lonely Crowd: A Study of the Changing American Character.* New Haven and London: Yale University Press.

Rimke, Heidi Marie. 2000. Governing Citizens through Self-Help Literature. *Cultural Studies* 14(1): 61–78.

Roland, Alan. 1996. *Cultural Pluralism and Psychoanalysis: The Asian and North American Experience.* London: Routledge.

Rosaldo, M. 1980. *Knowledge and Passion: Ilongot Notions of Self and Social Life.* Cambridge: Cambridge University Press.

Salaman, G. 1997. Culturing Production. In *Production of Culture/Cultures of Production,* Paul du Gay (ed.), pp. 235–72. London: Sage Publications.

Sharma, Aradhana and Akhil Gupta. 2006. Rethinking Theories of the State in an Age of Globalisation. In *The Anthropology of the State: A Reader,* A. Sharma and A. Gupta (eds), pp. 1–41. Massachusetts: Blackwell.

Wikan, Unni. 1990. *Managing Turbulent Hearts: A Balinese Formula for Living.* Chicago and London: University of Chicago Press.

Weber, M. 1958[1920]. *The Protestant Work Ethic and The Spirit of Capitalism: The Relationships between Religion and the Economic and Social Life in Modern Culture.* Trans. Talcott Parsons. Introduction by A. Giddens. New York: Charles Scribner's Sons.

6

Software Work in India: A Labour Process View

P. Vigneswara Ilavarasan

This chapter examines the nature of work and the workforce in the Indian software industry from a labour process perspective. Labour process is defined as '... the way we look at *how* work is done. It includes how workers relate to each other, how the work is organised, and most importantly, how the work process is controlled and coordinated' (Greenbaum 1988: 104). In the West, studies that focus on software work from a labour process perspective fall into two competing camps: the first view draws heavily on a Marxian framework and perceives software work as 'task fragmented' or 'deskilled', while the second view holds that software work is not task fragmented. Drawing on the arguments that have emerged in this debate and on data collected primarily from two software firms in Bangalore, the chapter examines software work and the nature of the workforce in the Indian context, with a focus on the question of deskilling.[1]

Software Work: Task Fragmented or Craft?

The academic literature on the software industry has been concerned primarily with the experience of the West, and there has been relatively little work on the Indian software industry from the point of view of labour. In the existing literature, two major competing views about software work have emerged. The first view is heavily influenced by Braverman's thesis on the deskilling of work and the degradation of labour under capitalism, as well as Marxian theory in general. According to this view, software work has been routinised through the fragmentation of tasks, as has happened in the conventional industrial workplace. Applying Taylor's scientific management principles, jobs are designed to achieve the maximum technical division of labour by dividing tasks into small or 'fragmented' pieces. Through task fragmentation, the planning or conception part of the work process is separated from the execution part, and skill requirements and job learning time are reduced to a minimum (Watson 1995). This system is known in the literature as 'Taylorism' or 'Fordism' (with regard to assembly line production) and is characteristic of the capitalist division of labour (Yates 1999). In the case of software work, task fragmentation means that low-level software workers perform routine tasks that do not require any analytical or creative skills, while higher-level workers perform the conception and design phase work that uses analytical or creative skills. Thus, according to this view, a perfect division of labour exists in the industry. The alternative view rejects this argument and asserts to the contrary that software work is still not routinised or task fragmented. According to this view, software work is not mechanistic in nature and has certain characteristics that defy the application of scientific management principles. Instead, it is pointed out that software work is a complex activity that is more intellectual than clerical in nature. In the following sections, these alternate views are explicated in more detail.

Using a Marxian framework, Greenbaum (1976, 1999) provides a historical analysis of the transformation of software work from craft activity to conventional industrial work, a move that took place in three phases—1950–65, 1965–70 and 1970–75. During the first phase, in the early days of computer use, there was no clear-cut division of labour and software work was more like a craft activity. During the second phase—'capital took control'—'programmers' were separated from 'operators' in the workplace and a new occupational sub-group—'systems analysts'—emerged. Systems analysts developed procedures to process information and find solutions to business problems, while programmers translated these solutions into a language the machine could understand. In this phase, a division of labour had emerged with different task sets, pay scales and training requirements.

As a result, the people occupying these different job categories were differentiated by class. Greenbaum (1976: 49) observes: 'While programmers were drawn from the college educated middle class and were paid annual salaries, operations positions required only a high school diploma and were paid hourly wages comparable to factory workers. Typically, operators were young men of working class families....' During the last phase there was an oversupply of software workers and '... the skills required for application programming were becoming less each year' (Greenbaum: 52). According to Greenbaum, this process of transformation of software work from craft to industrial work was associated with use of high level languages, the emergence of rigid hierarchies in software organisations, institutionalised training systems, and the separation of 'hand' and 'head' tasks in software work.

Kraft (1977, 1979), in his pioneering study, concluded that software work had been routinised and that certain occupational subgroups were being deskilled. He observed that software work was no more a craft activity and that activities involved in software work were divided into conception and execution tasks, bringing Taylorist management principles into the organisation (see also Kraft and Dubnoff 1986). He identified three instruments for the routinisation of software work: use of high-level languages, canned programmes and structured programming. According to him, through structured programming software development processes have been standardised. A project would be divided into smaller modules and each module would be given to a separate group of 'programmers'. These 'programmers' engage in activities that do not require any analytical skills. Moreover, a programmer working on a module would not have any knowledge about the other modules. In their historical analyses of the 'software factory', Cusumano (1989, 1994) and Matsumoto (1994) show that standardisation of the software development process was partly successful in late 1960s and early 1970s in certain kind of projects where new solutions are not required.

In the Indian context, the task fragmentation view is supported by Prasad (1998). She observed that activities required by the quality certifications (ISO 9000 series) of the International Organization for Standardization (Geneva) in the process of software production were used by Indian software companies to enhance managerial control rather than to improve the quality of the product being developed. The quality certification procedures in software organisations use structured programming, which has the same effect observed by Kraft earlier. For instance, one of the quality certification procedures insists that all the activities of the project should be documented. Documentation enables managers to seek solutions for new projects without consulting the workers, thus reducing dependence on workers' skills and implicit knowledge. When a worker leaves the project mid-way, a new worker can be inducted and is able to work on the basis of the documentation done by the previous workers, without halting the development process. '... the requirement that programmers document every step of their work means that any individual programmer no longer controls the production process, shifting control back into management hands in kind of 'invisible deskilling' (Prasad 1998: 444).

Routinisation of software work is reinforced by other institutionalised means such as the nature of training, and the pay and career structure available to software workers. There is a well-defined, differentiated structure of educational institutions that supplies workers to the software industry. Managers or high-level workers are from science institutes, specialists or middle level workers from engineering colleges, and coders and testers are from polytechnics. Similar differences in training have been found in other studies (for instance, Freeman and Aspray 1999) that showed that high-level workers had doctoral or master's degree and low-level workers had either high school or associates' degree. Moreover, according to Kraft, coders or low-level programmers are paid less and have limited career growth opportunities. Rarely do they become managers or technical specialists. The routinisation of work deprives them of the chance to learn and upgrade their skills, and they experience merely horizontal movement in the organisation. Technical specialists or programmer analysts are given 'virtual' promotions, in which they might get slightly increased pay or changed titles but the nature of work remains unchanged.[2]

Kraft (1977) also noted that the socio-economic background of different categories of workers differed. He observed:

> ... the parents of coders and low-level applications programmers were of modest economic and educational backgrounds. They were typically high school graduates and worked as blue-collar or clerical employees (1977: 47).

> The situation of analysts, managers, and high-level programmers was very different. Their fathers counted among their ranks professionals of various sorts (physicians, lawyers, research scientists, etc.) (1977: 48).

Similar differences are observed by Igbaria and Wormley (1995).

Another group of theorists have criticised the task fragmentation thesis, arguing that it is politically biased and fails to understand the nature of software work (Glass 2005; Orlikowski 1988). According to this perspective, software work is not task fragmented or routinised nor is it managed by Taylorist principles. These scholars argue that software work cannot be task fragmented or routinised like any other industrial work due to certain characteristics of the work. However, this argument does not have substantive empirical support from systematic studies such as those carried out by Kraft (1979) and Kraft and Dubnoff (1986). Instead, the arguments are based on reviews (Friedman 1990; Orlikowski 1988), descriptions by industry experts of personal experiences (Greenspun 2000; Glass 2001, 2005), and studies that focus on other issues but from which indirect inferences are drawn on this question (Aneesh 2001; Gaio 1995; Stinchcombe and Heimer 1988).

The ongoing debate on whether software work is deskilled or not is largely dependent on one's view of its nature, i.e., whether software production is a process that involves non-routine thought processes or whether it can be executed using routine processes. Based on a small sample of six graduate students, Glass et al. (1992) showed that more time is spent on intellectual than clerical tasks. Friedman (1986, cited in Gaio 1995) argues that Kraft's hypothesis of routinisation of software work and deskilling could be applied to the data entry activity of the software work. Data entry has been deskilled to the point of alienation, producing both physical and mental health hazards (Gaio 1995). However, data entry has become a different occupation that is better categorised as IT enabled work (Freeman and Aspray 1999).

According to Brooks (1975), a good software worker might be ten times more productive than an average worker. Unlike mass production work, the influx of more workers into a project does not guarantee that the project will be completed before time. Aneesh (2001) proposed that software work is less 'skill saturated' work. Even if tasks are relatively integrated, complete closure of the space for play in the structure of skills is difficult to achieve. Software work is such that the worker can solve the problem in many possible ways and an exact procedure for problem-solving is yet to be codified. Similarly, Stinchcombe and Heimer (1988) reason that software work is highly 'mental labour' intensive, and software work skills participate in both labour and capital markets. Also, absolute managerial control over workers is not possible because of the existing unequal relationship between expertise and experience in the work (Greenspun 2000). For instance, a worker with ten years of experience in Unix may be inferior in C++ based work.

Greenbaum and Stuedahl (2000) argue that the development of new media software products is not a linear process like that of software development in the earlier stages of the industry. This type of software development cannot be controlled or coordinated using traditional system development or project lifecycle techniques. This implies that software work has grown beyond the boundaries of a simple division of labour based on task fragmentation.

Cusumano (1989, 1991) observed that software firms are a new type of production organisation in which employees cannot be characterised as workers in traditional factories. He argued that task fragmentation is viable only in projects in which requirements and design are fixed and do not need any major changes at the later stages. But for totally new or innovative design projects, less structured organisational forms are needed to give software workers more freedom to invent and innovate (see also Greenspun 2000). Kunda (1995), in his ethnographic study of a computer firm in the US, concluded that systems of indirect or 'normative' control that shift responsibility for the execution of work onto the workers themselves are more important than forms of direct control employed in industrial organisations. Marks and Lockyer (2004) emphasise the role played by the team in knowledge acquisition by software workers within organisations. Based on a review of the literature, they conclude that '... as knowledge-intensive workers, their [software workers] primary interest is in the marketability of their own skills and knowledge in the external labour market instead of the well being of the organisation' (2004: 223). Based on research in the Australian software industry, Barrett (2001, 2004) offers a balanced view of the control of software workers. She concludes that software workers are not managed through any one system, systems of control instead depend on various factors like the nature of software work, whether it is a product or services company, the nature of the labour market, and so on.

In the light of this discussion, software work and the nature of the workforce in India are examined in the next section.

Work and Workforce in the
Indian Software Industry

The people factor has been very important for the growth of the Indian software services industry, because the industry works on the human resources (HR) augmentation mode. This means that the revenue of an organisation is directly related to the number of projects executed and number of people working on a project (Tschang 2001). In other words, the number of software workers is an indication of the revenue of the organisation. This is in direct opposition to software products companies, which have fewer employees but higher labour productivity. Software workers in India are highly paid (*Dataquest* 2001b), and software work is one of the most preferred occupations for the young (Akhilesh 1991; Spaeth 2000). But from the point of view of outsourcing companies, software labour is relatively cheap. It has been well documented by researchers (Arora et al. 2001; Heeks 1996; Kumar 2001; Nath and Hazra 2002) that Western countries prefer India for the outsourcing of their low skilled work due to low labour and other costs.

The Indian software industry is predominantly export-oriented and Indian firms mainly execute projects outsourced by Western clients. The 'support and maintenance' part of the software development cycle dominates the industry. A project is usually divided into four major stages: analysis and specification of software requirements, design of software, coding/writing and testing, and delivery and installation. The first two stages are completed 'onsite' (at the customer's site) and the third stage is outsourced to India. Cusumano et al. (2003) and Heeks (1998) claim that the 'waterfall' model of software development is followed by most Indian software firms. Also, India has the largest number of firms with quality certifications in the world, a fact that according to Prasad (1998) leads to routinisation of software work. Under these conditions, we may expect to find empirical support for the task fragmentation view. However, recent observations (Ilavarasan 2005; Parthasarathy and Aoyama 2006) suggest that there is an increasing amount of high skilled work flowing into the industry, a fact that tends to contradict this argument.

This study was designed to address six research questions:

1. Is there a clearcut division of the workforce into conception and execution workers?

2. Do execution workers participate in the conception part of the work?
3. Does the socio-economic background of different categories of the workforce differ?
4. Is the training for different categories of the workforce different?
5. Are career opportunities for execution workers restricted?
6. Do quality certification procedures enhance managerial control over work?

The data was collected during a two-month period in 2001,[3] primarily from a sample of two firms located in Bangalore—'A Tech' and 'B Tech' (pseudonyms).[4] Although the sample size was relatively small and may not seem to support wider generalisations, earlier studies (Arora et al. 2001; Nath and Hazra 2002) suggest that the nature of work performed in the Indian software industry is homogeneous across firms and thus meaningful inferences may be drawn even from a small sample.[5]

Division of Labour into Conception and Execution Tasks

According to the task fragmentation theory, activities involved in the software production process are divided into conception and execution tasks. The activities present in the first two stages of the software production process—'conception of idea for the software and preliminary analysis' and 'designing'—are conception tasks, while other activities involved in the later stages—such as coding, testing and maintenance—are execution tasks. Accordingly, one would expect to find software workers clearly divided into conception and execution workers. Conception workers are those who perform high-skilled activities while execution workers perform low-skilled activities.

Based on our analysis of work content, it can be argued that the software production process cannot be segmented into discrete stages of conception and execution. Factor analysis (principal component analysis with varimax rotation) was performed on 32 tasks listed in the task inventory.[6] Seven factors emerged which explained 68 per cent of the total variance of the data. The composition of the resultant six factors clearly indicates that they do not reflect discrete stages in the software development production process. For example, Factor 1 includes the following tasks: writing specifications, low-level designing, coding, debugging, programme testing, link testing, documentation and preparing housekeeping programmes. Within the same factor, tasks related to three different stages of software production, both conception and execution—designing, writing and testing—are present. Other factors also entail tasks from various stages of the software production process. This finding supports the alternative view (Orlikowski 1988) that the software production process is an iterative process in which discrete division into stages is not possible.

Software work is executed in the form of projects and each project involves certain roles. The roles in the project give a general outline of the activities to be performed by workers. There are usually four roles present in a project: developers, module leader, project leader and project manager. These four roles are almost constant in the industry, irrespective of the type of organisation. In some organisations, different labels are used—for example, module leaders may be called team leaders or technical leaders and project managers, business managers. Software organisations do not have definite role descriptions like ordinary job descriptions and there are no recorded or written guidelines to divide the work among roles in the project. Although role descriptions are absent, a general outline of activities associated with each role can be deduced. It was found that roles performed by workers in a project are taken more seriously than their positions or designations. As one worker said: 'I don't remember what my designation is. Here designations don't matter in work. The role matters in what you do in a project.'

In order to understand the nature of the division of labour based on work content, non-hierarchical cluster analysis (Ketchen and Shook 1996) was applied. This method classifies respondents based on their characteristics. In this case, workers were classified based on the frequency of activities they performed in the job. Based on the work content, workers can be classified into four categories, which approximates the roles described above (see Table 6.1).[7]

An analysis of the work content shows that all the workers perform activities related to both conception and execution tasks and there is no clear division between conception and execution workers. For instance, coding and debugging—two execution tasks—are performed by all categories of workers. On the other hand, high level

Table 6.1
Work Content for Different Categories of Software Workers

Frequency of Tasks Performed	*Activities of Categories of Workers with Approximate Roles Played in the Project*
Category 1 (Developer)	
Very frequently	Coding; Debugging
Frequently	Documentation; Programme testing
Sometimes	Writing programme specifications; Low level designing; Link testing; System testing; Internal reviewing
Occasionally	System architecture; Software architecture; Determining users' requirements; Estimating cost and time; Technical scoping; System specification in user terms; System specification in technical terms; High level designing; External reviewing; Preparing housekeeping programmes; User guide preparation; Training users; First level support to users; System maintenance and support; Training; Module Management
Never	Selling idea to users; Auditing; Recruitment; Evaluation of members; Firm-level policy making; Project management; General management
Category 2 (Module Leader/Developer)	
Very frequently	Nil
Frequently	Writing programme specification; High level designing; Low level designing; Coding; Debugging; Documentation; Programme testing; System testing; Internal reviewing
Sometimes	Determining users' requirements; Estimating cost and time; Module Management; System specification in technical terms; System specification in user terms; Technical scoping; Software architecture; Link testing; General management
Occasionally	Project management; Evaluation of members; External reviewing; First level support to users; Preparing housekeeping programmes; Selling idea to users; System architecture; System maintenance and support; Training; Training users; User guide preparation
Never	Firm-level policy making; Recruitment; Auditing; General Management
Category 3 (Module Leader/Project Leader)	
Very frequently	High level designing; Low level designing; Programme testing; Link testing; Internal reviewing
Frequently	Determining users' requirements; Estimating cost and time; Technical scoping system; Specification in technical terms; System specification in user terms; Writing programme specification; Coding; Debugging; Documentation; System testing; Module management; Project management

(Table 6.1 contd.)

(Table 6.1 contd.)

Frequency of Tasks Performed	Activities of Categories of Workers with Approximate Roles Played in the Project
Sometimes	Software architecture; Evaluation of members; External reviewing; First level support to users; Preparing housekeeping programmes; Selling idea to users; System architecture; System maintenance and support; Training; Training users; User guide preparation; Auditing
Occasionally	Firm level policy making; Recruitment
Never	Nil
Category 4 (Project Leader/Project Manager)	
Very frequently	Nil
Frequently	Determining users' requirements; Estimating cost and time; Technical scopng; System specification in technical terms; System specification in user terms; Writing programme specification; Coding; Debugging; Documentation; System testing; Module management; Project management
Sometimes	High level designing; Software architecture; External reviewing; Selling idea to users; General management; Recruitment; Module management; System specification in technical terms; System specification in user terms
Occasionally	Link testing; Low level designing; Programme testing; System architecture; System maintenance and support; Training; Training users; Auditing; Firm-level policy making; Coding; Debugging; Documentation; System testing; Writing programme specification
Never	First level support to users; Preparing housekeeping programmes; User guide preparation

Source: Survey data.

designing—a conception task—is also executed by all categories of workers (see Table 6.1). Although all these tasks tend to shift from 'very frequently' to 'sometimes' among respondents, none of the workers was found to exclusively perform either the conception or the execution part of the work.

Participation in Conception

According to the task fragmentation view, execution workers do not participate in the conception part of the project. Due to structured programming, the software development process has been formalised. A project is divided into smaller modules by managers using specialists, and each module is given to a separate group of coders and testers. The coders and testers are engaged in activities that do not need any analytical skills. Moreover, coders and testers working on a module do not have any knowledge of the other modules. By performing only the execution part of the work, they experience 'routinisation'. But the analysis presented above shows that in the Indian case, software workers are not divided rigidly into conception and execution workers and all the categories of workers tend to perform both types of activity. This implies that all the categories of workers participate in the conception part of the project. This finding is strengthened by in-depth analysis of the work distribution process.

When a project is contracted to an Indian firm, the skills required for the project are matched with the skills available. Workers with the required skills are selected to form a team. The selected workers could be those 'on the bench' (the period during which a worker is free after a project is completed and is waiting to be allotted work), or those who are working on other projects but are transferable. There is a separate department in software organisations that keeps an account of the skill sets of all the workers. Based on the availability of skills, work is allocated. If the required skills are unavailable, workers are trained to meet the demands of the project. During interviews it was revealed that there are no clear cut book-like instructions available for distributing the work in the project. Boundaries blur between a module leader and the developer.

The project leader and the module leaders divide the project into modules and allot work to the other team members. In most of the firms the core work is allocated to team members by the superordinate worker. In general, no worker is asked for his preference of work in the project. As a new worker said, 'They tell me to do the work, what they want me to do. I am never asked what I am interested in'. This is applicable to all categories of workers. But it was observed that workers are not asked for their preferences due to time and human resource constraints, rather than task fragmentation efforts. Most Indian firms provide services, and there is a need to deliver projects as quickly as possible. One project leader said: 'You can't really ask people what they want. Time matters a lot. If a guy wants to work on programme two, instead of one, I don't have any problem as long as I have some other guys to finish programme one. Otherwise, he has to do it.' Another project manager remarked, 'Work is allotted to the developers. We match the skill set of developers with the project requirements. They cannot just take the work that they want. We don't have that luxury here. We just want to finish off the work fast. There is severe crunch of people and not much time.'

There are, however, a few cases in which workers can choose their work. If the organisation is getting a project similar to an earlier one, the same team may be given the work. In this case, a worker could be given a preference. But under normal circumstances, a team is dismantled after the completion of a project.

Due to the export orientation of the industry, the participation of Indian workers in projects varies, from a limited role in conception to entire designing and execution. In certain projects, the client (abroad) completes the design and the rest of the work is done in India. In this case, Indian workers are primarily responsible for coding and testing. However, they have the freedom to suggest modifications to improve the design of the project. In most cases, during the design phase Indian workers are briefed about the ongoing work. It is common to see two parallel teams working both onsite and offshore for the same project, involving continuous interaction. As one worker said, 'Even when a project comes during a low level designing or coding phase, we have some participation in designing phase also. This helps us in coding better.'

In certain projects, work related to all the stages of software production is performed in India. These projects are known as development projects. In such projects, an internal review of the design is conducted before its execution. Any person in the team can suggest improvements in the design. All the team members have access to the specifications for the whole project, even though they work on a single module. As a developer said: 'The entire specification document is kept open for all team members. It is accessible to all. I can meet anybody to clarify the doubts. If I am able to prove that there is a mistake in designing, it will be corrected. I have the freedom to say that.' Another worker remarked, 'If I am interested in doing or participating in high level designing, I can do it. But I need to put extra time in my work. In fact the project leaders also insist on that, but the present work itself takes away all my time.' This shows that time is the only factor that limits a developer's participation in designing, not the structure or organisation of work.

Interestingly, when a 'bug' becomes too complex to solve within a team, help from outside is sought. The project leader contacts other project leaders who are working in similar areas. The team members are permitted to contact anybody inside the organisation. Information about the bug or the problem in the programme is emailed to all members in the organisation. Whoever is able to fix the bug or offer a solution is involved, irrespective of the membership in the team. In some cases, when a problem cannot be solved internally workers from other organisation are also contacted.

Information about all the projects is given to all via the intranet. All the workers know who is working in what project, what are the technologies used in the project and who are the clients. At various points in time, all the project members get an opportunity to interact either with the clients or the technical team of the clients. When video conferencing is arranged with the client, all the members attend it. Each knows their role in the project. Companies encourage employees to know about the whole project, including the other modules. The developers are expected to know about the links between modules. During the module integration and system-testing phases, all the team members are present. To quote a project leader: 'Everyone knows what's happening in the project. It's better to give the big picture to the developers. They can work better. It is very helpful in integration.'

There are periodic meetings among those working within specific modules and among those involved in the whole project. Module meetings are held more often than project meetings. In these meetings, the progress of the project is discussed, and any problems or issues related to the project can be raised by any team member. Members of one module team knows about the other modules. They may not know in depth the technical details of other modules, but they know about the logic of module functioning and how they are linked to the whole project.

Thus, it appears that all categories of workers participate in the conception part of software work. However, workers have limited freedom in the selection of projects in which to work: projects are thrust upon workers and the division of work is then decided within the project. Although there is a common perception that the role played by workers can change in subsequent projects, our findings reveal that the role played by individual workers remains constant. We did not find a single worker who performed the role of developer and then project manager in a subsequent project, or vice versa.

Differentiation of Workforce

According to the task fragmentation literature on the West, deskilling of work is reflected in the socio-economic background of workers. As noted above, studies showed that low-level workers are from lower class or middle class backgrounds while higher-level workers are from upper class backgrounds and their parents are professionals.

In the present study, workers were asked for their official social classification—General, Other Backward Class (OBC) or Scheduled Castes and Scheduled Tribes (SC/ST). This classification is primarily based on three indicators: educational status, economic status, and social/caste status. This classification forms the basis for many policy measures in the country. The general expectation is that a person belonging to the 'General' category would come from an upper caste, upper/middle class background and have a relatively better edu-cational background. Similarly, persons belonging to SC/ST categories hail from lower caste, lower class and poorer educational backgrounds (Chakravarti 2001). There could of course be exceptions.

Ninety per cent of the workers surveyed belonged to the General category and 10 per cent to the OBC category. There were no workers from SC or ST categories. Omvedt (2001a, 2001b) noted that OBCs and SC/STs are poorly represented in the Indian IT industry. These data suggest that software work is primarily an occupation of the upper class and castes. Thus, the study did not find any evidence for the hypothesis that different categories of workers in the industry come from different socio-economic strata.

This difference between the composition of the software workforce in India and the West may be due to differences in the social context. In the West, education is more evenly spread and the socio-economic class system is relatively stable, hence social stratification by class and education is reflected in the stratification of the software workforce. In India on the other hand, the middle class is a relatively homogeneous social stratum of educated, urban, and professional/managerial/white collar employees, due to its historical evolution. There may be less internal differentiation in this class that translates into stratification within the workforce. Moreover, given the large number of educated unemployed and especially the large number of engineering graduates, the IT industry is able to draw on people of similar educational backgrounds even for low-skilled routine jobs. The features that characterise the IT workforce—the predominance of engineering graduates (see below) and knowledge of English—tend to be a monopoly of the upper and middle castes and classes in India, leading to the relative social homogeneity of IT workers (Upadhya and Vasavi 2006).

Differential Training

According to the task fragmentation view, the training of IT workers differs among different categories. In the West, managers or high-level workers are from science institutes, specialists or middle level workers from engineering colleges, and coders and testers are from polytechnics. Also, high-level workers tend to have doctoral or master's degree and low-level workers either high school or associates' degree. Moreover, in-service training is restricted for low-level workers, and the training is tailored in such a way that it provides fewer opportunities for low-level workers to learn the tasks performed by high-level workers.

The study looked at the basic education and training of the workers and the training provided by software organisations. The former includes educational qualifications, the subject in which the respondent received his or her degrees or diploma, and the institutions where s/he studied. Educational qualifications were categorised into seven categories: (1) Bachelor of Technology (B. Tech.), Engineering (BE); (2) Master of Technology (M. Tech.), Master of Engineering (ME); (3) Master of Computer Applications (MCA); (4) Master of Science (M.Sc.); (5) Master of Business Administration (MBA); (6) Doctor of Philosophy (Ph.D.) and (7) other degrees or diplomas. Seventy per cent of the sample had BE/B.Tech. degrees and 12 per cent had ME/M.Tech. Only 1 per cent of the workers had other degrees or diplomas. Thus, educational qualifications do not differ across different categories of workers. The preference for engineering graduates (B.Tech./BE) in the Indian software industry is well known and has been attributed to the export orientation of the industry:

> Given the larger number of science and arts graduates, and the widespread availability of private training, the pool of potential software professionals is much larger than merely the engineering graduates. However, software firms are reluctant to tap this pool because of the potential negative signals to their customers (Arora et al. 2001: 1279).

Educational institutions from which the respondents graduated were grouped into four categories: (1) premier technology institutes (PTI); (2) premier engineering institutes (PEI) (3) state engineering colleges (SEC) and (4) others. This categorisation has an ordinal structure with PTIs leading in the quality of education offered. PTIs include the Indian Institutes of Technology, the Indian Institute of Science, the Indian Institutes of Management and the Tata Institute of Fundamental Research. PEIs include Regional Engineering Colleges (RECs) and the Birla Institute of Technology (BITS Pilani). SECs include engineering colleges run by the various state governments, while 'Others' includes private engineering colleges and other private colleges.

In the sample, 33 per cent were from the 'Others' category and 27 per cent were from SECs. Among all categories of workers, graduates from other educational institutions dominate, except in the category of project leaders/managers. The majority among project leaders/managers (38 per cent) are from PTIs. There are two possible explanations for this exception. First, project leaders/managers are the most experienced category of workers and had entered the industry when it was in a nascent stage and preferred graduates from PTIs. The second explanation supports the task fragmentation view that project leaders/managers are conception workers who are drawn from premier institutes. But qualitative observations contradict this surmise. An employee asserted, 'It's nothing like top people have come from top institutions, it's the experience and the expertise that matters'. Another worker opined, 'Generally people are from variety of institutions from reputed to less reputed institutions. But the commonality is all of them should have 70 per cent aggregate [marks] from 10th class to the final degree. Here, all are equal and hence no special filters are applied for higher positions.'

The study also collected information on the discipline in which respondents had received their degrees. These were divided into five categories: (1) computer science; (2) electrical and electronics; (3) other engineering disciplines; (4) sciences and (5) management. The subject classes were formed in terms of relevance of the discipline to software work. It was found that about 36 per cent of the workers were from engineering fields, 33 per cent were from the computer science stream, and 23 per cent were from electrical/electronics engineering field. A worker with any disciplinary background may attain the top position in the categories surveyed. Basic training does not differ for workers from different educational backgrounds.

Based on the content, trainings imparted by the companies can be broadly divided into two categories—technical and non-technical. Technical training involves imparting technical knowledge that is directly related to software work. Non-technical training involves imparting knowledge that is related more to the human aspects of the work. Technical training can further be divided into two categories—fundamental and specialised. Fundamental training is given to new recruits, and the main objective is to introduce software work to a person who is unfamiliar with it. It involves imparting all the fundamentals required to perform the work, and the period of training ranges from 30 to 90 days. A worker said: 'I knew nothing [about software work] before. All I am using or going to use is learnt from training in this firm. Anybody who enters the industry will be treated as an equal after executing a couple of projects. After a new trainee finishes his courses [training] here, he is on a level playing field.'

The nature of the training is driven by the market, i.e., organisations prepare their workers according to the needs of the contracted projects. Most of the trainings are 'need based'—when a firm takes on a project and does not have the competence to handle it, workers are trained in the relevant skills. There is no difference in the nature of the training imparted to various categories of workers, except for newly recruited workers who are given fundamental training. In this training, employees are not differentiated in terms of their subjects or degrees. Employees have no control over the nature of training they receive; it is largely driven by the clients.

Continuous training sessions are organised for all levels of workers. A worker states: 'Even when you reach the higher level, you need to update your skills. My project leader sits with me during training for VB 5.' Another worker said, 'The area was new. Even project leaders did not have prior experience in that. We all attended the training programme together for three weeks. Then we were told roughly about the things we are supposed to do. We worked on it for ten days and gave a presentation. Then the real work was allotted.' Often, 'low-level' workers are seen giving training to 'higher-level' workers. They give presentations to senior people about a new technology or technique that they have used for the first time in the organisation. These are known as 'knowledge sharing sessions' and seem to be held in all software companies.

Apart from initiatives taken by companies in training employees, there is constant pressure on workers to independently update their skills. In many cases, workers themselves take up training programmes. For example, during the bench period an employee is paid for doing nothing. But, according to a worker, 'If the period is long and uncertain, you cannot sit idle. You need to pick up something and try to learn in that period. When projects start coming in, you cannot coolly say, 'I was sleeping'. Moreover it is your life. It is better to learn something.'

Apart from formal training programmes, in some cases on-the-job training also takes place. On-the-job training is given in two ways: by inducting the new worker into an existing project or by assigning an internal project. When a worker is inducted into an existing project, s/he is allotted a small piece of work and is supported by the other team members. S/he learns the work by practical experience. In internal project cases, workers are allotted individual projects and expected to arrive at solutions with the help of a mentor. He learns through mentoring and through his own work.

In addition to technical training, workers are trained in the human aspects of their work. These programmes focus on corporate etiquette, presentation skills, team building, cross-cultural manners and effective email communication techniques. Training is given either by the in-house training department or by external trainers contracted by the firms. The in-house training is given by a specialised department or by other employees who have free time.

Career Opportunities for Execution Workers

According to the task fragmentation view, low-level workers have limited career growth opportunities; rarely do they become managers or technical specialists. The lack of career opportunities deprives them of the chance to learn and upgrade their skills and they experience only horizontal movement. Low- and middle-level workers get only 'virtual' promotions. They may get small increase in pay and their titles may also change, but the nature of work remains the same.

In the Indian case, it is observed that career opportunities are not restricted to any particular segment of the workforce. Most Indian software workers follow a similar career path, i.e., towards the managerial side. An informant compared his career path to that of a Western software worker:

> There you can see guys doing testing or coding for the last fifteen years. They have a proper ladder in that line itself [technical].
> I need to become a manager here. One cannot do much on

the technical side. We are more project based [i.e., engaged in software services rather than product development].

As mentioned earlier, the Indian software industry works predominantly on the HR augmentation mode. It needs many managers to coordinate projects between the Indian organisations and their parent firms or clients.

It was found that in the Indian software companies, the process of promotion is almost time-bound. All software engineers are promoted to the next level after gaining a certain number of years of experience in their current level:

> I joined as a fresher here. There was a performance appraisal after six months. It is for name's sake, to find out whether I am working or not. After that promotions are periodical. It is a twice a year affair.

> Performance appraisal is periodical everywhere. I need 18 months to shift to another grade. Then it will take at least six months more for next one. I was told that performance appraisal is quicker in the software sector. But I am yet to see it for myself.

For exceptionally good workers, promotions are announced in the middle of the year, but they will get a hike in pay only in the next financial year. Another study (Arora et al. 2001) also notes that Indian software workers are promoted to managerial positions based on seniority in the job rather than proven managerial capabilities. As observed earlier (*Dataquest* 2001b; Viswanathan 2001), after ten years of experience many Indian software workers tend either to settle abroad or start their own companies.

In summary, various categories of workers in Indian software companies do not form discrete divisions in the occupational pyramid of the industry. Rather, they are more like the layers of skin in an onion. The workers in the outer layer partly perform the activities of the inner layer along with the activities dedicated to their own layer. A new worker enters in the innermost layer and reaches the outer layers in a similar way. For each inner layer the next outer layer denotes more years of experience in the software industry, increasing skill levels, performing both managerial and technical activities and increasing salary.

Quality Certification Procedures
Enhance Managerial Control

It has been proposed that activities required by quality certifications
are indirectly aimed at task fragmentation. The ISO 9000 series of
the International Organisation for Standards and the Capability
Maturity Model (CMM) Levels of the Software Engineering Institute
are the two dominant quality certifications sought by Indian software
organisations. India has more firms with CMM certification than any
other country in the world (NASSCOM 2005). Apart from structured
programming, quality certification procedures insist that all the activities of the project should be documented. Documentation enables
managers to seek solutions for new projects without consulting the
workers, thus reducing dependence on workers' skills. When a
worker leaves the project in the middle, a new worker can be inducted
with reference to the documentation without halting the development
process. Thus a worker's control over the work is reduced and the
work itself becomes less labour intensive.

In contrast, the present study shows that workers are benefited by
the documentation activities prescribed by the quality certification procedures. As one worker remarked, 'I write thousands and thousands of
lines of codes. Documentation helps me when a problem arises. I can
always go back and check what went wrong.' With experience alone
one cannot solve all the problems of work in a software organisation, which is dynamic and complex. A less experienced worker may
have expertise in a rather narrow area in the work. It is difficult for a
person to keep track of all the developments in the software industry.
But the possibility of experienced workers understanding the new
development through their experience cannot be ruled out. One
worker said, 'My module leader generally knows what I am doing.
But during the system integration, when something goes wrong, I
need to be there to clarify or correct the things. It's very difficult for
him [the manager] to know in-depth what I am doing.'

Tacit skills (Wood 1987) of workers are often required and are
difficult to control. They resist attempts at standardisation. A project
manager observed: 'Guys don't do all the documentation they are
supposed to do. When they find some bugs, they fix it and don't care
to document it. We keep on devising something to control these kinds
of activities, but it's becoming difficult. We can tell them. We cannot
always stand behind them and look at what they are doing.' Thus

control over the work process remains divided between the managers and the workers. In fact, as noted by Cusumano (1991), dependence on the experience and skills of the workers increases in projects that are more unique, customised or even invented.

Several studies (such as Arora and Asundi 1999) suggest that Indian software firms use quality certifications more as a market ploy to attract customers than for any other reason. A worker opined, 'For companies to lure a big client and get a big project, SEI-CMM level or ISO certification plays an important role. The client gets assurance that whatever is being developed will be properly tested in certification companies.' However, doubts have been raised about the genuine nature of certifications in Indian software organisations. To quote a trade press report:

> Nexis search revealed four companies—Cognizant, Patni, Satyam and Zensar—claiming 'enterprise CMM 5', with no explanation of where the assessments were conducted or how many projects were assessed, or by whom. Dozens more companies trumpet their CMM levels with little or no explanation.

> Indeed, all of the services companies we interviewed for this story claimed that their CMM assessments applied across the company when in fact only 10 per cent to 30 per cent of their projects were assessed. That's partly because experts say that assessing every project at a big company would be too unwieldy and expensive (Koch 2004).

Also, in the Indian software industry there is a lack of application of computer aided software engineering tools, recycling and use of reusable components (Yourdon 1993). This also enhances the dependence of Indian software organisations on their employees.

Another activity suggested by quality certification procedures is reviewing, which involves cross-checking each others' work both within and between projects. In this process, a worker reviews the work done by other workers both in the same project and in other projects. The review process being followed in the organisations studied is more like supervising others' work. Thus, workers are given control over the work of their colleagues.

Quality certification activities are voluntary efforts pursued by Indian organisations to attract prospects. The nature of these certifications seems to differ with the nature of the markets they serve. The ISO series are considered more important in the European market and the CMM in the US market. Also, there is no consensus on the need for such models (Bach 1995) or the superiority of one or the other. Given this limitation, one may conclude that quality certification does not enhance managerial control over software work.

Conclusion

This chapter has examined software work and the structure of the workforce in India from the perspective of competing theories about the labour process in software production. Based on the literature, six research questions were identified for empirical study in the context of the Indian software industry. The findings show that all categories of workers perform activities related to both conception and execution phases of the development process. All categories of workers participate in executing the project, and participation in the conception part of the process is not limited to any person or position. Moreover, Indian software workers are predominantly from the upper socio-economic strata of society and different categories of workers do not differ in terms of their socio-economic background. Their education and the training given by software organisations do not differ for different categories of workers. All the categories of workers experience almost a similar career path. The study observed that workers are benefited by the documentation activities prescribed by the quality certification procedures. Also, control over work gets distributed among workers by review activities.

However, at a broader level, it can be argued that Indian software workers are controlled by external market conditions. They exhibit work autonomy within project boundaries that are controlled by forces external to them. For instance, the educational qualification (engineering degrees) of most employees, as required by the Indian industry, is a function of the overseas market. In addition, the nature of technical training programmes, the types of projects (either maintenance or development), and so on, are determined by external market trends and client demands. Within the international division of labour in the software production process, Western clients may be viewed as 'management' (in contradistinction to Indian software workers), as in the traditional task fragmentation view.

The conclusion that can be drawn from this discussion is that the position of the Indian software workforce in the labour process is similar to that described by Orlikowski (1988) with regard to Western software workers. She uses Derber's notion of ideological proletarianisation, in which '...professionals maintain an unusual degree of skill and discretion in carrying out specialised technical procedures, [but] they are increasingly stripped of authority to select their own projects or clients and to make major budgetary and policy decisions' (Derber 1983: 134). There is also a process of technical proletarianisation which indicates loss of control over the processes of work itself, similar to manufacturing assembly line workers:

> I would suggest that while DP [data processing] workers (unlike craft persons) [software workers] have always been ideologically proletarianised; there is no evidence that they have been subjected to technical proletarianisation to any significant or widespread degree. Given the growing importance of technical rationality in advanced industrial societies, the scarcity of DP skills relative to demand, and the ascendancy of DP workers to strategic positions, there is reason to doubt the likelihood of imminent technical proletarianisation of DP workers (Orlikowski 1988: 116).

Notes

1. In this chapter all the activities related to software production process or system development life-cycle (SDLC) of software are defined as software work. It is also commonly called programming.
2. These observations were based on a qualitative study conducted by Kraft (1977, 1979) using participant observation methods.
3. Data was collected through the triangulation method. The job inventory approach was used to examine the division of labour in the software workforce. A similar approach was used by Kraft and Dubnoff (1986) and Loseke and Sonquist (1979). This approach involves developing a checklist of tasks involved in software work and asking workers how frequently each task is performed in the course of their work. Sixteen tasks under four stages of software development were borrowed from the questionnaire framed by Bailyn (1989). Sixteen more tasks were added after consulting two experts. In the task inventory, each respondent was asked to mark how frequently each activity occurred in his or her work. Five options were given for each task: (1) never (2) occasionally (3) sometimes (4) frequently and (5) very frequently. A questionnaire consisting of questions related to the research issues, and the task inventory was prepared and tested through a pilot study.

Additional data was collected through semi-structured and open-ended interviews to supplement the quantitative data. Respondents were selected by incidental sampling method and efforts were made to include all categories of workers. Questions were related to what the workers do in their job, how they are trained, how the work is allocated, how they interact with others and the nature of tasks performed. An additional 13 unstructured, open-ended interviews were conducted with workers in firms other than the sample firms, to check whether the nature of work in the sample firms is similar to other firms in the industry. In all, 114 questionnaires were returned from the two firms, 60 from A Tech and 54 from B Tech. In addition, a total of 62 interviews were conducted, 33 in A Tech and 29 in B Tech.

4. 'A Tech' is a domestic company established in early 1980s in Bangalore with 21 offices worldwide. It earns 98 per cent of its revenue from software services and its major export destinations are the US and Europe. In the financial year 2000–01, it had a growth rate of 115.4 per cent and a turnover of US $540 million. According to *Dataquest* (2001a), a total of 9, 800 employees are working in A Tech. It has been rated as one of the top 10 software firms in India for the last four years. 'B Tech' is also a domestic company established in 1999 in Bangalore. It has co-headquarters in New Jersey and Somerset, USA. Nearly 66 per cent of its revenue comes from onsite work in the US. During 2000–01 it had a growth rate of 975 per cent and a turnover of US $14.6 million. According to the Human Resources Manager in B. Tech, the firm employed 1500 workers.

The firms were selected using the multistage cluster sampling method. One business unit with 450 employees from each firm was selected. In each unit, respondents were selected using quota sampling method from various hierarchy levels. Workers who are not involved in the software production or development process, such as from the administration and marketing departments, were not included in the sample. Each level was taken as a quota, and workers were selected using incidental sampling method within each category. In each firm, 80 workers were given the questionnaire. Finally, a total of 114 filled questionnaires were returned.

5. This chapter provides a comprehensive discussion of the study. Preliminary findings of it can be found in Ilavarasan and Sharma (2003).

6. Factor analysis is a data reduction technique that assigns numerous variables to groups.

7. For a detailed discussion see Ilavarasan and Sharma (2005).

References

Akhilesh, K.B. 1991. Vocational Choice Patterns of Urban Adolescents: A Case Study. *The Indian Journal of Social Work* 13(2): 265–74.

Aneesh, A. 2001. Skill Saturation: Rationalisation and Post-industrial Work. *Theory and Society* 30(3): 363–96.

Arora, A. and J. Asundi. 1999. Quality Certification and Economics of Contract Software Development: A Study of the Indian Software Service Companies. Paper presented at the NBER Conference on Organisational Change and Performance, Santa Rosa, CA. www.heinz.cmu.edu/project/india/index.html.

Arora, A., V.S. Arunachalarm, J. Asundi and R. Fernandes. 2001. The Indian Software Services Industry. *Research Policy* 30(8): 1267–87.

Bach, J. 1995. Enough About Process: What We Need are Heroes. *IEEE Software* (March). http://www.satisfice.com/articles/enough_about_process.pdf.

Bailyn, L. 1989. Toward the Perfect Workplace. *Communications of the ACM* 32(4): 460–71.

Barrett, R. 2001. Labouring under an Illusion? The Labour Process of Software Development in the Australian Information Industry. *New Technology, Work and Employment* 16(1): 18–34.

———. 2004. Working at Webboyz: An Analysis of Control over the Software Development Labour Process. *Sociology* 38(4): 777–94.

Brooks, F. 1975. *Mythical Man Month: Essays on Software Engineering.* Massachusetts: Addison Wesley.

Chakravarti, A. 2001. Caste and Agrarian Class: A View from Bihar. *Economic and Political Weekly* 36(17): 1449–62.

Cusumano, A.M. 1989. The Software Factory: A Historical Interpretation. *IEEE Software* (March): 23–30.

———. 1991. *Japan's Software Factories.* New York: Oxford University Press.

———. 1994. Software Factory. In *Encyclopaedia of Software Engineering,* J.J. Marciniak (ed.), 1208–20. New York: Willy Interscience Publications.

Cusumano, A.M., A. MacCormack, C. Kemerer and B. Randall. 2003. Software Development Worldwide: The State of the Practice. *IEEE Software* (November–December) 20(6): 28–34.

Dataquest. 2001a. The DQ Top 20, July.

———. 2001b. Reality? Not Anymore, May.

Derber, C. 1983. Managing Professionals: Ideological Proletarianisation and Post-Industrial Labour. *Theory and Society* 12(3): 309–41.

Freeman, P. and W. Aspray. 1999. *The Supply of Information Technology Workers in the United States.* Washington: Computing Research Association.

Friedman, A. 1986. Software Industry and Data Processing in the U.S.A: Work Organisation and Employment Structure. Report for the Directorate General for Employment, Social Affairs and Education, Commission for European Communities, Bristol.

———. 1990. Four Phases of Information Technology, Implications for Forecasting IT Work. *Futures* 22(8)(October): 787–800.

Gaio, J.F. 1995. Women in Software Programming. In *Women Encounter Technology: Changing Patterns of Employment in the Third World,* S. Mitter and S. Rowbotham (eds), London: Routledge.

Glass, R.L. 2001. A Story About the Creativity Involved in Software Work. *IEEE Software* 18(5) (September/October): 96–97.

———. 2005. The Plot to Deskill Software Engineering. *Communications of the ACM* 48(11): 21–24.

Glass, R.L., I. Vessey and S.A. Conger. 1992. Software Tasks. *Information and Management* 23: 183–91.

Greenbaum, J. 1976. Division of Labour in the Computer Field. *Monthly Review* 28(3): 41–55.

Greenbaum, J. 1988. In Search of Cooperation: An Historical Analysis of Work Organisation and Management Strategies. In *Proceedings of the 1988 ACM Conference on Computer-supported Cooperative Work*, Irene Greif (ed.), 102–14. New York: ACM Press.

———. 1999. On Twenty-Five Years with Braverman's Labour and Monopoly Capital (Or, How did Control and Coordination of Labour Get into the Software So Quickly?). *Monthly Review* (January). http://www.monthlyreview.org/1999greenbaum.htm.

Greenbaum, J. and D. Stuedahl. 2000. Deadlines and Work Practices in New Media Development, It's About Time. In Proceedings of IRIS 23 Laboratorium for Interaction Technology, U. Svensson, C. Snis, H. Sørensen, T. Fägerlind, M. Magnusson Lindroth, L.C. Östlund (eds), University of Trollhättan, Uddevalla. http://iris23.htu.se/proceedings/PDF/122final.PDF.

Greenspun, P. 2000. Managing Software Engineers. *ArsDigita Systems Journal.* www.arsdigita.com/asj/managing –software-engineers. Accessed on 18 January 2001.

Heeks, R. 1996. *India's Software Industry, State Policy, Liberalisation and Industrial Development.* New Delhi: Sage Publications.

———. 1998. The Uneven Profile of Indian Software Exports. Development Informatics Working Paper Series, No. 3, UK Institute of Development Policy and Management, University of Manchester. www.man.ac.uk/idpm.

Igbaria, M. and W.M. Wormley. 1995. Race Differences in Job Performance and Career Success. *Communications of the ACM* 38(3): 82–92.

Ilavarasan, P.V. 2005. R&D in Indian Software Industry. In *Managing Industrial Science Effectively,* Roli Varma (ed.). Hyderabad: ICFAI University Press.

Ilavarasan, P.V. and A.K. Sharma 2003. Is Software Work Routinised?: Some Observations from the Indian Software Industry. *Journal of Systems and Software* 66(1): 1–6.

———. 2005. I Don't Remember What my Designation is: Classifying Indian Software Workers. Proceedings of the Ninth Pacific Asia Conference on Information Systems, pp. 69-85. 7–10 July, Bangkok, Thailand. http://aisel.isworld.org/article_by_author.asp?Author_ID=8005

Ketchen, D.J. and C.L. Shook. 1996. The Application of Cluster Analysis in Strategic Management Research: An Analysis and Critique. *Strategic Management Journal* 17(6): 441–58.

Koch, C. 2004. Bursting the CMM Hype. *CIO Magazine,* March. http://www.cio.com/archive/030104/cmm.html.

Kraft, P. 1977. *Programmers and Managers: The Routinising of Computer Programming in the United States.* New York: Springer Verlag.

———. 1979. The Routinising of Computer Programming. *Sociology of Work and Occupations* 6(2): 139–55.

Kraft, P. and S. Dubnoff. 1986. Job Content, Fragmentation and Control in Computer Software Work. *Industrial Relations* 25(2): 184–96.

Kumar, N. 2001. Indian Software Industry Development: International and National Perspective. *Economic and Political Weekly* 36 (45): 4278–90.

Kunda, G. 1995. Engineering Culture: Control and Commitment in a High-Tech Organisation. *Organisation Science* 69(2): 228–30.

Loseke, D. and J.A. Sonquist. 1979. The Computer Worker in the Labour Forces: New Occupations and Old Problems. *Sociology of Work and Occupations* 6(2): 156–256.

Matsumoto, Y. 1994. Japanese Software Factory. In *Managing Industrial Science Effectively,* J.J. Marciniak (ed.), 593–604. New York: Willy Interscience Publications.

Marks, A and C. Lockyer. 2004. Producing Knowledge: The Use of the Project Team as a Vehicle for Knowledge and Skill Acquisition for Software Employees. *Economic and Industrial Democracy* 25(2): 219–45.

NASSCOM (National Association for Software and Service Companies) 2005. Business in India: Quality. http://www.nasscom.org/artdisplay.asp?cat_id=838.

Nath, P. and A. Hazra. 2002. Configuration of Indian Software Industry. *Economic and Political Weekly* 37(8): 737–42.

Omvedt, G. 2001a. Infosys and Microsoft–I. *The Hindu*, September.

———. 2001b. Infosys and Microsoft–II. *The Hindu*, September.

Orlikowski, W.J. 1988. Data Processing Occupation: Professionalisation or Proletarianisation. *Research in Sociology of Work* 4: 95–124.

Parthasarathy, B. and Y. Aoyama 2006. From Software Services to R&D Services: Local Entrepreneurship in the Software Industry in Bangalore, India. *Environment and Planning* A 38(7): 1269–1285.

Prasad, M. 1998. International Capital on 'Silicon Plateau', Work and Control in India's Computer Industry. *Social Forces* 77(2): 429–52.

Spaeth, A. 2000. India's IT Bonanza. *Time*, October.

Stinchcombe, A. and C. Heimer 1988. Interorganisational Relations and Careers in Computer Software Firms. *Research in Sociology of Work* 4: 179–204.

Tschang, T. 2001. The Basic Characteristics of Skills and Organisational Capabilities in the Indian Software Industry. *ADB Working Paper 13*, Asian Development Bank Institute, Tokyo.

Upadhya, C. and A.R. Vasavi. 2006. Work, Culture, and Sociality in the Indian IT Industry: A Sociological Study. Final report submitted to IDPAD. Bangalore: National Institute of Advanced Studies.

Viswanathan, V. 2001. Wipro's Offsprings. *The Week*, November.

Watson, T. J. 1995. *Sociology of Work and Industry*. London: Routledge.

Wood, S. 1987. The Deskilling Debate, New Technology and Work Organisation. *Acta Sociologica* 30 (1): 3–24.

Yates, D. M. 1999. Division of Labour. In *Encyclopedia of Political Economy,* A.P. O'Hara (ed.), pp. 219–23. London: Routledge.

Yourdon, E. 1993. *Decline and Fall of the American Programmer*. New Jersey: Yourdon Press.

7

Empowerment and Constraint: Women, Work and the Family in Chennai's Software Industry

C.J. Fuller and *Haripriya Narasimhan*

By 2005, over one million information technology (IT) professionals were employed in India and the number continues to rise rapidly. The industry is dominated by the young and the median age of IT professionals is around 27.5. Salaries are high by Indian standards, and graduates recruited in their early twenties on a starting salary of around Rs 15,000 per month in the major software and services companies can easily double it within a few years. IT professionals, especially employees of these software companies, are therefore prominent members of the new-rich middle class in contemporary India (Fuller and Narasimhan 2007). About one-third of all IT professionals work for software companies, and 24 per cent of them are women, although by 2007 this proportion is predicted to rise to 35 per cent. A similar number of people are employed in the IT-enabled services (ITES) and business process outsourcing (BPO) sector, where the work is more routine and less technical, and entry-level qualifications are lower; in this sector, women outnumber men by two to one (NASSCOM 2003, 2005a). Given gender inequality, these relative proportions are un-surprising. Nonetheless, although women are a minority among the software companies' 'knowledge professionals' (as they often call themselves), their presence in an industry at the leading edge of globalisation—as well as India's economic growth—is large enough to make it socially significant, at least among the middle class in Chennai where the research was conducted.[1]

Much of the literature on gender and globalisation in non-Western societies is about women's incorporation into the 'global assembly line' as workers in industries such as electronics and textiles, and its main themes include the exacerbation of gender inequalities, as well as the combination of empowerment, resistance, and exploitation experienced by women workers in relation to both the structures of global capital and domestic patriarchy (Marchand and Runyan 2000). To date, the most detailed ethnography of women in the global IT industry is Freeman's study (2000, 2002) of 'pink-collar' data processors in Barbados. She writes about empowerment and exploitation as well as resistance to the companies' tight disciplinary control. Although the two situations are far from identical (women form a minority of the workforce in Indian software companies, unlike in Barbadian data-processing firms), we can draw on Freeman's observation that sociological arguments about globalisation sometimes miss the '… active participation played by women workers … in both defining and reconfiguring "difference"'—as expressed in the sexual division of labour—amid the advance of global capitalism' (2000: 139). As we shall show, through their productive complicity with the demands of their work, women IT professionals have partially but significantly reconfigured gender relations and, as they themselves sometimes put it, have gained freedom and opportunities that their mothers never had.

Working for a Software Company

The top six software and services companies in India, as ranked by export revenue, are Tata Consultancy Services (TCS), Infosys Technologies, Wipro Technologies, Satyam Computer Services, Cognizant Technology Solutions (CTS) and HCL Technologies (NASSCOM 2005b). All six have branches in Chennai. Our research data on IT professionals comes mainly from interviews with a small and haphazard sample of twelve female and eleven male staff in one of these six companies, which we call Indian Computer Services (ICS). We also interviewed some people from the other five companies (two women and five men), as well as several small firms (five women and six men). All names in this chapter are pseudonyms.

Like other major software companies, ICS operates in several 'vertical domains'—such as financial services, insurance or retailing—and some professional staff are experts in particular domains. The majority, however, are software engineers who normally have a particular specialist expertise, and most of them are directly recruited from engineering colleges; about 20 to 25 per cent of new recruits are women. Starting salary at ICS is around Rs 15,000 per month. Most of the ICS staff work a 40- to 50-hour, five-day week according to a flexitime system, but managers in particular often work longer hours, especially when they have to complete a 'deliverable'—a specific task within a project that has its own deadline. Almost all work is done by teams of software engineers, plus a few domain specialists, who are supervised by team leaders and project managers; sometimes, technical specialists may belong to several teams. A team's size can vary from a handful to a hundred or so and some members usually work 'on-site' at the overseas client's office. Major IT firms such as ICS are part of a global industry, in which the US is the main market; overseas project assignments are an integral part of the job, and global software labour market opportunities to secure posts or earn money abroad are abundant. We should also note that the ICS staff predominantly belong to the 'Forward Castes', especially Tamil Brahmin, although no accurate figures exist and guesstimates of their over-representation in the company—and in Chennai's IT industry overall—vary greatly.

Like the other major software companies, ICS has office space in Tidel Park, an IT business park in south Chennai built by Tamil Nadu government agencies in 2000. ICS also occupies some older offices in the city as well as new premises on Old Mahabalipuram Road—now designated as Chennai's 'IT corridor'—which runs south from the Park. The IT companies' most modern buildings in Chennai—and still more those in Bangalore or Hyderabad—make Tidel Park look unsophisticated. But it is regarded as the hub of the city's IT industry and the Park's main building, a 13-storey white concrete and blue glass monolith, has become a prominent symbol of Chennai's emergence as a modern city.

Unlike the area surrounding it, Tidel Park is quiet, tidy and spacious, and its main building is always clean and cool inside. These qualities are greatly appreciated by IT professionals, especially women who describe the Park as a prestigious place to work. The main building contains a large 'food court' or self-service cafeteria where many of our interviews were conducted. We also spent time in ICS's offices and, from what we have seen and been told, the working space in all the modern buildings is much the same. A small number of senior managers have private offices and there are some meeting rooms, but most of the space consists of large open-plan offices of the standard modern type, which are divided by low partitions into individual workspaces, each containing a computer. People often decorate their workspaces with pictures, which may be religious. However, unlike in many other offices in Chennai, office walls or computer screens never display religious images or symbols.

Although the corporate ideology of IT companies tends to exaggerate the absence of hierarchies, in reality managerial hierarchies in IT companies are flatter than in more traditional companies. Particularly striking, compared with the latter, is the absence of support staff, especially the mostly female secretaries, receptionists and personal assistants preparing correspondence, answering telephones and serving male bosses.

Within ICS's virtually paperless, open-plan offices, team members, both male and female, work closely together. However, our evidence about work practices is superficial because security restrictions prevented us from carrying out participant-observation. Nonetheless, compared with the interactions observable in most workplaces or other social situations in Chennai, including those dominated by the young such as college campuses, conversations between men and women here—as well as their body language in each other's company—appear noticeably relaxed. In Tidel Park's cafeteria, too, groups of men and women mix freely when taking a break from their offices and it is not unusual to see obviously affectionate couples talking together at one of the tables.

Over 10,000 people work in Tidel Park; to operate the security turnstiles, they all have swipe cards, usually hung on chains around the neck, which have become the identifying markers of IT workers in Chennai. Entry into Tidel Park, like all IT offices, is more severely restricted than most other business premises. Apart from security guards, cafeteria staff and cleaners in the Park's semi-public space, IT professionals at work are insulated from the world outside and interact almost exclusively with each other, and are hardly ever seen by outsiders and subordinates—whether secretaries or peons—in their own organisation. These conditions significantly contribute to the unusually relaxed interactions between men and women, as one young single woman in ICS explicitly noted; we know, she said, that relations between the sexes are quite free inside Tidel Park, but outside it, even in the company of the same men—for example, at a team lunch in a restaurant—we have to revert to convention.

As mentioned above, ICS's staff operate on a flexitime system. The company's stated policy is that staff can start and finish the working day at any time, although they are required in the office between 10 a.m. and 4 p.m. Even if they are not working hard to finish a deliverable, many people stay in the office in the evening, often because that is when they have conference calls with American clients whose working day is just beginning. IT companies run bus services to the city's suburbs for the safe transit of their staff. Nevertheless, several young single women who live with their parents have told us that their parents become unhappy and anxious when they come home late, which adds to the concern that they already feel about their daughters working alongside so many men. However, many parents, we suspect, do not realise just how closely young men and women work together, and they have no way of knowing whether a deliverable really is due or is just an excuse to spend time with friends (or a secret boyfriend) at the office.

On the whole, while there seems to be a pervasive fear and suspiciousness about the moral conduct and sexual restraint of young, independent women who spend long and often late hours with men, the women interviewees never expressed any anxiety. Nor did any of them ever voice a concern about their reputation in the eyes of family members or outsiders. Complaints about sexual harassment by male colleagues are also remarkably uncommon; we have actually heard of only one such allegation, reported by a woman in ICS about an incident in another company. Moreover, IT companies, unlike older manufacturing companies, are not completely dominated by men and all the work is done inside offices; importantly, too, software engineers never do heavy, physical work alongside men of lower social class on external sites, all of which is typically seen as morally unsafe for women, particularly if they are unmarried. On the basis of research in Chennai in the 1980s, Mukhopadhyay concluded that, in comparison with pure science or medicine, the 'most socially dangerous field by far is engineering, both for the virtually all-male environment in which it is learned and the environment in which it is stereotypically practiced' (1994: 114). The rise of IT has radically altered this situation, for software engineering enables women to enter a high-status, well-paid technological profession without the dangers that did and still do attach to other branches of engineering.

Gender Equality at Work

As Béteille (1991) has forcefully argued, social equality can mean several things, but one crucial distinction is between equality as a right and as a policy. Béteille discusses this distinction mainly in relation to caste in India in comparison with race in the United States, mentioning gender only in passing. Nonetheless, the distinction formally applies to gender equality as well. Equality as a right primarily refers to individuals' rights and is exemplified in employment by 'equality of opportunity' for women and men (or people of different castes or races) in recruitment, remuneration and promotion. This is equivalent to gender neutrality or 'blindness', whereby women and men, as individuals, are all treated identically. Equality as a policy is primarily framed in terms of groups and is typically about 'affirmative action' designed to compensate for social and historical disadvantages suffered by certain groups, such as women vis-à-vis men or low castes vis-à-vis high castes. Indian IT companies, like other private firms, do not operate caste reservation policies; nor do they have affirmative action policies to employ or promote more women. In general, however, in ICS and other software companies, there is equality of opportunity for women and men as individuals, but women's ability to take advantage of this is materially affected by gender inequalities in the wider society.

Let us first consider equality among individuals. Almost without exception, our informants have insisted that there is no gender inequality in ICS or other major software companies. Thus, for example, Mala, a team leader in ICS, who is in her late twenties and unmarried, firmly insisted that the company has 'no gender gap'. By this she meant that gender is not a factor in recruitment, appraisal, promotion, salary levels, work allocation, project team composition or other significant issues.

A crucial element in attitudes towards gender is the fact that women and men have equal technical skills in software engineering, computer programming and other related fields, which is in turn linked to the assumption that both sexes are equally good at mathematics, science and technology. Particularly with respect to mathematics, widely seen as the pre-eminent academic subject in the curriculum, informants insist that there is no difference in ability between boys and girls; this finding is consistent with reports from Mukhopadhyay (2004: 476, 481) and Subrahmanyan (1998: 90). 'Women [in the West] are often presumed to be intellectually unsuited for science and mathematics', as well as '... both intellectually and physically unsuited for technology, which may require work in dirty, dangerous surroundings or distant locations' (Wright 1987: 17). Although Indians share the presumption about women's physical unsuitability for technology, they disagree about intellectual unsuitability. Thus the general argument about gendered science and technology (1987: 10–12, 16–17) is seriously biased by Euro-American assumptions (cf. Mukhopadhyay 2004: 482–88).

Parvati and her friend Sarojini, both in their early twenties, joked about the minority of young men in ICS who are fixated on their computers and stay late in the office, pretending to work. In an English software company where she did ethnographic research, however, Woodfield found that such fixation was commonplace and old stereotypes about male 'boffins' had not disappeared, which contributed to the fact that women in the company 'reported a double bind whereby they were either deemed adequately feminine but ... inadequate computer scientists' (2000: 95) or vice versa. Characteristically, these English women were often mistaken for secretaries, receptionists or cleaners. But this is not the case for women in ICS. More generally, Woodfield concluded that 'the degree to which skills were defined, recognised and assessed was more dependent on the sex of individual workers than on the explicitly stated business requirements of the organisation' (2000: 146). All this, as Woodfield shows, is consistent with prevailing assumptions that knowledge and skill are gendered and unequally distributed and she cites a range of sources showing that her conclusions hold more generally for companies in the West (2000: 146–58). When Woodfield's basic thesis was put to Parvati and Sarojini, however, they first looked bemused and then said firmly that it did not apply in India, and everyone else interviewed—apart from one or two naïve young men—seconded this. Furthermore, female software engineers in Chennai, unlike in England, are not seen as inadequately feminine by anyone, and the assumption that women and men bring the same technical knowledge and ability to the job crucially underpins the assertion that there is no gender inequality in software companies.

Women's individual equality with men is often linked to their 'empowerment'. Amrita, a married woman in her early thirties who works in ICS's public relations department, was the first person to talk about women's empowerment in IT. Amrita illustrated her point by saying that, unlike friends with other sorts of jobs, she does not expect to consult her husband about her work and she has no qualms about going home late when necessary. Our initial reaction was that 'empowerment' was part of Amrita's PR presentation, but we soon found out that the concept (and the word) is part of common parlance among IT professionals. Thus Anuradha, an ICS project manager, in her early thirties and married, believes that the IT industry has helped to empower women, especially by giving them choices that their mothers never had, and they are no longer looked down upon by men. And when we asked Revathi and her three friends, who are all single women in their early twenties working for ICS, they agreed that the IT industry has empowered women because it is 'knowledge-based' and therefore enables them to compete equally with men as individuals.

Men, too, sometimes talk about their empowerment. Thus Ravi, a project manager in ICS, who is married and in his early thirties, has found the IT industry empowering because it has given him a lot of autonomy and responsibility quite early, which would not have happened in a bureaucratic organisation. For women, given their normally subordinate role in Indian society, autonomy and responsibility are even more significant than they are for men. Lakshmi, although she placed the emphasis differently, illustrates this point. Lakshmi, in her early thirties, is a married assistant project manager in ICS. She specified that individuals, male or female, are selected 'on their strengths only' in ICS. She also talked about her 'empowerment' in detail. Thus, Lakshmi explained that she feels empowered when she represents ICS to customers abroad because it enables her to cope with pressure—which brings out 'one's inner ability'—and creates a sense of achievement that women can scarcely find outside the IT sector. She is also respected by her family members for what she has achieved. According to Lakshmi her empowerment also comes from her 'financial freedom'; although we did not ask about her salary, it is probably around Rs 40,000 per month. For women, empowerment through high earnings is particularly important because it can enhance their negotiating power in the family domain.

Lakshmi's feeling of empowerment as a representative of ICS is linked to her 'exposure', which is a common term in middle-class discourse in Chennai. 'Exposure', as we have discussed elsewhere (Fuller and Narasimhan 2006), mainly denotes the process of enhancing social skills and cultural knowledge through new opportunities, experiences, social contacts and sources of information. Exposure, inside and outside the workplace, primarily enables people to improve their career prospects, and also their overall life chances and those of their family members. Lakshmi moved to Chennai to join ICS in her early twenties and said that the exposure in the city—compared with the town in Tamil Nadu where she grew up—has been 'too good to miss'. For all IT professionals, the most vital form of exposure comes from working overseas on project assignments. In 2003, Lakshmi was sent to Britain for three months. It was 'tough', mainly because she left her young son behind, but the 'big exposure' directly contributed to the 'high level' of empowerment that she now feels.

In comparing IT companies with other organisations, our informants might be overstating their case about female empowerment. For instance, in government offices or nationalised banks, there have been a lot of women employees for a long time and many occupy responsible senior positions. For IT professionals, however, such comparisons are irrelevant, because they believe that in the bureaucratic hierarchies of government and the public sector, nobody does any real work, individual initiative is stifled and promotion is never on grounds of merit. In fact, a better comparison with IT may be medicine, a high-status, well-paid profession in which there are many women. Some of Caplan's middle-class informants in Chennai in the mid-1970s were doctors, but, she reports, women doctors wanting promotion are '... often seen as a threat by male colleagues, and many women commented that "You have to be at least twice as good as a man" before getting a higher position' (1985: 91). Thirty years later, male doctors' attitudes may have changed; in our experience, though, women IT professionals never make such comments and clearly expect to be treated equally as individuals with their male colleagues.

Under normal circumstances, almost all staff belong to mixed-sex project teams and everyone asked about team composition said that it depends on the skills that are needed, not gender, age, caste or regional origin (which matters because many non-Tamils work in ICS's Chennai offices). Moreover, almost everybody accepts the fact that women frequently supervise men. Some, men as well as women, say that women tend to be better managers than men because they are more sensitive to personal problems and social relationships within teams, and they argue that promotion should take more account of these qualities and depend less on technical attainment. Yet even women who comment in this way do not see gender bias in the company as the main issue. Thus Parvati complained about her insensitive male project manager, comparing him unfavourably with his female predecessor, but she made it clear that she was criticising him only for his poor managerial skills, which were exacerbated by his inefficient female assistant manager. Parvati was not suggesting that he had been promoted because he was male and was not accusing him of discriminating against women in his team—any more than he, as a Malayali, was discriminating against Tamils. Neela, a project team leader in another software company, complained that 'men have a problem with women bosses', but this is unusual. Moreover, Neela then explained that an older man in her team was troublesome mainly because of his age, and several others commented that managing older subordinates can be particularly difficult.

Team performance depends on cooperation between members and those who do not pull their weight are resented by others, who may complain about them to team leaders and managers. Women who take time off to deal with their children or other family responsibilities can provoke resentment from team members, especially if they are suddenly absent when a deliverable deadline is imminent. Women who spend too long answering telephone calls from over-anxious mothers typically irritate their colleagues as well, but so too do men who spend too much time chatting to their friends or sending them emails. Most complaints, though, are about particular individuals and generalised complaints about working with one sex or the other are rare.

Strain among team members is worst at the time of appraisal, especially during the annual appraisal that determines promotion (a more limited appraisal half-way through the year is less bothersome). The inescapable contradiction in the appraisal system is that team members are competing against each other, although their performance critically depends on how well they cooperate with each other. The situation is exacerbated by 'normalisation', whereby the human resources department standardises appraisal results, so that someone's score may be reduced if too many people in one team score too highly. In any event, a line manager responsible for appraisal may be accused of unfairness by those who have scored badly; the manager may have allegedly favoured his or her friends, and gender can then be an issue.

Team activities—such as lunches, which are fairly frequent—are designed to promote solidarity among all members, but informal socialising among male and female IT professionals has variable effects. Unmarried men, but also some married men, tend to stay in the office later than women and may then go out to eat or drink together, or play sport or engage in some other leisure activity. Groups of men often also socialise at weekends. Married women and single women living with their parents normally go home directly from the office; single women living in rented accommodation, usually with female friends, may socialise after work, but much less than men. At weekends, groups of single women often get together, over a meal or at the cinema, but they rarely if ever drink alcohol. Mixed-sex socialising among groups of IT professionals may occur, but nobody mentioned it. During the working day, some men—but no women—also leave their offices together to smoke. Because of these differences, bonding between male managers and men in their teams is often fairly strong, whereas it is weaker between female managers and other women, and weakest between managers and team members of the opposite sex. This can give men some advantages—for example, in lobbying male managers for overseas assignments—but the effect on appraisal is not clear-cut, because although male managers may reward their friends at this time, they may also do the opposite to avoid potentially damaging accusations of favouritism. In any case, male managers tend to be regarded, especially by women, as less reliable, so that they do provoke some concern about fairness. The real impact, if any, of different socialisation patterns on appraisal and promotion is unclear and nobody has ever cited any particular case in which they believed that gender bias had unfairly affected somebody's career.

Marriage

'Women have constraints', agreed Parvati and Sarojini, which in practice means that gender inequality within the wider society can significantly affect women's ability to take advantage of equality at work. Marriage and children are the most important considerations and we focus on them, although Papanek (1989) rightly emphasises the larger work of 'status-production' for the family often done by women, noting that the conflict between family and work (as discussed below) might be better seen as one between '*old* obligations and *new* demands' (1989: 109; emphasis original).

In some professions, such as medicine and teaching, career-minded single women were and are not unusual in Chennai. In 1974–75, when Caplan studied professional women in the city, she found that only half her sample were or had been married, with a significant proportion remaining single, mainly through personal choice, a need to support the natal family or lack of suitable men for 'overqualified' women (1985: 88–91). In contrast, we have neither met nor heard of any women IT professionals in their thirties or forties who have remained single while pursuing their careers and all the single women we know assumed that they would get married eventually. In fact, there probably are some older, single women in software companies, but they are certainly a small minority. One reason is that attitudes to employed women, married or unmarried, have become more relaxed in Chennai in the last three decades, especially for IT professionals in companies like ICS, who enjoy a high occupational status and do not suffer the disdain or disapproval that Caplan described. Another reason is that most women IT professionals come from fairly well-off middle-class families, whereas in some of Caplan's cases families depended on daughters for financial support and therefore blocked their marriages. Furthermore, because the women have plenty of money themselves, marriage expenses rarely pose problems, whereas they do, for example, for some educated professional women from poor families in Karnataka who opt to remain single (Ullrich 1994: 208).

It is also important that IT professionals can usually be more confident than most other women about their marriage prospects, as we shall briefly discuss. At first sight—and as young women's parents fear—large software companies look like the ideal environment for love marriages in which people can freely choose their own partners. Many informants have told us that love affairs quite often develop between young, single people who work closely together. Sometimes these romances lead to marriage, and this is most likely when the couple would be suitable partners for an arranged marriage in any case. Some young women believe that love marriage is better in principle, but because finding a suitable partner by oneself is risky, difficult and time-consuming, arrangement by parents is the normal practice; others say that love marriage is a bad idea.

Amrita, who had an arranged marriage, claimed that women's empowerment was promoting love marriage, but the opposite view is more common. Thus one senior company manager who had an

arranged marriage said that women IT professionals 'are more practical and mature; because they are empowered, they do not go for
love marriages'; his wife, who was then a lecturer in mathematics,
laughed but did not disagree with him. By the same token, some
men say that 'empowered' single women in IT are 'hard to catch'
and consistently refuse advances from their male colleagues. The
key consideration here is that women IT professionals are confident
of their value as potential partners and hence are sure about their
parents' ability to find them good husbands. Moreover, many young
women (and men) believe that their parents are wiser than they are
and should be involved in, or even responsible for, choosing their
partners. A few women complain that parents, worrying about 'over-
qualified' daughters 'left on the shelf', put pressure on them to marry
too soon. Yet most women are also confident that they will have a
full say in the selection process so that no unwanted man will be
forced upon them.

In addition, women—even more than men—are aware that family
life as well as a continuing career will be very hard after a love marriage which is opposed by either set of parents and, even when talking
about arranged marriages, some single women are less concerned
about prospective husbands than about the parents-in-law. Therefore,
women IT professionals mostly favour arranged marriage in practice,
if not always in principle, and arranged marriages are the norm.

A few women leave the IT industry after marriage because it is
their 'community tradition' that wives do not work outside the home.
The majority, however, do not resign and single women consistently
say that they want a husband who will let them choose whether to
continue working after marriage. They also say that they want someone
who understands the industry's special conditions, such as the need
to work late or go abroad, although they typically assume, more or
less explicitly, that they must adjust to their husband's and parents-
in-laws' needs, not vice versa. Nonetheless, these wishes indicate
that most women prefer a husband who is also an IT professional. In
contrast, most male IT professionals are (or hope to be) married to
non-working and 'home-loving' wives. Presently, there are apparently
enough men in the minority to satisfy women IT professionals, and
the discrepancy in preferences is not a noticeable problem.

Marriage does not necessarily affect a woman IT professional's
working life. If her husband is not based in Chennai, however,
she may move to a job in another place and overseas postings are

usually more problematic for married women—or indeed married men—than for singles, with only very lucky couples managing to go abroad together. Marriage entails a major restructuring of relationships and responsibilities for Indian women, more than it does for men, especially if, as is often the case for our informants, the wife moves into her husband's home and has to learn to live with his family, particularly his mother. In some households, wives work a 'double shift' before and after office hours; exploitation by mothers-in-law certainly exists, although our fieldwork data are too thin for reliable conclusions about its extent. Nonetheless, as some married women IT professionals in Chennai have told us explicitly, a key aspect of their empowerment is that they can resist demands from their mothers-in-law, partly because they are away at the office for the greater part of the day, but more importantly because their large salaries contribute immensely to the household budget.

Children and Family Responsibilities

However empowered they are or feel, almost all women IT professionals still give their families higher priority than their work and—like nearly all women in India and much of the rest of the world—they do not regard paid work as 'any part of women's normal *duties*' in the way that it is for men (Sharma 1986: 129; emphasis original). Conversely, largely because it is seen as a duty, women—especially married women—consistently assume more familial responsibility than men. Thus, for example, a woman is far more likely to take time off work to care for a sick parent or parent-in-law than a man. Once they have children, women's familial priorities and responsibilities move up to a new level, so that childbirth, rather than marriage by itself, usually has the greater impact on women IT professionals' working lives. As yet, hardly any of these women are old enough to have teenagers, so that the discussion below is entirely about young children.

Very few mothers rely wholly or mainly on paid caregivers. Our sole clear-cut example is Mary, the manager of a small software company in her early forties. Mary is a Keralite Christian married to a Tamil Hindu with whom she has one young son. Mary and her 'very cooperative' husband, who runs his own IT business, live as a nuclear family and they employ a full-time help to look after their son as well as a driver who takes him to and from school. In an emergency, Mary's parents-in-law help in childcare. In Mary's experience as a manager, most mothers lack a proper 'support system', so they continually ask for time off work. Many women resign when they marry or have children; thus, money spent on training them is wasted.

Among all the female IT professionals we have met, Mary's battling determination to succeed in her career—as well as her lack of sympathy for other women workers—is exceptional. But so too is her childcare system. Gauri, a senior manager in a major software company and in her late thirties, also employs a full-time help to look after her young son, but she and her husband live with his parents so that they too play a part in their grandson's care.

Mary and even Gauri are extremely unusual, for most mothers— and other members of their families—will not entrust children to employed caregivers, except on a limited, part-time basis; instead, mothers depend heavily on their parents-in-law and often their own parents as well. Lakshmi is a mother using part-time childcare whose unusual arrangements provide an intermediate case. Lakshmi, who was mentioned earlier, is married to a manager in a data transcription company and they have one son, aged five. Lakshmi's parents live far away from Chennai; she has two married sisters and one married brother, who is also in IT and lives in Chennai. Lakshmi's parents in-law live in the next street. In the morning, she takes her son to school and after school, in early 2004, he used to go to her parents-in-law, who looked after him until she returned home. Later that year, she decided to employ a personal tutor for her son, not because he really needs tuition but so that her parents-in-law are not over-burdened with childcare, for they also look after their daughter's son. During the working week, Lakshmi rarely cooks; in the morning, food is delivered to her house and in the evening it is usually provided by her in-laws. At weekends, she goes to work only if absolutely necessary, so that she can catch up with housework and spend more time with her son. She said that because it was so hard to leave him when she went to Britain for an assignment, she might not go abroad again.

Lakshmi regards ICS as an excellent employer and praised its flexi-time system, which helps her—occasional stressful crises apart—to manage the balance between family and work through 'proper planning' and 'working effectively'. Yet Lakshmi is very anxious about her son and did consider a career break because she felt that she was neglecting him. She is also unhappy that her husband often eats in his parents' home because she has not cooked an evening meal. Lakshmi and her brother have been trying to persuade their parents to move to Chennai, so that they could help her and reduce her reliance on her parents-in-law, towards whom Lakshmi seemed ambivalent. She emphasised that her parents-in-law are supportive and she lets her son visit them frequently, but she also complained about depending on them. Lakshmi has made it clear that her job at ICS must limit her responsibilities as a dutiful daughter-in-law; she says that her husband's parents have accepted this, partly because their married daughter works and they therefore understand the circumstances, but partly also because her 'financial empowerment' has made them 'adjust' to her position. Lakshmi said that in the future, when she has met her financial needs and personal ambitions, she intends to find a less demanding job outside the IT sector.

Anuradha is more fortunate. Anuradha, an ICS project manager, is married to another IT professional and they have a very young daughter; they stay with his parents and her parents live in the same apartment block. After marriage, Anuradha, who had previously worked in two other software companies, moved with her husband to the United States for two-and-a-half years, where she joined ICS. But she never wanted to live abroad, and had made it a condition of her marriage that she and her husband would return to Chennai after making some money. Because of her child, Anuradha now refuses to go abroad on project assignments and said that this is not a problem because she needs no more 'exposure'. She does not find her job stressful and never works at weekend; she is close to her family, finds living with her parents-in-law easy, and can always rely on them and her parents to care for her daughter during the working day. Mainly because Anuradha's childcare arrangements are assured, she has easily been able to balance her family obligations and her work commitments.

Jayashree, in contrast, eventually recognised that she could not cope. An assistant project manager in 2004 (when we interviewed her), she is in her mid-thirties and married with two children; her husband also works in the IT industry and they live near his parents. After their daughter's birth in 1992 they went overseas to earn more money and spent three years there. On returning to Chennai Jayashree took a job in ICS, about which she was pragmatic rather than enthusiastic. Jayashree explained that her parents-in-law mainly care for her toddler son, but sometimes she employs a baby-sitter. Periodically, when her parents-in-law visit her brother-in-law in the

United States, then her parents, who live in a different part of Chennai, look after her son. Thus, she described herself as a 'nomad' moving between houses. Jayashree said that she kept her weekends free unless a crisis erupted, but she complained that her husband did not do his share of household chores, many of which, she joked, have been 'outsourced'; thus, take-away meals are now a routine. She talked about the pressures of combining family life and work and, unlike Anuradha or even Lakshmi, Jayashree found herself heavily burdened with the problems familiar to many working mothers across the world. She dwelt on her guilt about neglecting her son, who had seen so little of her and seemed more attached to his paternal grandparents. Eventually she resigned from ICS as she wanted to spend more time with her son. She now does contract work at home for the company.

Mothers commonly leave their jobs or take career breaks for reasons like Jayashree's; several such cases were mentioned to us. If the manager is unsympathetic to requests to go home early or take time off, resignation is probable. But many women (though we cannot estimate the proportion) decide to leave their jobs when they have children, and even some young, enthusiastic software engineers say that they want and expect to become full-time mothers later. Mala, for instance, who was quoted above on the lack of 'gender gap', hoped to marry soon and, despite wanting to continue working for some time, she also expected to retire early. 'Working women give less attention to children', Mala said, but 'there should be no compromise on children, life is short, so family is more important'. Mala's perspective is widely shared: for example, by Revathi and her friends. Emphasising a woman's primary responsibility for children, and her empowerment and gender equality at work, is common and is not seen as inconsistent, as it would be by many professional women in the West.

For the vast majority of women IT professionals with young children, the provision of childcare by their husband's and their own parents primarily determines whether they can balance the demands of their job with those of their family. These women's empowerment may place them in a relatively good negotiating position vis-à-vis their parents-in-laws in particular, but it does not actually diminish their reliance upon their husbands' and their own parents, given general unwillingness to employ full-time childcare. Husbands—whether described as supportive or not—are mostly irrelevant, because they rarely assume any serious responsibility for childcare or other familial or domestic duties. A psychiatrist in Chennai, whose practice includes work for a major software company, revealed that her overburdened married women patients typically complained that whereas 'I am not like my mother' (because a woman's role and expectations have changed so much), 'my husband is like my father'.

Once men become retired grandfathers, they often do help to look after their grandchildren, but the responsibility still falls mainly on grandmothers who, in middle-class circles, now undertake much more childcare and other domestic labour than their own mothers or mothers-in-law did in their old age. In many respects, indeed, it is grandparents, especially grandmothers, who provide family labour to support IT professionals. According to Donner (2005: 121–24), like their peers in Kolkata older women sometimes resent becoming hard-working childminders for empowered daughters-in-law and daughters, especially when they had expected a dutiful, 'home-loving' daughter-in-law to serve them. Not all grandparents, therefore, agree to help with childcare and, in such a case, a mother's ability to manage the balance between family and work may be seriously jeopardised. A similar problem arises if a mother relies for childcare on the same sets of parents as her own and her husbands' siblings. Satisfying all parties can be difficult, even if they live in the same vicinity, but it becomes still harder if they are scattered across Chennai. It is particularly complicated when a set of siblings, all with young children, live in completely different places, especially if some are overseas, where they may be visited for extended periods by one or other set of parents. As we have seen, this situation was faced by Jayashree before she left ICS and it is not unusual in our informants' mobile, professional middle-class families, whose ramifying networks structure a mother's opportunities and constraints.

Conclusion

To recapitulate, among IT professionals in Chennai the position of single women and even married women without children differs relatively little from that of men, but it becomes very different for women when they have children. Unlike men, women put responsibilities towards the family, especially their children, well ahead of their work and career, and their ability to manage the balance between family and work critically depends on childcare support from their parents-in-law and parents. For the majority of women, therefore, equality among individuals at work becomes progressively circumscribed or counteracted by gender inequality in the wider society.

When we met the CEO of ICS, he said that the company has to accept that Indian women do not balance family and career like Western women do, although he also acknowledged that ideally the 'attrition rate', especially high among married women with children, should be better controlled. He did not go into details, but longer maternity leave or more opportunities for working from home are typically suggested by all managers, male or female, when this issue is raised. Plainly, more 'family-friendly' policies could be introduced by ICS and other companies, which have mixed reputations for their attitudes to women and their family obligations. Some people, such as Jayashree, complained that ICS used to be more accommodating towards women, but now refuses to accept excuses about children; Lakshmi on the contrary praised the company for its flexibility and willingness to listen to women's problems.

As is well known, there are very few women among the software companies' senior managers, but many of our informants took the line that the normal course of promotion will raise the number markedly, because the proportion of women in the workforce is now much higher than a decade or more ago. Some ambitious young women expressed this opinion forcefully, but just as many others said that they had no desire to become senior managers and, in the future, they expected to be married with children, who would take priority over promotion. Hence any change in company policies can only slightly affect women's career paths if many or most of them firmly put their responsibility towards the family first, particularly when this means that mothers or grandmothers (not employed outsiders) should care for children according to the norms of a 'patrifocal family structure and ideology' (Mukhopadhyay and Seymour 1994: 3–4).

Yet the case of women IT professionals in Chennai is not just another example of global capitalism reinforcing gender inequality. The equality between women and men as individuals in ICS and other software companies is a social reality that means a lot to these women; it also gives them a degree of personal autonomy and empowerment within their families and social circles that their mothers—and the vast majority of Indian women—have rarely enjoyed. Very significantly, too, men IT professionals learn to treat women as equals. None of these developments will revolutionise gender relations throughout middle class Chennai, let alone the rest of India, but they are profoundly important to the many thousands of young professionals now working in the software industry.[2]

Notes

1. The research in Chennai was carried out for about twelve months between August 2003 and August 2005 by Haripriya Narasimhan; Fuller worked with her for about two months. Although the text of this chapter was written by Fuller, it represents the joint views of the authors. The research was supported by the UK Economic and Social Research Council as part of a research project on 'Regionalism, Nationalism and Globalisation in India' in the Department of Anthropology at the London School of Economics. We thank Henrike Donner, Carol Upadhya, A.R. Vasavi as well as participants at the Bangalore workshop for useful comments on an earlier draft of this chapter.
2. The data collected in Bangalore and discussed in other chapters in this volume suggest some significant differences between IT professionals in the two cities, although some of the variation may be due to small samples of informants or observers' biases. Nonetheless, there appears to be more competitiveness, stress and alienation at work, and more disillusion among women about unrealised gender equality, in Bangalore than in Chennai. We suggest, at least as a hypothesis, that this may be partly because staff in the major Indian software companies like ICS securely occupy the top of the IT job ladder in Chennai. In Bangalore, however, these companies operate alongside multinational companies engaged in research and development, product design, etc., as well as business services, so that the software industry is more diverse and more heavily influenced by western business norms, which in turn probably promote more competitiveness—along with its negativities—among individuals working in it.

References

Béteille, André. 1991. Equality as a Right and as a Policy. In *Society and Politics in India: Essays in Comparative Perspective*, pp. 192–214. London: Athlone Press.

Caplan, Patricia. 1985. *Class and Gender in India: Women and their Organizations in a South Indian City*. London: Tavistock.

Donner, Henrike. 2005. Children are Capital, Grandchildren are Interest: Changing Educational Strategies and Parenting in Calcutta Middle-Class Families. In *Globalising India: Perspectives from Below*, Jackie Assayag and C.J. Fuller (eds), pp. 109–26. London: Anthem Press.

Freeman, Carla. 2000. *High Tech and High Heels in the Global Economy: Women, Work, and Pink-Collar Identities in the Caribbean*. Durham: Duke University Press.

———. 2002. Designing Women: Corporate Discipline and Barbados's Off-Shore Pink-Collar Sector. In *The Anthropology of Globalisation*, Jonathan X. Inda and Renato Rosaldo (eds), pp. 83–99. Oxford: Blackwell Publishing.

Fuller, C.J. and Haripriya Narasimhan. 2006. Engineering Colleges, 'Exposure' and Information Technology Professionals in Tamil Nadu. *Economic and Political Weekly* 41(3): 258–62.

———. 2007. Information Technology Professionals and the New-Rich Middle Class in Chennai (Madras). *Modern Asian Studies* 41(1): 121–50.

Marchand, Marianne H. and Anne S. Runyan. 2000. Introduction. In *idem* (eds), *Gender and Global Restructuring: Sightings, Sites and Resistances*, pp. 1–22. London: Routledge.

Mukhopadhyay, Carol C. 1994. Family Structure and Indian Women's Participation in Science and Engineering. In *Women, Education, and Family Structure in India* Carol C. Mukhopadhyay and Susan Seymour (eds), pp. 103–32. Boulder: Westview Press.

———. 2004. A Feminist Cognitive Anthropology: The Case of Women and Mathematics. *Ethos* 32(4): 458–92.

Mukhopadhyay, Carol C. and Susan Seymour. 1994. Introduction and Theoretical Overview. In *idem* (eds), *Women, Education, and Family Structure in India*, pp. 1–33. Boulder: Westview Press.

NASSCOM (National Association of Software and Services Companies). 2003. Facts & Figures: Indian IT Software and Services Market. www.nasscom.org

———. (2005a). Indian Scenario: Profile. www.nasscom.org.

———. (2005b). Press Releases. www.nasscom.org

Papanek, Hanna. 1989. Family Status-Production Work: Women's Contribution to Social Mobility and Class Differentiation. In *Gender and the Household Domain: Social and Cultural Dimensions,* Maithreyi Krishnaraj and Karuna Chanana (eds), pp. 97–116. New Delhi: Sage Publications.

Sharma, Ursula. 1986. *Women's Work, Class, and the Urban Household.* London: Tavistock.

Subrahmanyan, Lalita. 1998. *Women Scientists in the Third World: The Indian Experience.* New Delhi: Sage Publications.

Ullrich, Helen E. 1994. Asset and Liability: The Role of Female Education in Changing Marriage Patterns among Havik Brahmins. In *Women, Education, and Family Structure in India,* Carol C. Mukhopadhyay and Susan Seymour (eds), pp. 187–212. Boulder: Westview Press.

Woodfield, Ruth. 2000. *Women, Work and Computing.* Cambridge: Cambridge University Press.

Wright, Barbara D. (ed) 1987. Introduction. In *Women, Work, and Technology: Transformations,* Barbara D. Wright, Myra Marx Ferree, Gail O. Mellow, Linda H. Lewis, Maria-Luz D. Samper, Robert Asher, Kathleen Claspell (eds), pp. 1–22. Ann Arbor: University of Michigan Press.

8

'Serviced from India': The Making of India's Global Youth Workforce

A.R. Vasavi

They can be identified easily: in the malls and supermarkets with their electronic swipe ID cards hung around their necks; inside company organised taxis that ferry them from their homes to their offices during odd hours of the day and night; in the long lines to use the ATMs at various junctions in the cities; in hotels and cafes in small and large groups and in clinics and counselling centres bearing signs of fatigue and stress. They are the new youth ITES (Information Technology Enabled Services) brigade—employees of the many ITES companies that have mushroomed in the Indian metropolitan cities of New Delhi, Chennai, Mumbai, NOIDA/Gurgaon, Bangalore, Pune and Hyderabad, and are now springing up in towns such as Coimbatore, Tiruchirapalli and Mangalore.

Ranging in age from 19 to 25 years, the youth ITES workers stand distinct from workers in other occupations in their work culture, identity and sociality. Individually and collectively, they embody their subjected positions in the global high technology work regime and bear the cultural marking of the global consumer industry. As participants in and carriers of this new global consumer economy, the Indian youth ITES workforce has been forged through a series of interlinkages between educational institutions, recruitment and training industries, the ITES companies that employ them, and the consumer economy that caters to and grows through them. Oblivious of their position as 'workers', an identity that is yet to be recognised or reckoned with by them, ITES youth are imbricated in and negotiate through networks of work, new socialities and identities, and pre-scribed family and community compulsions.

In the making of this new brigade of youth global subjects/ workers is the coming together of state, industry and market, each of which deploys markers to constitute them. As urban, middle and upper middle class youth emerge as global workers on India's na-tional economic and cultural terrain, they constitute an unanticipated category of worker-consumers who rupture many established and ascribed roles and norms, and signify the potential reordering of urban Indian family structures, inter-generational relations and the positioning of youth. The end product is a transnational information service subject, whose constitution, presence and agency (which is yet to be fully articulated and represented) will have bearings on the nature of globalisation in the 21st century.[1]

The Emerging Global Youth of the 21st Century

The growing presence and agency of youth as actors in the global social and economic canvas has produced varied understandings of their predicament. Challenging the West's naturalised representation of youth, in which the inevitable physiological condition of 'storm and stress' was accepted as universal and inevitable, there is increas-ing recognition of the varied and social construction of youth across cultures and nations (Larson 2002). Recent studies have gone beyond the emphasis on youth as a social problem and are now focusing on the forms and processes through which youth are engulfed by the circuits of globalisation, and their varied responses to and engagement with it (Vasavi 1998; Zhen 2000; Liechty 2003; Nilan and Feixa 2006). One result of globalisation has been the emergence of what Larson identifies as 'new adolescences' and 'new adulthoods' (2002: 22), even in non-Western countries, resembling trends of the West. Much of this has been made possible by the expansion of secondary educa-tion, delay in the age at marriage, urbanisation, entry into industries, and more recently engagement with the hegemonic global media and consumer culture and its attendant youth cultures. Such 'hybridised world kids' (Besley 2003: 153) have become the subjects of studies that focus on their subjectivities and identities in varied socio-economic and cultural worlds (Nilan and Feixa 2006). But, the spread of such a hegemonic culture has also induced increasing '... disjunctions between public symbols of affluence and private experiences of deprivation' (Vasavi 1998: 30) among youth. Similarly, Comaroff and Comaroff (2001) detail conditions in which youth are subject to unemployment, disruption, displacement, and are victims of the loss of culture and overarching anomic conditions, due to economic and cultural disembedding in the postcolonial and newly globalising nations. In the West, changing economic and family structures, shifts in welfare policies, and demographic denouement of an aging population, all signal trends in which youth prolong their stay in the parental home and are experiencing increasing unemployment and underemployment. Further, the impact of immigration has led to ethnic differences between generations, with more youth coming from immigrant communities giving rise to forecasts and portrayals of imminent tensions (Larson 2002). Referring to the new spaces that immigrant youth occupy in the advanced capitalist countries, Maira (2004) writes of 'youthscapes' to highlight the spaces and forms by which youth negotiate and constitute new identities and citizenship. The beginning of the 21st century is, therefore, for most youth a period of intense fragmentation and disjunction more significant than that experienced by the older generations (Brown et al. 2002).

The mark of the latest phase of globalisation, based on flexible capital and advanced communication technologies, also imprints youth. The spread and growth of information and communication technologies (ICT) are altering the micro and macro worlds of youth, and in some cases such as Japan, leading to the marking of youth as 'adolechnic' or adolescents who by making extensive use of ICTs create and engage in a subculture that marks them out from the otherwise homogenous Japanese society (Holden 2006). Although accessibility to ICTs remains problematic in most industrialising countries, in certain regions and contexts ICTs have enabled access to a larger world that largely excluded once disadvantaged and excluded marginal groups, thereby contributing to the development of new transnational linkages among youth.

In these studies and representations, which flag the positioning of youth in the global economic and social scenario, little attention has been paid to the emergence of youth as a specific segment of workers in the new global economy and to the ways in which their labour, identity and sociality are altered.[2] In India's growing ITES industry or what should be referred to as the 'technology mediated tertiary labour' sector,[3] youth have become the single biggest source of labour. Their amenability to training and their availability in relatively large numbers feed directly into the global ITES industry's need for cost-effective and customer-oriented labour.[4]

Tapping the Pool of Available Youth

Although India's ITES industry emerged as an offshoot of the success-ful outsourcing and offshore information technology (IT) or software development services industry, it has grown in leaps and bounds since the late 1990s, crossing figures and setting trends that were mostly unanticipated. The industry grew at a rate of 37 per cent during the fiscal year 2005–06, generated revenue of 7.2 billion dollars (of which 6.3 billion was from exports), and employed approximately 400,000 persons.[5] As companies seek to set up base in various Indian metropolitan centres, and as news about the 'positive outlook, people skills, ability to work under pressure' (Taylor and Bain, 2005: 274) of the workforce and the efficiency, cost-effectiveness and reliability of the services spreads, the industry is expected to employ about one million workers and generate a revenue of 25 billion dollars by 2008 (Seshu 2006). A range of companies, from in-house or captive organisations that are wholly-owned subsidiaries of large transnational companies, to Indian 'third party' organisations that cater to different clients, have taken root and are close competitors for the pool of available youth workers. The ITES sector includes not only call centres that provide a range of 'voice' services[6] but also business process outsourcing (BPO), back-office non-voice services, technical support services, finance, ticketing, telemarketing, legal and accountancy ser-vices, insurance and tax processing, medical transcription and a range of other office related work—giving rise to India's reputation as the 'back-office of the world'. More recently, drawing on the availability of math and science teachers, some companies have initiated online tutorial services, thereby inviting cartoons such as the one that figures an American father chastising his child that he cannot outsource his homework to India! Most ITES companies cater to markets and clients in the USA and the UK, and few include services to Australia and other English-speaking countries.

The popular media tends largely to celebrate the ITES industry in the same manner that it does the IT industry—it identifies its potential to 'leapfrog' India into a post-industrial service economy and resolve the problem of widespread unemployment, especially of the educated youth. Some critics, albeit few and far between, have labelled ITES as 'the global beck and call service' and the workers as 'cyber coolies', underscoring the servile nature of the work and the subservience that it signifies.[7]

Recognising and building on the economic opportunities that ITES companies offer, the Government of India has earmarked ITES as a prime industry. In order to cater to the industry's need for 'flexible labour', the government offers a range of incentives such as declaring tax holiday for a specific period; modifying rules to permit women to work on night shifts; de-licensing working hours to permit round the clock and throughout the year (24x7) work; providing facilities such as subsidised land, uninterrupted power supply, broadband and direct overseas cable connections; increasing the Floor Space Index in cities such as Mumbai, and even attempting to declare ITES work as essential services so as to prevent employees from going on strike (Government of Karnataka n.d.; Government of India 2003; Focus on the Global South 2005). The state is promoting the ITES industry through other measures such as developing a database on workers to strengthen security, empanelling training agencies and so on. More recently, catering to the demand to professionalise the industry, a new certification programme has been launched to create 'a robust and continuous pipeline of talent'.[8]

To make Indian ITES a global brand name, the government has coined the slogan 'Serviced from India' as equivalent to the 'Made in India' brand (*Business Line* 2006). In this campaign and global marketing blitz, the singlemost important selling point is the availability of a large pool of trainable labour, hence the now popular refrain that 'India has the largest English-speaking talent pool in the world—over 440,000 engineering degree and diploma holders, approximately 2.3 million other (arts, commerce and science) graduates and 300,000 post-graduates are added each year' (NASSCOM, n.d.).

This sudden attention to youth and to their training and employment is directly linked to the need to absorb them into the growing ITES workforce. India has one of the largest proportion of youth population in the world,[9] but it is only recently that issues of youth

and their education, training and employment have received attention from the state. An education system that is largely exclusive,
where there has been no planned effort to address issues of
vocational education, training and employment generation, and in
which only 6 per cent of the cohort of 18–24 year olds has access to
higher education,[10] has meant that issues pertaining to youth, their
opportunities, and their agency in the national context have been
neglected. But the demand for ITES labour has stimulated discussions
on the state of youth, and egged on by the IT and ITES industries
that are keen on absorbing them there is now an intense focus on
revamping vocational and college education to cater to the global
demand for service workers. An additional boost to legitimising
and making ITES industry and employment acceptable to the larger
public, and ensuring continuous support from the government, has
come from widespread reports and analyses of data which reiterate
that India will face an 'unemployment explosion' in the future, with
youth between the ages of 15 and 29 years accounting for as much
as 211 million unemployed by the year 2020.[11] This spectre of masses
of unemployed (and therefore dangerous and potentially disruptive)
youth feeds into promoting programmes that seek to make quick
and effective ICT and ITES related training available. The recent
attempts at introducing computer education at all school levels,
vocationalising secondary education with a focus on ITES and ICT
training, and ensuring improvement in soft skills such as English
language and communication abilities in all educational programmes,
feed into the development of the ITES labour force.[12] The results is
that the ITES workforce in India is predominantly young, and unlike
call centre workers in the West which consists of mixed age groups
and of relatively less educated persons, the Indian workforce consists
largely of college graduates.

Although the ITES industry and the government seek to legitimise the spread of ITES on the basis that it will help resolve the problem
of the large numbers of educated unemployed, the ITES industry
will not solve this problem. The largest proportion of unemployed
or underemployed youth are from rural areas. They are non-English
educated and primarily without the cultural capital to gain entry into
such work; thus, they are distanced from the new ITES jobs. This
explains why this booming industry finds it difficult to access sufficiently large numbers of suitable young workers.

Selling Jobs Tailored for Youth

The industry deploys a range of strategies in search of youth workers to be transformed into ITES 'agents', 'associates', 'consultants', 'representatives', 'customer service representatives' and 'desk engineers'— all designations that disguise the routinised nature of the work for which they are employed. Advertisements present preppy looking youth who beam confidence and bear all the signs of success—good clothes, poise and working in plush environments.[13] Work contexts and going to work are represented as fun, and photographs display employees in postures of casual swagger and confidence. Youth with a bag swung casually on the shoulder and a strident swing in the walk are meant to signify the cool attitude that is part of the work. Advertisement texts call the young to 'reach out to the world' and join companies that can turn them into 'professionals' without bearing the burden of the usual trappings of being a gold medallist or having an MBA or a chartered accountant degree. As a training consultant noted, '... IQ and degrees are the last things required. The job entails talking while your fingers work, it needs a certain aptitude. Which is why it appeals to a large pool of young people who are not necessarily very highly qualified. They are told to wear a smile on their voice'.[14] Promising them careers that will enable them to become 'mature and all-rounded persons', advertisements entice youth for 'not a job, but a career'. And in what is a cruel distortion of failed aspirations to have a medical career, some advertisements seek to recruit youth to medical transcription by indicating that medical transcription is another way of being a doctor!

Drawing on the popular desire to travel to 'foreign countries' (as the widespread expression that actually refers to the West goes), advertisements seek to integrate those with even 'just graduate degrees' into the new global village where they can 'excel and find their place in the sun'. Cashing in on the peppy tone of teenage talk, one advertisement called for 'customer jockeys' who should 'get set to rock 'n talk'. Although the focus is primarily on youth between the ages of 18 and 26 years, advertisements also seek to attract people from a range of social positions. To youth, the jobs are presented as 'opportunities to earn while they learn', for retired persons it is the 'recognition of their experience' and for the housewife, it is an opportunity to show that she is 'more than just a homemaker'. Recent trends indicate a focus on recruiting women, who are being increasingly recognised as more appropriate for ITES work because it entails personalised touches, and the ability to be more appeasing and responsive to customers.[15]

Given the ubiquity of such advertisements, and the widespread media reports of the success of the ITES industry and the improved lifestyles it offers to youth, it is not surprising that for the majority of educated youth across the country, joining the IT and/or ITES industry tops their choice of careers. A national survey of adolescents' career choices (Arulmani and Nag-Arulmani 2006) indicates that a career in computers ranked the second highest choice among all students—a choice that signals a significant shift in preferences from medicine, engineering and administrative services, which for years were the top choice for many young people. Given the limited chances of such large numbers entering professional engineering or computer science education programmes, the chances that they will enter the ITES industry instead are high.

Desperate for a large pool of labour to feed this growing industry, many companies hold open or walk-in interviews where young people are encouraged to come with their resumes, and take a test and an interview. Reception areas of these companies often contain crowds of youngsters, some accompanied by anxious parents, who seek to gain employment without going through the anxiety of the typical long-drawn 'application to final decision' processes. Campus recruitments, until now a privilege enjoyed only by the premier institutes of technology and business management, are now conducted in many English-speaking undergraduate colleges, and companies vie with one another to recruit the best students.

Complementing these campus recruitments are periodic ITES job fairs, often sponsored by one or more companies or media organisations, where companies seek to recruit large number of workers within a span of a couple of days. Many students, including those from rural and metropolitan areas, attend these fairs hoping to join companies whose advertisements they are unable to access. Presenting just their biodata and taking a test—often only for English and pronunciation—fresh graduates, the unemployed, and those seeking a quick change in jobs or a higher pay package throng these fairs. Although the interviews are supposedly focused on aptitude and general communication skills, the key eliminating factor for call centres is the inability to speak acceptable and standarised English, and those with heavy regional or Indian accents—what is referred to in the industry as 'Mother Tongue Influence' (MTI)—are weeded out.

Those who are recruited are hired as trainees and undergo training usually for a period of three months, and after the probation period are absorbed into the company as regular employees. Such 'job fairs' and the demand for English-speaking personnel have led to a mushrooming of institutes and centres in cities and Tier Two towns that provide quick spoken English courses. Supplementing these is the extensive ancillary industry of training and placement services for ITES jobs that has sprung up in the metropolitan centres where the ITES industry has a presence. Offering English language and communication skills training as well as more ITES-specific training, these centres also act as placement services for ITES companies in their hunt for workers.[16]

New Opportunities, New Life: Youth Access ITES

Bombarded by advertisements, job fairs, recruitment drives and a media that celebrates the new global jobs that have become available at the nation's doorstep, the youth themselves offer varied reasons for joining the ITES industry. For many, the relatively high salaries, especially compared with their parents' earnings and what is offered by other jobs, provide them an opportunity to be economically and socially independent. In an economy in which absorption into companies through trainee apprenticeship or focused development of a workforce is largely missing, ITES jobs come easy. They are available without the stiff competitive exam regime that governs other employment avenues and to which only a fraction of students gain entry. Unlike most jobs that require family contacts, influence, networks, and/or payment of bribes, ITES jobs are based on 'objective' criteria that the industry considers valuable, such as the ability to speak standard English, to excel in communication, and to be pleasant and adaptable persons. Such demands reinforce among the youth the need to be trained, skilled and oriented in these markers.

For a large pool of graduates with basic degrees, who lack opportunities to be integrated into professional or higher education programmes or to be absorbed into regular and established employment, ITES work flags their employability. As one placement officer puts it, 'They are typically people who are getting nowhere in life and they come for it, whether they like it or not. The pay is good'. For many, it is primarily the salaries, or what Krishnamurthy (2004) in her study of ITES workers in Pune noted to be the attraction of their purchasing power, the opportunity to work in an MNC (multinational company), the 'freedom to earn' rather than be dependent on their parents, and an opportunity for 'time pass',[17] that account for their presence in the ITES workforce. For some, this kind of work is seen as a step towards a job in the more respected and accepted software industry. Some students, unable to afford the increasing costs of higher education, see ITES jobs as a way to earn money to pay for their higher education courses. Since English-speaking skills are typically available only to those who have studied in private schools (where English is the medium of instruction), such jobs then become, by default, available primarily to the higher socio-economic group. As a result, only a relatively small proportion of those employed in the ITES sector actually supplement their families' income or are the key breadwinners.[18]

In many cases, ITES salaries provide the springboard from which many youth, especially boys, break from the economic, social and emotional bondage of their families. For long, the stagnant economy, the stiff competition to enter professional educational tracks, and the inability to gain secure employment have forced youth into conditions of prolonged dependence on parents and other family members. In many cases, independence from the family came only after gaining full-time, respectable employment, a condition that was not assured even if one was married. For many youth, ITES jobs have enabled an earlier break into independence; it is not unusual to come across ITES employees sharing apartments as a way of being independent of their families. Their consumption oriented lifestyles, facilitated by their high salaries and independent living, are a contrast to, and in many ways contravene, the cherished Indian values of saving for a rainy day, of family and kin based sociality, and community and caste dictated gastronomic preferences. Dating, being able to engage with a culture of consumerism, and entry into the new youth subculture are added attractions.

Training as Inculcation of New Dispositions

The period after recruitment sees the army of fresh recruits placed into intense training workshops and programmes that may last from three weeks to four months. Split into modules, each training programme focuses on providing technical and domain knowledge of the work, and in the case of call centres, an overarching focus on learning American or British English, culture and accent, and customer service norms. A 'bridge week' sees the assessment and the placement of each trainee onto the floor or work process, and an assigning of their designations and work responsibilities. Some companies opt for 'boot camp' style intense off-site training programmes in order to induct employees into the culture of the company and the norms and practices of the work, and to create bonding among the workers. Much of the training is aimed at producing fully socialised and trained service workers, incorporating them into the company's culture and its policies of customer service. Aimed at creating new dispositions in workers in which efficiency, reliability, communication styles and work norms are drawn from Western culture, the offshore ITES worker is sought to be made into a near visible service worker whose physical absence and social difference are sought to be compensated with additional affects of politeness and concern.

Training inculcates a set of 'dispositions' that, as Bourdieu notes, includes the engendering of '… aspirations and practices objectively compatible with … objective requirements' (1977: 77). In this case such training serves to internalise among the youth the need to be efficient, reliable, competent and endowed with the qualities of being a service worker. In all of this, training seeks to negate the cultural origin of the worker and attempts to make each into an acceptable global service worker, 'a citizen of the company catering to the needs of the global customer'[19]. And in the case of the call centres, where employees interact with a range of customers predominantly from the West, they are taught to be polite, to listen carefully, to built rapport, to sell, persuade or dissuade, and to be solicitious and considerate. Such demands, more explicit in call centres, are representative of 'emotional labour' (Hochschild 1983) or 'affective labour' (Hardt 1999), which draws on human contact and interaction in both real and virtual worlds and which seeks to induce a '…feeling of ease, well-being, satisfaction, excitement and even passion, a sense of connectedness or community' (Hardt 1999: 96). Despite the overwhelming ways in which the content of the trainings focuses on disseminating and inculcating the culture of the West, there are instances in which training draws on Indian culture to legitimise ideals of service. In one instance, the trainer exhorted the trainees to draw on the Indian ideal of *athithi devo*—the Indian cultural norm of treating the guest as god—and to treat customers as guests whom they must serve with devotion and sensitivity. Several features of the training are internalised by ITES employees, and they tend to valourise these as endowing them with life skills, improved communication abilities, better work norms, more professionalism and career consciousness.[20] If such trainings, and the continued orientation and inputs provided to the youth, are seen as forms of education, then work itself is located within a space and a process in which it is made to be seen as a combination of education, employment and entertainment.

Education, Employment and Entertainment

ITES Work as Lifestyle

Consisting of an average of nine hours per day (typically with one half hour break and two fifteen-minute breaks), ITES work comes with a regimen that seeks to extract the most of the youth's labour on the key logics of cost-efficiency and customer-orientation (Taylor and Bain 2005).[21] New technologies monitor, measure, and evaluate the work output in terms of volume and time, and induce each worker to maintain the standards and norms set by the company (Winiecki 2004). But beyond the deployment of the 'electronic panopticon',[22] represented in most cases by an intricate and complex combination of the use of computer technology and hidden cameras to monitor workplace behaviour, are sophisticated psychological and organisational behaviour practices that combine with new micro-management techniques to integrate the individual worker into his or her work environment.

In an effort to camouflage the rigour, monotony, repetitiveness and the overall stressful nature of the work,[23] ITES companies create work environments, processes and new socialities that combine to present and represent work as lifestyle rather than as conventional labour. The work spaces, despite their rows of uniform cubicles and array of IT and communication technologies, are designed to recreate a college-like atmosphere. The interiors of some offices are festooned with symbols of youth culture such as posters of popular media icons and party stringers that are used to decorate large work spaces. Through such strategies, ITES companies seek to defray the intense, demanding and often demeaning work in which workers are engaged. In some companies, the fifteen-minute break is an occasion for the 'fun officer' to conduct games and stimulation exercises, and the availability of Western fast food, and casual clothing are reminiscent of college canteens and campuses. In many companies there is a 'Rewards and Recognition Department' that provides incen-tives and awards to high performing individuals and encourages intense inter-team competition. The rewards and treats reinforce the consumption-oriented lifestyle. 'Halloween nights' with the 'Grim Reaper' visiting them on the floor; celebration with gifts at New Year's and Christmas; outings to bowling alleys and go-karting tracks; dinner treats at expensive restaurants; and prizes of coveted electronic goods such as DVD players, stereos, televisions and mobile phones, all compound the varied ways in which employment is masked as entertainment and the workers are integrated into the circuits of consumerism, which subsequently feeds into the formation of a new identity.

The strategies used to lessen the monotony of the work—the periodic recreation and social activities provided by ITES companies—are processes through which new forms of sociality and culture are constructed. Much of this new sociality substitutes for the loss of sociality that results from prolonged working hours (an average of 11 hours, if two hours of commute are added to the nine hours of work that is the norm), and lack of synchrony between their work timings and those of their families and friends. One result of the combination of the trainings and re-orientations, the new sociality generated at and outside the workplace, and the promotion of the culture of consumption and new communication styles, is an alter-ation in the personal affects of ITES youth. The casual but designer wear, the new found confidence, the altered gastronomic choices, and new socialities mark them individually and collectively, and enable them to engage in the larger consumption culture and global youth subcultures that are emerging in large metropolises.[24] Ashim Ahluwalia's documentary film *John and Jane* captures this well, highlighting the altered lifestyle and personalities of several ITES workers in Mumbai who attempt to translate the virtuality of their work and its Western culture into a reality in their everyday life. Work compels one to enter the circuits of global consumerism and consists of visiting bars, discos, international food chain restaurants, and in donning international fashion wear and accessories.

The alterations in dress (with an emphasis on owning a range of designer wear and accessories including the now indispensable cell phone) and the shift in attitude, language, accent, and orientation of the workers are often sources of discontent and tension between parents and ITES youth. Parents critique the altered sociality, health problems, and the stress and strain that their children experience. For some, it is the very culture of the industry, its encouragement of consumerism, and its strongly westernised and individualised orientation that fosters a new sociality of which they do not approve. When they become financially independent, many youth disengage from the authority of their parents, leading parents to seek counselling to learn how to handle their newly independent children who otherwise would be obedient and accommodating offspring. Girls particularly are seen as being susceptible to a culture of westernisation in which their dressing styles, habits of smoking and drinking, and new attitudes of defiance are commented upon.[25] One fallout of this construction and representation of the altered and unacceptable youth ITES person is the trend in which ITES women are increasingly stigmatised and are not regarded as suitable brides.

Contra Shome (2006: 107),[26] ITES work represents not the 'new logics and formations of race' or a 'transnational governmentality' (which assigns an all-subsuming dominance over the body and mind of the worker), but an 'entanglement' in which each party or agency seeks to fulfil their own individual agenda (Thomas 1991). Herein, the industry seeks to appropriate, utilise and maximise the skills, time and orientation of the youth, and the youth in turn seek to draw economic benefits, social identities and cultural markers from their engagement with the industry. In this entanglement lie multiple logics in which for the youth it is the employment opportunities, their attendant economic and social independence, and the forging of new identities as 'professionals', that make the industry attractive, and which complements the industry's need for a large pool of young, trainable and disposable labour. This seconds Liechty's observation of Nepali youth's imbrication in the circuits of global consumerism where a cultural compromise is forged leading to '... the inextricable simultaneity of using and being used, telling and being told' (2003: 252), between global and the local cultural processes.

This entanglement and appropriation into a transnational economic order then means that youth must negotiate between three differing and compelling contexts/logics. First, they must negotiate with the virtuality of their labour, which unlike the production of a good is not visible, and which requires them to assign meanings, come to terms with, and submit to the mediation of high technology and its surveillance system. Second, work entails a lifestyle and results in the imbrication of the worker into a cycle of materiality that signifies their new identity and sociality, and to sustain which they require this job. If the expensive cell phone, the new motorbike, and the designer clothes were required to fit into the social circle of ITES persons, then soon the need to sustain this lifestyle and the world of goods associated with it becomes the reason for staying on in the job. Finally, they must negotiate between the demands of family-ascribed sociality—in which they must interact and interrelate with persons on the basis of family norms and expectations—and the new sociality generated at the workplace, which is vastly different from that at home. Located within these three circuits of scripted work mediated by technology, consumerism and new sociality, these workers experience and express identities and subjectivities that indicate their relational position in the matrix of work, family and society.

The discord that results from either substituting one set of norms for the other, or attempting to integrate all, or in the confusion among the options, is manifested in the increasing cases of stress, burn-out, tension and the high rate of absenteeism and turnover. Narratives and biographies of youth workers testify to this deep ambiguity associated with work and its impact on them: 'We have the money but there is no satisfaction with what we buy'; 'I've changed a lot, everyone tells me so. Only I can't seem to see how'; 'I spend a lot of money on smoking and drinking. I have to, to fit in with the crowd'; 'Our team manager told me that I have to change my personality if I was to become successful. I don't know how to'; 'I've learnt a lot from my job but everyone tells me that I have changed'; 'This job has made me a professional but I am not sure how long I can work like this'. These expressions echo Hochschild's summative statement on the imprint of emotional labour: [27]

Those who perform emotional labour in the course of giving service are like those who perform physical labour in the course of making things: both are subject to the rules of mass production. But when the product—the thing to be engineered, mass produced, and subjected to speed-up and slowdown— is a smile, a mood, a feeling, or a relationship, it comes to belong more to the organisation and less to the self (Hochschild 1983: 198).

ITES Youth as Transnational
Information Service Subjects

Despite their criticisms of the long-term impact of the work on themselves, youth ITES personnel also highlight the ways in which they
are integrated into the company. Expressions such as 'It's a cool
job', 'I'm now a global employee', 'Being there for people makes
me feel good', or 'Many times I have helped people and that is very
satisfying', indicate the industry's ability to sell the work as non-
work and as education, employment and entertainment. Youth also
underscore their allegiance to the industry: ' In becoming a team
player your world becomes the company', 'I'm now a global citizen
as I speak to people from different parts of the world', etc. The result
is that youth ITES workers craft their working selves as professionals,
independent persons and visible consumers. Imbricated into the
rationale and logics of the workplace as well argued by Winiecki
(2004), youth workers in technology-mediated tertiary work become
particular kinds of subjects as they internalise the discipline and
rationalisation of the workplace. While Winiecki focuses on the ways
in which the subjective strategies and forms of control are deployed
and rationalised as objective (which are also relevant for India),
here the formation of the subject position in the context of the larger
acceptance of the rationale of the industry is also significant. This
subject position is constituted by the regime of global, high-tech work,
which marks its workers not as 'workers' but as subjects who both
objectively and subjectively subscribe to the logics of the industry.
Such a process of 'subjectification' is made possible by a range of
factors that reinforce the general observation that youth workers are
weakly attached to the labour force. Yet, this constitution is a result
of the characteristics of work and of the diffused work conditions
that combine education, employment and entertainment; the training
that integrates the youth into a world of goods, altered lifestyles and
personalities; the individualised bargaining and mobility within the
work system and the construction of work as primarily transient.

Although the work is onerous, burdensome and not what most
would choose to retain as their career or profession, there is little
that marks them as 'workers' in the popularly accepted sense of the
term. Several factors account for this negation/non-recognition of an
identity as workers. For one, the very nature of the work, the plush

work environments, the office setting, and the use of high technology diffuse typical constructions of workers and work contexts. The initial intensive training and the periodic training programmes create an orientation in which they are marked and identified not as 'workers' but as skilled and trained employees/professionals whose potential will be recognised by the company and who can reap the benefits of being continual learners within the organisation. Here youth ITES workers share with the women informatics workers of Barbados the '...aura of professionalism [which] helps to blur the boundaries of class identification and to diminish the [workers'] sense of class' (Freeman 2000: 237). Added to this is the fact that most of the youth ITES employees come from middle class, urban backgrounds, and for many the job is seen as transient and transitory. As a result, issues of worker identity and rights are not pressing concerns and most problems associated with the work are sought to be dismissed or are borne stoically as the job is considered to be temporary. Recognising their power, as demand outweighs supply and as multiple jobs chase them, youth workers choose to vote with their feet, and high levels of attrition—in many cases up to 70 per cent of the workforce in a year—are not unusual.[28] In the constitution of this non-worker identity and the subjection of ITES youth to the culture of the industry and its associated circuits of consumerism and lifestyle itself, Castells' observation that '...as work is globally integrated, labour is locally fragmented' (1996: 421) is apposite. The Indian ITES workers do not recognise themselves as either 'virtual proletariats' (Poster 2002) or as 'cybertariats' (Huws 2003). As the industry is in a nascent phase, the need for collective bargaining remains unrecognised and contested.[29] These workers share their work conditions and its imprint with the low-status, temporary workers of the industrialised West, who in their conditions of work are 'despatalised, de-socialised, and de-politicised' (McRobbie 2003: 112). And as several scholars have noted, workers do not necessarily embed themselves within the singular identity of being workers, but rather are embedded and marked by multiple identities that draw from the larger culture in which they are located.[30] Among youth ITES workers, it is their embeddness in the overwhelming culture of the industry, its imagery, its logic, and its associated links to the world of goods, altered lifestyles and new socialities, that predominantly accounts for the '...production of new subjectivities that become embedded in the archive of knowledge, subjectivity, and subjectification' (Winiecki 2004: 92). The end product is not a typical worker marked as a worker but a transnational information service subject who acts and interacts on the logic of an entanglement.

The historical transformation of the Indian peasant into the industrial worker has been documented by scholars (Chakrabarty 1989; Nair 1998; Joshi 2003), and sociological studies have focused on the retention of the social structure and culture of caste even in the new contexts of industrial work (Parry 1999; Chari 2004). As the 'grand transformation' (Poster 2002: 339) from the primacy of the agricultural and manufacturing sectors to the spectral rise of the global, high-technology led service industries takes place in India, we are witness to the emergence of enclave economies which, in their integration into the global circuits of capital, labour and commodities, stand out as markedly different from the earlier non-global work culture and orientation. Inasmuch as ITES work is emblematic of the new global high-technology service work, the workers, who are predominantly youth, are increasingly becoming subjectified as the carriers of this economy and its associated consumer culture.

In numbers and specificity, the growth and significance of the global youth subjects/workers[31] can be compared with the emergence of female labour in the export-oriented industrialisation of the New Industrial Economies of the 1970s and 1980s. Women became key agents and subjects of these industrial regimes, which incorporated and built on the constructions and reification of women's inherent qualities such as their reliability, docility and nimble-fingered abilities (Fuentes and Ehrenreich 1984; Ong 1997; Mills 2003). A range of factory discipline and managerial tactics were deployed to constitute a mass of women factory workers who worked to sustain the profitability of these transnational industries. An emphasis on fashion, beauty and commodified leisure marked them as consumers rather than as productive labour, and they reproduced themselves in the images in which they were absorbed and retained in the work.

Subsequently, as women became the rank and file of such industries it led to the feminisation of export industries in Southeast Asia and Central America and to the complex positioning of women in their social and work worlds. An extension of such imbrication of women within the circuits of global consumerism has also been documented among women in offshore ITES services in the West Indies (Freeman 2000). Occupying positions and identities that are neither white collar or blue collar, women ITES workers in the Caribbean are constituted by and represent themselves more as 'pink collar' worker-consumers whose identities and subjectivities as well-dressed, independent women negotiating ascribed cultural logics are prioritised over their identity as workers. Such constructions highlight how '…local and transnational processes of production and consumption not only converge but also reshape each other' (Freeman 2000: 261). If women emerged as 'the paradigmatic subjects' of transnational industrial work of the 1970s and 1980s, then perhaps youth can be seen as the new 'paradigmatic subjects' of the transnational information economy.[32] Their availability, trainability and dispensability fit well into the logics of flexible capitalism, which requires a large supply of cost-efficient, trainable and dispensable labour. Enticed into the circuits of capitalism and consumerism and as new workers without the identity of being workers, the ITES youth negotiate the varied processes of subjection that absorbs their skills and knowledge; use and deploy their relatively high salaries to assert their independence and identity on the social scene; and compromise and sacrifice their familial and ascribed sociality while forging new socialities that integrate them as the new global subject-consumers of the 21st century.

Notes

1. This essay is based primarily on data collected for the research study, 'IT Professionals in India and the Netherlands: Work, Culture and Transnationalism', carried out at the National Institute of Advanced Studies, Bangalore and supported by the Indo–Dutch Programme on Alternatives in Development, The Netherlands. The key sources of data are observations and discussions from on-site visits to training sessions, work shifts, follow-up interviews with about forty informants and their family members and details from discussions (and some confidential notes) with counsellors. Detailed and follow-up data from key sources was difficult as many of the workers were hesitant about having their lives documented. My gratitude to Carol Upadhya for largely bearing the responsibility of conducting the research (and egging me on to complete this essay) and to Sahana Udupa, Sarita Seshagiri, Pallavi Bhatt, Rakesh Mehar and Pratish N. for their assistance in conducting the field research. A month-long fellowship at the International Institute of Asian Studies (IIAS), Amsterdam branch, helped provide the much-needed space for reading and reviewing related literature. I am grateful to IIAS and IDPAD for this support and to Peter Van der Veer for making it possible. Special thanks to Donald Winiecki for sharing his papers and for inputs to this article.

2. Recent reports, such as one by the International Labour Organisation, highlight the problem of unemployment of large numbers of youth who form a significant proportion of the world's population. See http: //www.ilo.org/trends.

3. Winiecki (2004) uses this term, which is more appropriate than Information Technology Enabled Services (ITES) as it captures both the technology and service dimensions. But the term ITES is retained for this chapter as it is widely used in India.

4. Studies such as those by Remesh (2004), Ng and Mitter (2005), Shome (2006) and Taylor and Bain (2005) have focused on call centre work in India. However, none have emphasised the centrality of youth as workers or elaborated on the sociological specificity of their identity, its implications for the political economy of work or its socio-cultural impact. Krishnamurthy's (2004) work on call centres in Pune does elaborate on strategies and processes through which youth craft their identities.

5. NASSCOM, 'ITES-BPO Factsheet', www.nasscom.org. Data for the industry varies among agencies and sources. NASSCOM data is cited here because it is the IT and ITES industries' primary representative body.

6. Between the years 1999 and 2005 (the peak years of the establishment of the ITES industry in India), voice related services accounted for 85 per cent of the work. However, by 2006 voice related work accounts for only 35 per cent of the work. Many companies are now offering strategic consultancies on design, management and deployment of services ('India, not just Calling', *Business Standard*, October 30, 2006).

7. See Geetha Seshu, 'The Global Beck and Call Services', www.indiatogether.com, May 8, 2006. Also see Remesh (2004) for details on the stress and insecurities of call centre workers, based on which he refers to them as 'cyber coolies'.

8. Launched in November 2006, the BPO certification programme seeks to support the industry by providing a pool of persons with certified skills. See www.nasscom. in/aspx.

9. Precise figure of the youth population are unavailable from the Census data. However, several reports such as that by the ILO note the large number of youth who constitute the bulk of the population in this country.

10. For a critique of the lack of vocational education and the crisis it has created, see Yasmeen (2006).

11. A report by a private company, TeamLease Services (2006), takes a higher rate of population increase than that of the government and academic sources and highlights such figures.

12. See www.nasscom.org.

13. All the above terms are from advertisements published, between the years 2004 and 2006, in the Employment and Opportunities sections of leading English newspapers such as *The Hindu, The Times of India, Deccan Herald,* and *New Indian Express.*

14. www.indiatogether.com

15. Ibid.

16. Joining this pool of workers, drawn primarily from the metropolitan cities and two-tier towns, are a growing number of expatriate employees. As ITES work has declined in Western countries and jobs have been 'Bangalored', workers have come from the United Kingdom, the United States, Ireland and other countries. They are referred to as 'adventure workers' and are billed by the government as part of the new 'brain gain', in contrast to the 'brain drain' of the pre-liberalisation period.

17. Popular phrase for ways to kill or pass time, often associated with urban youth.
18. This is confirmed by data collected from our study in Bangalore (Upadhya and Vasavi 2006) and also by Remesh (2004).
19. From the stated objectives of a training programme of an ITES company.
20. Ng and Mitter (2005) also confirm this and indicate how ITES workers in Delhi appreciated their training as endowing them with new skills.
21. A number of studies (Remesh 2004; van den Broek 2004; Taylor and Bain 2005) describe the labour process in the ITES industry (particularly in call centres) in India. This essay does not focus on this aspect but concerns the implications of the working conditions and culture for the identities of workers, their construction of the work and their resulting subjectivities.
22. There is a large and interesting literature on the 'electronic panopticon' of modern information technology and computer-driven workplaces; see Bain and Taylor (2000) for details.
23. Because several studies have detailed the working conditions and forms of surveillance in ITES companies (Freeman 2000; Winiecki 2004; Remesh 2004), this essay does not focus on this aspect.
24. A larger culture of consumption is available within the metropolises, as a result of the newly liberalised and globalising economy, in which youth are key participants (see Saldanha 2002).
25. The actual proportion of girls who do transform in this way may not be significant. However, it is the visibility of the few who do and the strong disapproval that it invokes that is the basis for the widespread view that women ITES workers are changed by the ITES culture and money.
26. Shome's essay (2006) is representative of the kind of cultural studies that is based primarily on secondary data and on the author's interpretation of it. With data that is neither primary nor reliable (as most of the materials are from mainstream media reports), absence of any research methodology or a critical review of existing textual and theoretical categories, Shome seeks to represent ITES work (primarily call centres) as representative of a 'new racial logics', as seen in the ways in which workers are subject to a reworking of their 'aurality' and to regimes of disembodied work. By drawing on such theoretical concepts and representations, ITES work is fitted into the current discourse of cultural studies, an approach that fails to throw light on the political and economic contexts and the social and cultural specificity and complexity of ITES work and its implications. Further, Shome fails to take into consideration the fact that ITES work even in the West draws on similar disciplinary and surveillance strategies, and is therefore not racist in its intent.
27. Hochschild's (1983) seminal work factors in the social dimension and thereby the social management of emotional labour and its subsequent collective imprint on the US society, where 'natural feeling' is now collectively reified. Much of Hochschild's observations about the extraction, training and management of emotional labour by organisations need to be reviewed in the context of ITES work in non-Western countries, especially in voice-based work. We need to study such emotional labour when it is deployed in cross-cultural contexts, and if and how emotional labour and its management are culturally refracted.
28. Data from the NIAS–IDPAD study (Upadhya and Vasavi 2006) indicate attrition to be about 70 per cent per year on average. The *Business Standard* (October 2006) cites levels up to 75 per cent in the ITES industry.

29. The anti-union perspective is entrenched in the new political economy of neo-liberalism, and the state strongly supports the industry's anti-union stand. Sandhu (2006) also notes this among ITES companies and in NASSCOM, the industry's trade association. It is only recently (November 2006) that West Bengal, ruled by the Communist Party of India (Marxist), has encouraged the establishment of an 'association' for IT employees (*The Hindu*, November 14, 2006).
30. See Nair (1998) and Ong (1987) for details on miners and mill workers' identities and women workers in international export industries, respectively.
31. The Philippines has a large and growing number of youth ITES workers, and much of the contexts, trends, and ways in which they are constituted as a workforce and integrated into the global circuits of IT work, consumerism and lifestyles are similar to those observed in India.
32. Ong (1997) calls attention to the use of this term by Gayathri Spivak, but also rejects its validity as it fails to account for the varied and multiple positions and characteristics of different working women. However, the term has relevance as it draws attention to the centrality of certain subjects in the different phases and contexts of capitalism.

References

Arulmani, Gideon and Sonali Nag-Arulmani. 2006. Work Orientations and Responses to Career Choices—Indian Regional Survey. Draft Report. Bangalore: The Promise Foundation.

Bain, Peter and Phil Taylor. 2000. Entrapped by the 'Electronic Panopticon'? Worker Resistance in the Call Center. *New Technology, Work and Employment* 15(1): 2–18.

Besley, A.C. 2003. Hybrid and Globalised: Youth Cultures in the Postmodern Era. *The Review of Education, Pedagogy, and Cultural Studies* 25(2): 153–77.

Bourdieu, Pierre. 1977. *Outline of a Theory of Practice*. Trans. Richard Nice. Cambridge: Cambridge University Press.

Brown, Bradford, Reed Larson and T.S. Saraswati. 2002. *The World's Youth: Adolescence in Eight Regions of the Globe*. Cambridge: Cambridge University Press.

Business Line (2006). Serviced from India, July.

Castells, Manuel. 1996. *The Information Age: Economy, Society and Culture. Vol. 1* of *The Rise of the Network Society*. Oxford: Blackwell Publishing.

Chakrabarty, Dipesh. 1989. *Re-thinking Working Class History: Bengal 1890–40*. New Jersey: Princeton University Press.

Chari, Sharad. 2004. *Fraternal Capital: Peasant Workers, Self-Made Men and Globalisation in Provincial India*. New Delhi: Permanent Black.

Comaroff, Jean and John Comaroff. 2001. Millennial Capitalism: First Thoughts on a Second Coming. In *idem* (eds) *Millennial Capitalism and the Culture of Neoliberalism*, 1–56. Durham: Duke University Press.

Fuentes, Annette and Barbara Ehrenreich. 1984. *Women in the Global Factory*. Boston: South End Press.

Freeman, Carla. 2000. *High Tech and High Heels in the Global Economy: Women, Work and Pink-Collar Identities in the Caribbean*. Durham: Duke University Press.

Government of India. 2003. Task Force on Meeting the Human Resources Challenge for IT and IT Enabled Services. New Delhi: Ministry of Communications and Information.

Government of Karnataka. n.d. *The Millenium BPO Policy*. Bangalore: Department of Information Technology and Biotechnology.

Hardt, Michael. 1999. Affective Labour. *Boundary* 26(2): 89–100.

Hochschild, Arlie. 1983. *The Managed Heart: Commercialisation of Human Feeling*. University of California Press: Berkeley.

Holden, Todd. 2006. The Social Life of Japan's Adolechnic. In *Global Youth? Hybrid Identities, Plural Worlds*, Pam Nilan and Carles Feixa (eds), pp. 72–90. London: Routledge.

Huws, Ursula. 2003. *The Making of a Cyertariat: Virtual Work in a Real World*. New York: Monthly Review Press.

Joshi, Chitra. 2003. *Lost Worlds: Indian Labour and Its Forgotten Histories*. New Delhi: Permanent Black.

Krishnamurthy, Mathangi. 2004. Resources and Rebels: A Study of Identity Management in Indian Call Centers. *Anthropology of Work Review* 25(3–4): 9–18.

Larson, Reed W. 2002. Globalisation, Societal Change, and New Technologies: What they Mean for the Future of Adolescence. *Journal of Research on Adolescence* 12(1): 1–30.

Liechty, Mark. 2003. *Suitably Modern: Making Middle Class Culture in a New Consumer Society*. Princeton: Princeton University Press.

Maira, Sunaina. 2004. Imperial Feelings: Youth Culture, Citizenship, and Globalization. In *Globalisation: Culture and Education in the New Millennium*, Marcelo M. Suarez-Orozco and Desiree Baolin Qin-Hilliard (eds), pp. 203–34. Berkeley: University of California Press.

McRobbie, Angela. 2003. From Holloway to Hollywood: Happiness at Work in the New Cultural Economy? In *Cultural Economy*, Paul du Gay and Michael Pryke (eds), pp. 87–114. London: Sage Publications.

Mills, Mary Beth. 2003. Gender and Inequality in the Global Labor Force. *Annual Review of Anthropology* 32: 41–62.

Nair, Janaki. 1998. *Miners and Millhands: Work, Culture, and Politics in Princely Mysore*. New Delhi: Sage Publications.

NASSCOM (National Association of Software and Services Companies) n.d. Indian ITES_BPO Industry-Factsheet. www.nasscom.org.

Ng, Cecilia and Swasti Mitter. 2005. Valuing Women's Voices: Call Centre Workers in Malaysia and India. *Idem.* (eds), In *Gender and the Digital Economy; Perspectives from the Developing World*, pp. 132–58. New Delhi: Sage Publications.

Nilan, Pam and Carles Feixa (eds). 2006. *Global Youth? Hybrid Identities, Plural Worlds*. London: Routledge.

Ong, Aihwa. 1987. *Spirits of Resistance and Capitalist Discipline: Factory Women in Malaysia*. New York: SUNY Press.

———. 1997. The Gender and Labour Politics of Postmodernity. In *The Politics of Culture in the Shadow of Capital*, Lisa Lowe and David Lloyd (eds), pp. 61–97. Durham: Duke University Press.

Parry, Jonathan. 1999. Lords of Labour: Working and Shirking in Bhilai. *Contributions to Indian Sociology (N.S.)* 33(1&2): 107–39.

Poster, Mark. 2002. Workers as Cyborgs: Labor and Networked Computers. *Journal of Labour Research* 23(3): 339–54.

Remesh, Babu P. 2004. 'Cyber Coolies' in BPO: Insecurities and Vulnerabilities of Non-Standard Work. *Economic and Political Weekly* 39(5): 492–97.

Saldanha, Arun. 2002. Music, Space, Identity: Geographies of Youth Culture in Bangalore. *Cultural Studies* 16(3): 337–50.

Sandhu, Amandeep. 2006. Why Unions Fail in Organising India's BPO–ITES Industry. *Economic and Political Weekly* 41(41): 4319–22.

Seshu, Geetha. 2006. The Global Beck and Call Services. www.indiatogether.com.

Shome, Raka. 2006. Thinking through the Diaspora: Call Centres, India and a New Politics of Hybridity. *International Journal of Cultural Studies* 9(1): 105–24.

Teamlease (2006). *India Labour Report 2006*. Bangalore: Teamlease. http://www.teamlease.com/images/reports/PR_%20TL_ILR06.pdf.

Taylor, Phil and Peter Bain. 2005. 'India Calling to the Far Away Towns': The Call Centre Labour Process and Globalisation. *Work, Employment and Society* 19(2): 261–82.

Thomas, Nicholas. 1991. *Entangled Objects: Exchange, Material Culture, and Colonialism in the Pacific*. Massachusetts: Harvard University Press.

Upadhya, Carol and A.R. Vasavi. 2006. Work, Culture and Sociality in the Indian IT Industry: A Sociological Study (Final Report submitted to *IDPAD*). Bangalore: National Institute of Advanced Studies.

Vasavi, A.R. 1998. Fashion, Pepsi and Harshad Mehta: Westernization or Modernization? *Voices* 2(1): 28–30.

van den Broek, Diane. 2004. 'We have the Values': Customers, Control and Corporate Ideology in Call Centre Operations. *New Technology, Work and Employment* 19(1): 1–13.

Winiecki, Donald J. 2004. Shadowboxing with Data: Production of the Subject in Contemporary Call Centre Organisations. *New Technology, Work and Employment* 19(2): 78–95.

Yasmeen, Summiya. 2006. Criminal Neglect of Vocational Education. *Education World* 8(8): 52–58.

Zhen, Zhang. 2000. Mediating Time: The 'Rice Bowl of Youth' in fin de siecle Urban China. *Public Culture* 12(1): 93–111.

9

Work Organisation, Control and 'Empowerment': Managing the Contradictions of Call Centre Work

Babu P. Remesh

The global business order has undergone a massive transformation in recent years with a marked upsurge of the technologically embedded information economy. Rapid advancements in the fields of digital information processing and telecommunications have provided considerable impetus to outsourcing and the relocation of work—especially services—to cheap labour destinations. As a result, offshore outsourcing—in which firms from the developed nations (mostly in the West) outsource work processes to auxiliary firms in developing countries—has assumed unprecedented prominence.

A new organisational logic behind the competitiveness of business in the global information society is the creation of value chains based on inter-organisational networking. This new philosophy of work organisation *inter alia* implies alteration of the knowledge and skill base of jobs, and the means and practices of organising work and control relations within organisations (Kolehmainen 2004). Modern service sector firms in developing countries provide ample evidence of this temporal transformation, with their distinct characteristics that are hardly amenable to conventional norms and forms of work and work organisation.

In the service sector, customers are considered integral to the work organisation, either due to simultaneous production and use of many personal services or due to a strong client-led definition and even co-production of the actual services. The customer-oriented nature of the work often challenges traditional conceptions of control and coordination, especially those of manager–worker control relations.

In addition, 'informatisation' of work creates possibilities for novel modes of conceptualising and organising work, leading to discernible changes in work cultures.

How does the customer orientation of services shape the work and working conditions in service firms in the 'information society'? How independent and autonomous is the work in these firms? What are the forms of control? To what extent does technology define and dictate the work organisation in modern firms? What are the empowerment strategies and caring mechanisms resorted to by managements to overcome the adverse impacts of technological surveillance and to manage 'emotional labour'? These are some of the issues that are addressed in this essay, which discusses in particular the dynamics and contradictions of technology-based service sector work in the case of Indian call centres. The central focus of this essay is on the logic and nature of on-site work organisation and the management of the resultant contradictions of call centre work. Accordingly, an attempt is made to explain the deep-seated paradoxes arising out of the mutually competing dual goals of cost efficiency and customer orientation that are pursued by these firms.

The major data sources for preparing this essay include a survey of about 277 call centre employees in NOIDA (Remesh 2004a)[1] and interviews with around 40 agents working in various call centres in the National Capital Region (NCR). This information is further supplemented by the inputs gained from discussions with management executives, Human Resources (HR) heads and team leaders in the industry.

All the call centres selected for the study had less than six years of experience in the business. All were third party centres and were dealing with international customers and outsourced work in the areas of customer care, sales support and help desk (see Table 9.1). At the time of the survey, it is estimated that all these firms together employed 6,010 customer care agents, 62 per cent of which were men. Around 90 per cent of the agents were engaged in voice-based work.

Profile of the Call Centre Workforce

The portrayal of 'work as fun' and 'workplace as yet another campus' is the central technique through which potential workers are attracted

Table 9.1
Details of the Firms Surveyed

Number of Firms	6
Type of Firms	All third party centres; involved in international and outsourced work
Experience in BPO business (years)	2–5 years
Major activities	Customer Care
	Sales Support
	Help Desk
*Number of agents**	
Male	3,705 (61.7)
Female	2,305 (38.3)
Total	**6,010 (100.0)**
Process*	
Voice	5,364 (89.3)
Non-voice	646 (10.7)
Total	**6,010 (100.0)**

Note: *Estimated based on information provided by the respondents.
            Figures in parentheses indicate percentage.
Source: Survey data, 2003.

to the BPO (business process outsourcing) or the ITES (IT enabled services) sector. The superior image of work and the vibrant ambience of the workplace—with sweeping glass and concrete buildings, factory rows of jazzy computers, the company of smart and trendy peers—help to draw educated and fun-loving youngsters from the urban middle class, who are fascinated by western ways of living and modern work environments.

A review of employment advertisements for BPO companies reveals that the preferred profile of a call centre agent is: 'a fresh young graduate with good English-speaking and comprehension ability.' Normally, the upper age limit specified for entry ranges from 26 to 28 years. These firms, in their advertisements, flag the bright ambience of the workplace as the prime aspect of attraction. A modern work environment with state of the art equipment and other indoor facilities such as cafeteria, internet kiosk, recreation centre, gym, clinic and so on, enable these firms to impress potential youngsters from the urban 'creamy layer'.

The fact that these jobs are easily accessed (because they do not require a lot of experience or high educational qualification) also attracts youngsters. Computer literacy, good typing and communication skills and good command over English, are the basic requirements.

Perceptions of higher career prospects, both within and outside the firm, also motivate youngsters to join this industry.[2] The atypical work hours of the BPO firms, due to their dependence on international clients, also tempt another group of youngsters to join BPOs in anticipation of continuation of studies alongside work.

The superior designations that are attached to BPO work also add to its acceptability among youngsters. Though a newly recruited agent is essentially engaged in a job that is only slightly better than that of a receptionist/computer operator or a telephone operator, BPO firms label these jobs with very attractive titles such as Customer Care Officer, Call Centre Executive, Customer Care Executive, Contact Centre Representative, Customer Support Executive and so on.[3] All of these factors lead to favourable supply conditions in the labour market and the emergence of a new genre of workers, who stand apart from workers in the conventional manufacturing/service sectors in terms of their socio-economic and demographic attributes.

Out of the 277 respondents of the survey, 97 per cent were in the age category of 20–30 years. The mean and median ages of the work-force were found to be 25 years. The educational profile of the agents was also impressive: 97 per cent had a minimum qualification of a college degree and the average number of years of education was seventeen. Almost all the respondents (98 per cent) had completed their higher education in institutions situated at urban centres. The schooling of 233 (84 per cent) respondents was in English medium public or convent schools. Ninety-four per cent of them had completed their last academic course with either first class or distinction. Most of the agents in the sample had entered the job a few years after completing their graduation. Also, many of them had some prior experience in BPO before joining their current jobs. Thus, these survey results challenge the widely conceived notion that call centre agents are mostly 'freshers' who have just completed their graduation or even undergraduates.

Educational and occupational status of parents also shows an im-pressive picture, with 94 per cent of fathers and 63 per cent of mothers being graduates. The fathers are mostly in government jobs (56 per cent), business (27 per cent) or professional services (13 per cent) in urban centres. In 28.5 per cent of the cases, the mothers are also employed, mostly in government sector jobs. Caste-wise enumeration of respondents (see Table 9.2) also confirms the argument that most

Table 9.2
Profile of the Respondents

	Male No. %	Female No. %	Total No. %
Sample size	178 (64.3)	99 (35.7)	277 (100.0)
Age			
Below 20	–	4 (4.0)	4 (1.4)
20–25	107 (60.1)	71 (71.7)	178 (64.3)
26–30	68 (38.2)	15 (15.2)	83 (30.0)
31–35	3 (1.7)	8 (8.1)	11 (4.0)
Above 35	–	1 (1.0)	1 (0.3)
Caste category			
Forward Caste	171 (96.1)	96 (97.0)	267 (96.4)
Backward Caste	5 (2.8)	1 (1.0)	6 (2.2)
Others	2 (1.1)	2 (2.0)	4 (1.4)
Marital status			
Married	28 (15.7)	8 (8.1)	36 (13.0)
Unmarried	150 (84.3)	87 (87.9)	237 (85.6)
Widowed/Separated	–	4 (4.0)	4 (1.4)
Education			
Intermediate	2 (1.1)	6 (6.1)	8 (2.9)
Graduates	132 (74.2)	76 (76.8)	208 (75.1)
Post graduates & above	21 (11.8)	8 (8.1)	29 (10.5)
Professional training	23 (12.9)	9 (9.1)	32 (11.6)

Note: Figures in parentheses indicate percentage.
Source: Survey data, 2003.

workers belong to the 'creamy layer'; the majority of the respondents (96 per cent) belong to forward castes.

On the whole, the picture that emerges is one of a new genre of workers with strikingly different characteristics, which in turn is reflected in marked changes in employment relations and institutional features of the labour market. The superior work environment, use of the state of the art technology in day-to-day work, better salary structure, catchy designations, smart and young peer workers, etc., lead the workers to believe that the job they are doing is that of an executive or a professional.

Given the comparatively bright profile of the work and workforce in the BPO sector, one would naturally expect an increased supply of job aspirants; this is confirmed by the survey findings. The favourable supply conditions in the labour market allow the firms to evaluate the candidates in several rounds of interviews and tests—on language, communication and 'hospitality' (customer service) skills—and to hand-pick the best of the lot, through various modes. The stringent recruitment practices followed by call centre firms suggests that one of the major objectives of outsourcing in this sector is to minimise costs by recruiting well-qualified personnel, which also leads to reduced training costs.

Modes of Recruitment and Training

The emerging profile of the call centre workforce seems to be beneficial to the firms, due to its cost-minimisation implications. Given the sharp competition in the field and the non-viability of reducing labour and infrastructure costs, the only option left to these firms to minimise production costs is to cut down on training costs. A scrutiny of employment advertisements suggests that they are targeting mainly those youngsters who potentially could be fine-tuned to the job with minimal training. Unlike their developed country counterparts, BPOs in India invest only limited resources in in-service training of employees.

The recruitment is mostly conducted through direct selection. In this method, potential candidates are short-listed through walk-in-interviews, scrutiny of curriculum vitae or telephonic interviews. The interviews are conducted on the firm's premises, though some other convenient locations (such as deluxe hotels and guest houses) may be selected during periods of pressing demand. BPO firms recruit workers as and when required, which largely depends on the quantum of their assignments. Separate recruitment divisions were found to be functioning in four out of the six firms, year round.

Recruitment through placement agencies is the other prominent mode of selection. In this case, the firm places a bulk order for its manpower requirement to these agencies and the latter do the recruitment and even some preliminary fine-tuning of the candidates. At the time of the field survey, there were more than a dozen recruitment agencies functioning in NOIDA, most of which provide generic placement services. Normally, these agencies charge a recruitment fee from the client equivalent to one month's salary of the recruited employee. The placement agencies also carry out a series of tests on the language aptitude and communication skills of the candidate. In addition, some of these agencies offer some career counselling services to prepare youngsters for this employment.

Candidates are also selected through call centre colleges/call centre training courses. In fact, one of the BPO firms studied was known as a 'call centre college'. This firm engages both in placement (for other firms) and recruitment (for the firm itself). The label of 'college' allows it to attract appropriate candidates who are keen on learning the work. Workers are also recruited through various crash course-training programmes too, and in some of these courses the organisers place the candidates in companies. Yet another mode of recruitment is through employee referral schemes, in which agents are rewarded for directing suitable youngsters to the company. The incentive package ranges from Rs. 3,000 to 5,000 per person recruited,[4] amounts that in some cases are disbursed in monthly installments. The firms view referrals as an ideal mode of recruitment because the candidates are hand-picked by the agents and so are sufficiently oriented and fine-tuned to meet the requirements of the firm. To minimise training costs, firms give preference to candidates with some previous experience. The job advertisements of the BPOs testify to this strong preference for experienced workers. The survey findings also support these arguments, with 43 per cent of the respondents having some prior experience in BPO.

Irrespective of the mode, the recruitment process entails several rounds including written tests, group discussions, aptitude tests on language and communication skills and interviews. The tenure of engagement is normally linked to the project, which allows the management to get rid of workers who fall short of expectations. The high attrition rate[5] in the industry could also be related to this rejection of workers after the first trial.

The post-recruitment training normally includes four to eight weeks of in-house orientation in voice/accent, soft skills and accent training. Exposure to American TV shows and Hollywood blockbusters and reading English fiction are some of the techniques used to familiarise the new recruits with Western culture and etiquette. Further, agents are specially trained in their specific job tasks ('processes') with the aid of process training manuals. Outsourcing of training in soft skills training and grooming of the workforce is not significant in this industry. Apart from trainers, experienced agents also train newly recruited employees.

Understanding Call Centre Work

Unlike their developed country counterparts, most Indian call centres concentrate on low-end operations in information processing and transfer, although this pattern is fast changing and higher-end work (or 'knowledge process outsourcing') is also on the rise. Call centres engage agents to interact with customers on either outbound or inbound calls, on activities as diverse as sales and telemarketing, product and service information, customer care and support, after-sales services, banking/insurance services, and information sharing, as per the requirements of their national or transnational clients.

The operations in BPO companies are divided into 'voice' and 'non-voice' processes. The former category, which is comparatively more prominent in the Indian ITES sector, includes customer support in sales and helpdesk activities. The latter includes work being carried out via the internet such as email help lines, email correspondence, insurance claims processing, medical transcription and so on. Irrespective of the category, the work is further divided into specific processes that are entrusted to separate teams of around ten to thirty members. The requirements of the work vary across processes, so the agents are given detailed training/orientation with the help of specific training manuals. As the cultural backgrounds of the agents and the customers differ greatly, a major focus of training in Indian call centres is on styling the accent, and familiarising employees with western customs and manners.

Agents are recruited either for a specific project or are on probation for 6–12 months. Only a small proportion of the recruited employees are eventually confirmed. Sixty-two per cent of the respondents in the survey were 'regular'. Fifty-three per cent of the respondents were receiving a monthly salary above Rs. 10,000 and another 19 per cent received between Rs. 8,000 and 10,000. These salaries are comparable to those of the more qualified hands in alternative jobs in manufacturing or service industries. However, this status is only titular, as the agents themselves know that they can be expelled any time. The only advantage that 'regular' agents have is in terms of their entitlement to some additional benefits such as paid leave, Provident Fund and so on. The duration of engagement of the agents in their present job supports the argument that having a 'regular' status is meaningless. Only 13 per cent of the agents was found to have been in the same job for more than two years. Further, 57 per cent of the respondents had less than one year of experience.[6]

The work organisation in BPOs is atypical in terms of working hours and work patterns. Unlike the conventional service sector and manufacturing firms in India (and elsewhere), the work in Indian BPOs is mostly done in night shifts in order to suit the requirements of the clients in the western countries. As the work is organised through a tight integration of computer and telecommunication devices, the technology often demands and dictates the work pattern and intensity—a common characteristic of BPO firms world over. Further, the customer-oriented nature of the work challenges the conventional notions of control and coordination, especially those of manager–worker control relations.

A typical BPO operates 24 hours a day, 365 days a year. To enable this, these firms practice flexibility in working patterns: agents' work schedules do not have any fixed days as weekly holidays. The same flexibility is practiced in the case of shift patterns, where the agents are expected to be flexible and amenable to work on any of the shifts, as per the requirements of the firm. It is quite paradoxical that to follow rigid working hours and inflexible work patterns, the firms are practicing 'flexible' arrangements with the workforce! The firms surveyed had a 48-hour workweek for all their employees. Except for one firm that follows a three-shift pattern (of eight hours each), all the firms had shifts of nine and half hours duration. To avoid any disruption in staffing, agents are encouraged to avail of transportation facilities arranged by the firm. During the working hours agents are entitled to 30–40 minutes meal break and two small breaks of 10–15 minutes for tea and refreshments, for which records are maintained.[7]

Call centre agents can avail of leave to which they are entitled[8] only with the prior consent of the team leader or manager. Agents revealed that there have been situations in which they found it very difficult to get even a few days leave. Availing of leave without prior consent is treated as unauthorised absence, which is a sufficient reason to terminate the services of the agent.[9] Even if an agent is sick, it is mandatory to get the consent of the team leader at least 4–6 hours before the shift, failing which the absence would be considered as 'unscheduled leave'.[10] All these types of leave (except casual leave) are not available to probationers. Further, as call centres function according to the time schedule of the clients, the employees are usually not eligible for Indian national holidays.

The design of the workplace in call centres is also unique. As per the organisational hierarchy, there are separate floors or wings for top executives, managers and process teams.[11] Within the work area of process teams, the space is organised into rows of clean, bare cubicles, each of which houses a computer and a telephone with designed headsets. The team leaders are usually positioned in a central point for easy supervision. To help agents to deal with international customers, international timings are displayed on the monitor of the PCs or through electronic boards positioned at central locations.

There are contradictory conceptualisations of the nature and quality of work in call centres. On the one hand, the optimists (mostly employer organisations, management representatives and so on) construe call centre work as an opportunity for skill upgradation and training, in which one gets ample scope for working with employees who are resourceful and committed to delivering quality services. Further, the ambience of the workplace and the work environment are regarded as enabling and 'empowering'.[12] On the other hand, a growing body of academic literature portrays call centres as 'modern sweatshops' or 'bright satanic offices', where exploitation of labour is ensured through increased rationalisation and Taylorisation of work (Baldry et al. 1998; Taylor and Bain 1999; Callahan and Thompson 2001). Despite this lack of unanimity in the understanding of call centre work, there exists a wider consensus that this type of work is characterised by several deep-seated contradictions—contradictions of pleasure and pain in the experience of work and conflicts arising out of the competing logics of customer orientation and rationalisation.

World over, there are two major drivers for the organisation of work through call centres. First, the outsourcing of work to BPOs allows a drastic reduction in cost per transaction, compared to the conventional customer interface modes involving person-to-person interaction. Second, it adds more quality to customer service through flexibility (for instance, allowing round-the-clock customer service) and extra opportunities to the customers (for example, one-stop point for multiple transactions and queries). However, the dual goals of cost efficiency and customer orientation is one of the underlying dilemmas of call centre work. It was evident from the survey that a major task of Human Resource (HR) managers is to find a balance between these twin objectives, in a cost optimising manner. In view of this, the subsequent discussion focuses specifically on the aspects of work rationalisation and customer-oriented nature of work in call centres.

Rationalisation of Work, Technology-aided Surveillance and Systems of Control

As per the standard classifications followed in the literature, the forms of production organisation in Indian call centres more or less conform to that of a 'mass-production' or production-line model, which is normally expected in situations where the work is mostly low-end information processing (Deery and Kinnie 2004). The logics of production organisation in 'mass production centres' are rationalisation and cost minimisation, where jobs are designed according to Taylorist principles and are usually unskilled, repetitive and monotonous. Agents are supplied with tightly scripted dialogues and are required to follow highly defined and detailed interactions ('scripts') when dealing with customers. This system enables management to examine the performance of the employee quantitatively—through average call time, number of calls and so on—besides allowing the supervisor to listen remotely to the agent's call, with or without the knowledge of the employee, to ascertain whether the work is being done according to the stipulated norms and standards.[13]

Typically, call centre agents are found sitting at their workstations, attending calls through headsets and inputting or retrieving information into or from their PCs or terminals. They follow a set of detailed and specific instructions while interacting with the customers, whose information is readily available in their computer monitors. Calls are distributed to the workers with the aid of specially designed devices. The agents are provided with precisely scripted information, which is prepared and organised in advance to anticipate all possible aspects of the customer–employee interaction. This leaves hardly any scope for the agent to deviate from the overall frame of interaction, which is pre-designed by the management. The workers are subjected to a work regime that is based on a high degree of computer–telephony integration. The use of such technology along with standard scripts allows firms to keep 'free time' between calls to bare minimum.

Technology-aided Controls

A unique feature of work organisation in call centres is the high degree of monitoring and the extensive use of technology-aided control mechanisms. Technologically aided controls and surveillance mechanisms allow firms to pursue the twin objectives of rationalisation (cost minimisation) along with standardisation (quality check). The technology-induced efficiency at work requires agents to submit to a highly controlled work regime, which is more akin to assembly line manufacturing (Standing 1999). The technology of call management in Indian firms is more or less similar to that of their Western counterparts. Accordingly, Automated Call Distribution (ACD) and Predictive Dialling Technologies are engaged to automatically transfer queued calls to available agents and to keep the free time between calls to the bare minimum. According to a respondent, this pre-designed framework of call distribution enables the firm to dump 'a day's work in an hour' onto the agent. Unlike a conventional office, a typical call centre will see their staff spending their entire day seated at their respective cubicles, receiving calls through headsets and inputting information into (or extracting from) the PCs in front of them. Work is monitored on the spot and after working hours with the help of specially designed software,[14] computer networks and closed circuit cameras. The respondents testify that it is very difficult for them to make or receive personal phone calls as the system of telephonic interaction in the firm is also pre-designed, leaving no space for personal communications. The domination of technology over labour is evident in all aspects of workplace design and organisation, such as surveillance and monitoring, fixing and maintaining targets and evaluation of performance of the employee.

Surveillance

According to some observers, the degree of surveillance at work in most call centres is comparable to the situation of 19th century prisons or Roman slave ships. (Bibby 2000). Workplace interactions are continuously recorded/taped, which are randomly checked by the manager/team leader. To some of the respondents, the feeling of being observed continuously itself is a psychological torture. Technology allows close observation and assessment of the entire gamut of activities carried out by an agent, from their entry into the workplace to the lunch break through to the end of the shift. Employees are restricted to their own work areas and the common spaces earmarked for recreation and refreshment.[15] For each entry into and exit from the work bay, agents have to swipe their electronic identity cards. The data collected in this way is often subjected to analysis by the team leader in order to assess punctuality and attentiveness. During the working hours, the agents are directed to observe punctuality in taking the admissible breaks, which are also tracked through the computer system. Agents are required to be logged in and attend calls for a certain number of hours per shift, which prevents them from taking too many breaks. For each break, agents are required to log off while leaving the work bay and log in again at the time of resuming work. Those who are away from the work bay for longer durations or unable to attend calls for more than the stipulated number of minutes are instantly warned through intranet messages.

Targets

The agents are supposed to meet daily targets, which are stipulated in terms of number of calls or non-voice transactions successfully attended. These quotas are often fixed at such a high level that the agent has to burn out to fulfil it. For instance, an agent who attends 80 calls a day would be assigned 100 calls by the HR division after a performance review meeting. The team leaders/managers undertake regular 'target meetings' and one-to-one meetings, in which agents are repeatedly reminded of the importance of meeting targets. Targets are set on an individual basis and are linked to career prospects and perks (such as promotion, increments and gifts). To promote a competitive spirit among agents and teams, their performance statistics are periodically displayed on the workstations and on the floor. In some cases, apart from individual targets, teams are also assigned targets (which are also linked to incentives—such as group parties, picnics and so on). These strategies generate peer pressure as well as individual incentives to attain higher levels of productivity. Further, this mix of individualisation and teamwork allows managements to regularly evaluate, consolidate, and compare the performance of each agent against their own 'perceived potential levels of productivity' and with those of 'good' workers in the process team.

Performance Appraisal

Performance is rated in terms of productivity (quantum of work done) and quality.[16] A long list of 'defects' is prepared by firms pertaining to every aspect of work. Mistakes in work invite immediate warnings and other corrective measures. Track cards/warning cards are maintained to record the daily ratings of the agents. Normally, three errors a day could lead to a warning and zero points and three consecutive zeros to counselling or termination notice. Keeping the daily track/warning card free from red marks is a difficult task for agents, since for any mistakes, including those made outside of the work area or beyond the control of the agent, are treated as 'defects'. For instance, reaching the pickup point late by more than five minutes would be marked as 'transport defect',[17] while availing of leave without prior permission would be counted as 'unscheduled defect'. Similarly, taking more than the stipulated time for a lunch break is a 'defect', despite the fact that on many occasions agents lose considerable time in queuing for lunch.

Daily performance appraisals are consolidated from time to time (either weekly or monthly) and the cumulative scores of each agent are displayed on a board on the floor or on the workstation.[18] A commonly followed system for performance appraisal is that of a five-point rating, in which an agent who scored 'excellent' throughout the year gets maximum of five points. A fair monthly score is linked to incentives in cash and kind.[19] The annual increments in salary as well as the vertical mobility of the agent in the firm are also linked to this rating. A cumulative score of five points leads to a total yearly benefit of Rs. 20,000–30,000 in the salary, four points to Rs. 15,000–20,000 and so on. In the matter of promotion also, the annual scores carry some weightage. Linking performance with incentives/punitive actions creates continuous stress on agents.

From the field study, it was evident that only few agents could attain a five point rating in the preceding year of the survey, but a large number attained three or four points. Those who were able to obtain five points explained how difficult and strenuous it was for them to achieve it. None of them was fully confident that they could retain this achievement in the coming years. Those who failed to achieve five points also explained the difficulty of attaining it, as any unanticipated aberration (such as sick leave or urgent family requirements) may result in a lower score. Though aware of the hidden stress and strain with this system, many of the respondents expressed satisfaction with it because it assured some increase in salaries, based on their performance.

Overall, the technology allows the firm to introduce efficient controls and surveillance systems, which to a great extent facilitates the rationalisation of work through effective checks on quality and quantity of work and standardisation of services.

Customer-oriented Bureaucracy

Along with the use of a high degree of technological surveillance, call centres employ several traditional bureaucratic controls and methods of human resource management, based on complex and comprehensive systems of reporting, warnings and rewards. However, it is not completely correct to conceptualise these as bureaucratic controls in the conventional sense. Due to the customer-oriented nature of work, control systems in call centres are often supplemented by customer-related norms. For instance, in the survey the firms were found to rely on feedback from customers or random checks of the quality of calls (with an eye on customer satisfaction) while assessing the quality of work carried out by the agents. Thus, the systems of control in call centres are largely based on 'customer oriented bureaucracy and values' (Korczynski 2002), in which the form of work organisation involves two potentially contradictory logics at play. On the one hand, the firm strives towards routinisation and efficiency. On the other hand, it needs to focus on customer and customer satisfaction.

Agents are regularly informed of the attitudes and behaviours required for the job through intranet communications and other means (such as discussion in target/review meetings, messages flashed on the monitors of the PCs, posters displayed on the workstations or recreation rooms and so on). In a bureaucracy, control rests primarily on measurement of output and of process behaviours, particularly regarding adherence to hierarchically imposed procedures and rules. But in call centres, to cater to the irrational and sometimes astonishing behaviour of customers, agents may have to go beyond pre-designed procedures. In view of this, agents are repeatedly reminded of the importance of carrying forward the interaction with self-control (based on customer related norms) in order to attain the corporate goals. For instance, in some of the selected firms for the study, the process orientation manuals supplied to the agents include some messages reminding the employee of the benefits of quality work and the consequences of bad work.

BPO firms also encourage workers to familiarise themselves with the cultural background of customers, through various means. Unlike call centres in the West, this aspect assumes importance in India because firms must groom their workforces to cater to the requirements of customers who belong to a different culture. This need for cultural sensitivity *inter alia* puts additional burden (of being culturally sensitive and appropriate) on the workers in India, as the onus of learning about the culture of the customers ultimately falls on them.

Managing Emotional Labour: 'Empowerment' and 'Structured Socialisation'

Similar to any other 'caring' occupation, work in call centres demands substantial levels of customer oriented 'emotional labour'. Agents are expected to display customer oriented attitudes and feelings to facilitate smooth interaction. Here, the emotions of the employees are often combined with the product information to enhance the levels of customer satisfaction. The agents are required to 'manufacture' relationships. As the agents are the virtual ambassadors of their clients, the firms attach considerable significance to ensuring that all of the transactions are fair and meaningful.

As discussed earlier, any deviations from the 'defined' framework of interaction are conceived as 'defects'. Quite often, aspects such as the mood of the agent, facial expressions and choice of words are subject to monitoring. Agents are even forced to either express some feelings that they do not feel or to suppress certain feelings that they genuinely want to share. In both the cases, the employees find the job depressing and leading to emotional turmoil. In addition, agents often have to cope with abusive and irate customers from the West, who are particularly annoyed with the poor quality of services that they attribute to cultural or linguistic reasons. Even after detailed training and painful preparations, quite often the awareness of agents about the cultural, socio-economic and geographical backgrounds of the customers is too weak to deliver quality service. This 'cultural constraint' is an additional stressful dimension of call centre work in India, compared with that in Western countries.

Emotional exhaustion adds to the physical and mental strain of the workers, leading to higher levels of stress and burnout under the electronically monitored work and tightly bureaucratised work regime.[20] There is ample evidence in the literature that one of the major determinants of the alarming attrition rates of workers from call centres is the strain of emotional labour along with high levels of physical and mental exertion.[21] Managing emotional labour assumes added importance, given the limited scope for socialising in call centres.

The extensive use of emotional labour demands that firms resort to systematic application of human resource policies right from the recruitment stage. Accordingly, pro-customer attitudes and values among candidates are given priority in recruitment decisions. Firms are keen to select ideal employees who possess 'positive' values and attitudes.[22] An analysis of vacancy advertisements of call centre firms in India suggests that 'positive qualities and attitudes' are among the most desirable qualifications enlisted by employers. The competence of the candidates to deliver deep, committed emotional labour is often tested through simulations of the work situation and role-plays. For instance, many of the interviewees explained that at the time of recruitment they had to participate in work simulation exercises in which they were asked to handle various types of calls—those that involve dealing with irate and abusive customers, telemarketing, as well as routine information sharing.

Further, BPO firms seek to infuse customer-oriented values and the corporate ethos into employees through cultural and 'normative' controls. These values are further strengthened through customer orientation training sessions,[23] training manuals[24] and performance assessments. Performance appraisals and counselling are often used as opportunities to impart the managerial ethos to the agents. This helps the company to alter the image of management from that of 'control' to one of employee 'development'. For instance, unlike conventional work regimes, here managements rely more on 'counselling' those employees who fail to meet their targets rather than resorting to a formal procedure of disciplinary action.

In order to relieve stress and stem employee attrition, BPO companies have designed and introduced various coping processes and situations of 'structured socialisation'—i.e., promotion of the collectivity and socialising within certain pre-designed constraints, which helps the firm to 'optimally' re-energise workers without really empowering them. Accordingly, a major task for HR managers in call centres is to create avenues for the workers to overcome the stress of emotional labour. HR departments are entrusted with organising consultative forums (such as intranet discussion forums) and group activities for recreation (such as competitions, get-togethers, parties and picnics) and so on. Some firms provide 'down time' and 'off-stage areas' where employees can drop their corporate masks and engage in friendly talk with their colleagues, in order to temporarily free workers from the stress of continual scrutiny and supervision. However, these opportunities are often designed and integrated within the overall framework of control and work organisation. Such shock-absorbing mechanisms are thus only meant for 'healthy' recreation and for re-energising agents.[25] In essence, through 'structured socialisation' managements ensure that the creativity and productivity of the workers are effectively tapped to strike the 'right' balance between work and fun, thereby creating a 'productively docile' workforce.

Providing an illusory sense of empowerment is yet another method that helps to create an environment that enables agents to cope with the demeaning effects of emotional labour and the close controls imposed by electronic surveillance. Accordingly, managements project 'work as fun' and the 'workplace as yet another campus', in order to retain skilled hands and to prevent undesirable levels of attrition. The positive images of superior work,[26] the vibrant ambience of the workplace, attractive designations, impressive salary structure, etc., are effectively used to cultivate confidence and to create a sense of 'empowerment' among the workers. Further, visits by high-level managers, corporate gatherings, public reading of appreciation letters (from top management, clients and customers) and other such methods are used as tools to manage and motivate BPO workers.

A closer analysis thus reveals that in call centres, personnel management policies are increasingly used to enable employees to cope with the pressures and pains of emotional labour. These policies are implemented through various techniques including fanciful situations of 'empowerment' along with pre-designed controls and systems of subordination. Allowing some freedom to take on-the-spot decisions while dealing with customers (without consulting the team leader) is a commonly followed technique for 'empowering' the agents.

Simultaneously, firms clearly specify the limits to this 'free' decision-making so as to ensure control over the workers. In other words, while managing emotional labour, BPO companies blend 'soft' and systematic personnel management policies along with the rather hard and inflexible controls imposed by the electronically enabled management and surveillance systems.

Space management is yet another feature that adds to the creation of an 'enabling' and 'empowered' environment. Along with defining entry limits for each category of the employees within the firm, the HR Department allows employees to organise their allotted space according to their taste. Employees are free to keep wallpapers of their choice on their monitors or to clip photographs of their friends and relatives on the flip chart. Thus, employees are 'free' to make their small, clean cubicles 'virtually spacious'. Insisting on a strict dress code on paper but permitting workers to wear outfits of their choice is one of the most widely adopted HR strategies to make workers happy with no additional costs. Similarly, HR managers design codes of conduct that are actually meant to be violated rather than complied with, thereby enabling workers to enjoy 'freedom' and 'flexibility' at the workplace![27] Thus, providing illusory freedom and flexibility is central to managing call centre agents.

On the whole, call centres represent a marked shift in the HR paradigm vis-à-vis that found in conventional manufacturing/service sectors. Here, HR managers are vested with the task of camouflaging work as fun. Accordingly, workplace strategies are designed to provide situations to de-stress employees and to allow them to air their grievances with least damage to the firm.

Insecurities and Vulnerabilities[28]

Employment in BPOs implies a host of insecurities and vulnerabilities that are partially reflected in the high attrition rates. Despite getting salaries and facilities that an ordinary graduate in India could never imagine in any other job, attrition rates in the industry are quite high: various estimates suggest they are in the range of 40–60 per cent.

In our survey, push attrition was found to be a significant feature. Separation is mostly due to the expiry of the contractual term, increased stress and lack of career prospects within the firm. Growing push attrition rates clearly indicate the employment insecurities associated with short-term employment contracts, the demanding and stressful nature of the work, and lack of bright career paths in this sector. On the one hand, workers are expelled regularly due to the firms' desire to retain only the most productive hands and to get rid of long-term commitments towards employees. On the other hand, the nature of work is so stressful and demanding that often agents quit. Further, some quit the job after an initial trial when they realise that the chances of vertical mobility are bleak.[29]

Agents, especially those who work on voice processes, are forced to live as Indian by day and as Westerners after sundown. Further, the job is fairly demeaning since some call centre operations demand acquisition of even a new persona.[30] Work can get frustrating at times, especially when dealing with irate and abusive customers. Even the most positive and alert agents report that there were times when they lost their temper and had to cry or curse in order to vent their frustration. Many of them agree that frustration is one of the primary factors that force workers to consider quitting. The close monitoring and continuous work assessment followed in BPOs also add to the frustration, and agents often find these systems demeaning. In performance assessment, the past track record of the agent is not taken into account; it is often done 'objectively' with the aid of computer software. Some workers find this mechanical and impersonal way of evaluation of their contributions unfair, and complain that the recognitions and rewards for work are very short-lived, as today's mistakes and poor performance are not discounted in view of a good past track record. Because working hours are artificially created, they obviously conflict with the natural rhythms of the human body.[31] Unearthly hours and over-exertion take a heavy toll in terms of health (both mental and physical) and job performance. The results are twofold—increased healthcare costs on the one hand and frustrations at the workplace on the other. Odd work timings usually lead to disturbances in personal and social life. There are problems related to maintaining friendships, keeping in touch with relatives, accomplishing household duties and finding time for sound family relations. Employees are not even entitled to national/ religious holidays, as ITES companies work according to the clients' calendar.[32]

Respondents reported several symptoms of mental and physical ill health such as nervousness, chronic fatigue, body ache, insomnia, nausea, anxiety, restlessness, irritability and even depression. Some of them pointed out that working in shifts even causes psychoneurotic disturbances such as depression. Respondents also reported frequent occurrence of gastrointestinal problems, with digestive problems such as constipation, peptic ulcer, indigestion, diarrhoea, excessive gas formation, abdominal pain and heartburn. It was also noticed that workers develop poor eating habits as well as smoking, excessive drinking of coffee and so on, to cope with psychological and physical stress.[33]

Insecurity of Representation

Despite the predominance of 'voice-based' work, call centre firms are characterised by totalisation of labour control or the 'end of employee voice'. None of the respondents in the study was a union member, nor was there any active union presence or contact with other union members or representatives. The complete absence of trade union activities could be due to a host of reasons, which include the unique profile of the workforce, the unusual patterns of work and workforce organisation, the newness of the occupation, lack of union history, high rates of turnover and so on.

Due to their differently conceived identity as 'professionals' or 'executives', most of the respondents did not find their issues and problems similar to those of conventional manufacturing/service sector workers. Further, because most of them are not primary bread-winners of their families they do not entertain any long term plans to stay in their current occupation. Many consider this job as transitory and stopgap. This short-term approach *inter alia* leads to undermining of long-term considerations at the workplace, such as organising and collective representation.

The dualistic pattern in the workforce (in which a major proportion of workers have insecure employment) allows firms to check any initiatives towards mobilising and organising. Further, the 'inherent' rigidities in the work organisation, which are camouflaged as 'flexibilities', enable firms to observe a close watch on agents and discard the possible 'trouble-makers' from time to time. While designing punitive measures towards the 'organisers', firms use these 'inflexibilities' as an effective mode of control.

The unique design of the workplace in BPOs also provides clear vision and easy access for the management to closely monitor agents' work, which itself acts as a block to organisational efforts as these are normally treated as against the interests of the firm. Further, the firm ensures that the agents are left with no free time for such 'undesirable dealings'. The work is designed in such a way that agents work continuously in the endless pursuit of targets, and in many cases they do not even find time to think of collectivity and trade unionism.

Individualisation versus Collectivity

The philosophy of work organisation in BPOs is based on individualisation. Agents are moulded to act as individuals who report to and are monitored by another individual. Even in project-based teamwork, this is the core principle that structures work relationships. This norm is widely internalised by call centre agents, for instance that salary is a personal matter that should not be shared with peers in the workplace. The firms in their codes of conduct highlight that discussing salary and related matters with fellow workers would invite warnings and disciplinary action.

Promoting individualised situations leads to greater isolation and lower likelihood of establishing networks of information and support. The scope for agents to interact among themselves and with similar employees outside is limited, and employees often do not have any chance to mingle with outsiders as their entire movement right from their doorsteps till they return home are planned by the firm.[34] Even within the firm, the world of the agents is mostly confined to the process in which they are involved. Despite their 'highly educated' status, the understanding of agents about similar organisations that are engaged in BPO work within NOIDA and on the trade union presence is abysmally low. Even within the firm, agents' orientations are mostly confined to the process in which they are involved.

BPO firms are keen to nip any sprouts of dissent in the bud. Those agents who are vocal against management decisions are forced to quit their job, through carefully planned retrenchment mechanisms. A frequently used mechanism is to isolate and depress the employee.[35] Firms reiterate to employees that the decision of management is final and more or less irreversible. Also, it is made clear to the workers that their vertical mobility on the job ladder is linked to their healthy relations with the management more than to their performance ratings. Any move on the part of agents against the interests of management is viewed seriously and is followed by punitive measures. All these factors prevent agents even from attempting to organise themselves, even if they find some time or ways to do that.

BPO firms also ensure a lively environment of competitive spirit among the agents, which works against forging strong bonds of collectivity and cooperation. For instance, periodic display of performance statistics helps the management to promote competition (in terms of productivity) among the workers, which promotes individualisation.

Responses to Non-representation

Given the lack of trade unions, firms provide some alternative mechanisms for employee 'voice', primarily as a safety valve. These are designed to create avenues for the workers to air their grievances with least damage to the firm. The creation of such 'empowering' situations to compensate for the absence of trade unions is central to the changed paradigm of human resource management in the new economy. Accordingly, HR divisions organise consultative forums (such as intranet discussion forums) and group activities for recreation (such as competitions, get-togethers, parties, and picnics) and so on. These shock-absorbing mechanisms are, however, only meant for 'healthy' recreation and reenergising the agents. It is believed that any 'misuse' of these consultative facilities would eventually lead to punitive measures. Thus, the 'collectivity' and 'solidarity' in the viewpoint of management assumes a narrow meaning, which is directly related to productivity enhancement. Due to this 'controlled socialisation', it was found that the intranet discussion forums in the firms studied were mostly used for circulating jokes and tips for 'productivity improvement'. HR departments also organise several group efforts in the workplace to divert the attention of workers away from organising.[36]

In the absence of a formal collective mechanism such as trade unions, issues such as authoritarian managerial styles, excessive workloads, inflexible break timings, and unreasonable rosters lead to some forms of informal/formal and individual/collective resistance. During times of intense frustration, agents confront the management in other ways as well. For instance, agents often challenge management's discourse about care, quality and teamwork by subjecting it to derision. Making fun of management style is also a form of resistance. Agents sometimes disregard the organisation's scripted conversational rules. Searching for weaknesses in the organisation's control systems and constructing free spaces for themselves, which provide an amnesty from normal emotional labour, were other strategies observed. Some agents admitted that at times they deliberately redirect calls to other service operators, enter misleading activity codes into the system or simply hang up on offensive customers, in order to resist the management's authoritarian regime in the absence of any effective device for grievance representation.

Summary

An underlying aspect of work organisation in call centres is the centrality of computer-telephony integration, which enables ample possibilities for cost reduction through rationalisation, routinisation and deskilling of professional work. However, unlike in conventional manufacturing firms, the unique nature of work requirements in call centres do not allow the observance of a 'mass production model' along traditional bureaucratic lines. The consumer-oriented and emotional labour-based nature of the industry demands the integration of certain levels of normative control, 'empowerment' opportunities, and personnel care to prevent attrition and absenteeism. Thus, the success of human resource management, and of the industry as a whole, depends on the competence of firms in balancing the competing goals of technologically enabled rationalisation and quality enhancement in service provision, alongside managing 'emotional labour'.

There is a growing paradox in the work organisation of call centres. Despite the fact that the work is supposed to be characterised by innovations, flexibilities and freedoms, at the core it denotes a relatively inflexible form of work organisation. This inconsistency *inter alia* has resulted in the creation of a new class of workers, with distinct features and differently conceived identities, eroding even basic rights at work. Many of the contradictions embedded in call centre work in the Indian context are equally found in similar workplace situations of the Western world. Nevertheless, the findings of the present study suggest that the contradictions and tensions in call centre work in India are much more complicated due to the interplay of several other factors, including atypical work hours and the additional burden placed by different cultural backgrounds of workers and consumers.

Notes

1. This essay is based on a research study, 'Labour in Business Process Outsourcing: A Case Study of Call Centre Agents', conducted by the author at the V.V. Giri National Labour Institute (Remesh 2004a), and information gathered for a forthcoming study, 'Labour in the Information Economy: A Study of Work Organisation, Controls and Empowerment'. The NLI study was a micro study conducted in 2003, based entirely on the responses of call centre agents in a limited geographical cluster. The study was aimed at objectively evaluating the perceptions of the work experience of call centre agents in order to throw light on the potentialities and possible problem areas in human relations and to strengthen the sustainability of the industry in long term. The views expressed in this essay are that of the author and do not represent those of the Institute where he is employed.

2. It is widely perceived that for industrious and committed workers, there is a good chance to enhance their salaries and upgrade their designations within a short time of joining a firm. Also, it is believed that gaining some experience in the BPO sector provides a chance to migrate to better firms, both within and outside the country.

3. An examination of the advertisements of the BPOs reveals that more than a score of designations are used to denote almost the same type of work.

4. Further, in one of the firms agents are given a VCD player if they provide five successful referrals.

5. A detailed account of attrition is provided in the subsequent section.

6. Most of the respondents were not bothered about job security. This is partly because of their attitude towards the job as a transitory one and partly due to the realisation that the company would retain most of them even though they are replaceable (because of the high attrition rates and the ongoing rivalry among firms in recruiting the right candidates).

7. All these breaks are tracked continuously by the computer system. This enables the team leader or manager to generate statements of time utilisation of the employees at any point of time.

8. The number of casual leaves permitted varied from seven to twelve per year. Other leaves include medical leave, privileged leave, optional leave, study leave and maternity leave.

9. During the survey period we came across about half a dozen cases of termination due to 'unauthorised absence'.

10. Any dispute regarding attendance could be crosschecked with the data sheets corresponding to the electronic identity cards of the agents, which are also used for recording attendance.

11. Although there are certain differences in this matter across firms, the explanation here is more or less that of a 'typical' firm that was covered in the field study.

12. This observation is based on an analysis of the contents of position announcements of BPO firms as well as the viewpoints expressed by their top executives, HR managers and representatives of employer organisations (such as NASSCOM—National Association of Software Service Companies), in both print and electronic media.

13. In contrast, in the other major form of production organisation in call centres, i.e., the 'empowerment model', employees are given much more control over their work and are allowed to blend their individual skills and information while interacting with customers. Unlike the mass production firms, where monitoring and surveillance are normally realised through automated controls, empowerment firms ensure better performance through wider systems of training, coaching and performance management (Deery and Kinnie 2004).

14. BPO firms use specifically designed software to analyse the performance of employees and generate grade sheets.

15. There are certain differences across various firms in this aspect. However, this is the common inference that one could arrive at while analysing the spatial design of the sample firms. As all the firms are third party firms with internationally outsourced work, segregation of different processes and functions of the firms are justified on account of security reasons. However, this need not be true for all the call centre firms in India. There are reports that many of the captive firms follow a more 'democratic' use of space.

16. In quality check, attention is given to the manner in which the calls/mails are attended—accent, alertness, attitude and aptness of the response (for the voice process) and grammar, punctuation and right information (for the e-mail process).

17. If the employee fails to report for work due to 'transport defect' of the firm, it would be treated as a paid holiday. Even in this case, the employee's monthly rating would fall due to these non-working days.

18. The firms prepare the daily performance record of each process, which are shared with the clients on a routine basis.

19. Incentives in kind include awards in the form of gift coupons, sponsored dinners and picnics, and expensive gifts.

20. The stringent monitoring and surveillance mechanisms build up tremendous pressure on the employees, as they are aware that their work is being measured, monitored, regularly evaluated and compared with the performance of their peers. This surveillance often leaves agents mentally, physically and emotionally exhausted. Further, linking performance with incentives and punitive action creates additional stress. An overall five points score thus implies an intensive pattern of work and continuous stress.

21. Of late, an increasing body of literature suggests that a considerable proportion of the workforce in Indian call centres is in the grip of an exhaustion syndrome, which is popularly referred to as BOSS (Burn Out and Stress Syndrome).

22. An analysis of the advertisements of various call centres in electronic, print and other media (for instance, wall advertisements and banners) reveals that the desirable attributes for call centre workers include 'pleasant manners', 'positive attitude' and 'service minded nature'.

23. Immediately after recruitment, candidates are given a few weeks' training, a major part of which focuses on preparing them for customer-oriented service work.

After induction as well, regular refresher modules are organised to reinforce the customer-oriented culture.

24. The process training manuals, apart from orienting agents on the specific process of the project they are working on and serving as a reference for trouble shooting, are used extensively by the firms to orient and reinforce employees on the benefits of good work and the demerits and consequences of poor work.

25. Due to this 'controlled and structured socialisation', most of the intranet discussion forums are used primarily for circulating jokes and tips for 'productivity improvement'.

26. Though call centre agents are engaged in what is essentially a receptionist/computer operator or a telephone operator's job, call centre work is often represented as technologically savvy and enabling work that is suited for bright and industrious youngsters.

27. This includes organisation of group work and competitions—such as floral arrangements, hanging of colourful balloons and so on.

28. The discussion in this section is largely based on an earlier paper of the author (Remesh 2004b).

29. Instances of massive attrition soon after the announcement of promotion results are widely reported by agents.

30. In some cases, agents have to assume other names to suit the requirements of the customer.

31. As human alertness is controlled by the biological clock, which is designed to have sleep at night and alertness during the day, workers naturally cannot function at peak alertness and performance during odd hours.

32. To quote an employee: 'We are not getting a holiday on Independence Day, but there would be a holiday on George Washington's Birthday!'

33. These preliminary findings point to the desirability of undertaking a detailed epidemiological study of these atypical occupations.

34. In some of the firms, the arrangements are made in such a way that the vehicle would pick up the agents from their homes and drop them directly inside the firms' premises. Since refreshment and recreation faculties are provided inside, the workers have no reason to go out of the company premises.

35. The company isolates the person from all colleagues by making him/her sit without any work (but with pay) for several days.

36. Several perks/facilities offered to the employees such as conveyance arrangements, providing in-house facilities such as credit card collection boxes and ATMs and so on, are also aimed at enhancing the intensity of work by freeing the agents from day-to-day worries.

References

Baldry, Chris, P. Bain and P. Taylor 1998. 'Bright Satanic Offices': Intensification, Control and Team Taylorism. In *Workplaces of the Future*, P. Thompson and C. Warhurst (eds), pp. 163–83. Basingstoke: Macmillan.

Bibby, Andrew 2000. *Organising Financial Call Centres*. Discussion Paper, UNI, http: // www.andrewbibby.com

Callahan, George and Paul Thompson 2001. Edwards Revisited: Technological Control and Call Centres. *Economic and Industrial Democracy* 22(1): 13–37.

Deery, Stephen and Nicholas Kinnie (eds) 2004. *Call Centres and Human Resource Management: A Cross-national Perspective.* New York: Palgrave Macmillan.

Kolehmainen, Sirpa 2004. The Dynamics of Control and Commitment in IT Firms. In *Information Society and the Workplace: Spaces, Boundaries and Agency,* Tuula Heiskanen and Jeff Hearn (eds), pp. 83–102. London: Routledge.

Korczynski, Marek. 2002. *Human Resource Management in Service Work.* New York: Palgrave Macmillan.

Remesh, Babu P. 2004a. Labour in Business Process Outsourcing: A Case Study of Call Centre Agents. NLI Research Studies Series No. 51. NOIDA: V.V.Giri National Labour Institute.

———. 2004b. 'Cyber Coolies' in BPO: Insecurities and Vulnerabilities of Non-standard Work. *Economic and Political Weekly* 39(5): 492–97.

Standing, Guy 1999. *Understanding Global Labour Flexibility: Seeking Distributive Justice.* London: Macmillan Press Limited.

Taylor, Phil and Peter Bain 1999. 'An Assembly Line in the Head': Work and Employee Relations in Call Centres. *Industrial Relations Journal* 30(2): 101–17.

Editors

Carol Upadhya, a social anthropologist, is currently Fellow at the School of Social Sciences, National Institute of Advanced Studies, Bangalore. Her research interests focus on contemporary Indian society and culture, globalisation, economic anthropology, the history of anthropology and sociology in India, and anthropological theory. Her most recent work has been on work, workers and entrepreneurs in the Indian information technology industry. Earlier, she has written on the social impact of the Green Revolution and the emergence of a new business class in coastal Andhra Pradesh. She is co-editor, with Mario Rutten, of the volume *Small Business Entrepreneurs in Asia and Europe: Towards a Comparative Persective* (1977). She has a doctorate in social anthropology from Yale University and had taught sociology at SNDT Women's University in Mumbai.

A.R. Vasavi, a graduate of the Department of Sociology, Delhi School of Economics, holds a doctorate in social anthropology from Michigan State University; and is currently Professor at the School of Social Sciences, National Institute of Advanced Studies, Bangalore. She has taught at Michigan State University, Tufts University and the Indian Institute of Management, Kozhikode. Her early research work focused on the sociology of India and she is the author of a book, *Harbingers of Rain: Land and Life in South India* (1999). In addition to coordinating a project on elementary education in Karnataka, she is working on an edited volume of translations of Kannada writings on society and culture and a volume of her collected writings on agrarian change in India. Her research interests also include the sociology of education and the new cultural economies of globalising India.

Contributors

Chris Fuller is Professor of Anthropology at the London School of Economics. His current research,with Haripriya Narasimhan, is on Tamil Brahmans and modern change, and previously he worked on aspects of globalisation in Tamil Nadu. For many years he conducted research in the Minakshi temple, Madurai. His most recent books are *The Renewal of the Priesthood: Modernity and Traditionalism in a South Indian Temple* (2003, 2004); *The Camphor Flame: Popular Hinduism and Society in India* (revised edition, 2004); and *Globalising India: Perspectives from Below* co-edited with Jackie Assayag (2005).

P. Vigneswara Ilavarasan is Assistant Professor in the Department of Humanities and Social Sciences, Indian Institute of Technology (IIT), Delhi. He has BSc in physics from Madras University, MA in sociology from Pondicherry University and PhD in sociology from IIT, Kanpur. He held a two-year post-doctoral fellowship at the International Institute of Information Technology, Bangalore. He has taught at the Central University, Pondicherry, for a year. His research interests are in sociology of work and industry; science, technology and society; and the Indian information technology industry.

Marisa D'Mello has a doctorate from the Centre for Technology, Innovation and Culture (TIK Centre), University of Oslo, with a dissertation entitled 'Understanding Selves and Identities of IT Professionals: A Case Study from India'. Her thesis examined how identities of Indian information technology (IT) workers were constructed and related with globalisation processes, mobilities, culture, gender and organisational practices. She has postgraduate degrees in psychology from India and the USA. She was a Lecturer in Psychology before working as an Human Resources professional in the Indian IT industry for several years. Currently, she is a consultant in Mumbai and is associated with the TIK Centre, University of Oslo and the Department of Sociology and Anthropology, St. Xavier's College, Mumbai.

Sanjukta Mukherjee is currently pursuing Ph.D. in geography and Certificate of Advanced Studies in Women's Studies at Syracuse University. She holds a Masters degree from Jawaharlal Nehru University, New Delhi. Her areas of expertise in research and teaching broadly traverse feminist, economic, and development geographies and revolve around contemporary processes of global capitalist transformations, gender and uneven development. Based on extensive field research in Bangalore and Delhi, her dissertation, entitled 'Producing the Indian IT Miracle: Gender, Geography and the Neo-liberalising State', examines the factors that have contributed to the increasing significance of India in the global software industry and its potential for progressive social change.

Haripriya Narasimhan is Research Fellow in the Department of Anthropology at the London School of Economics. She has a Ph.D. in Anthropology from Syracuse University. She has worked with Chris Fuller on two ESRC-funded research projects in Tamil Nadu.

Babu P. Remesh is Associate Fellow and Coordinator, Integrated Labour History Research Programme and Archives of Indian Labour at the V.V.Giri National Labour Institute, NOIDA, India. He completed his M.Phil. in Applied Economics and Ph.D. (Economics) from the Centre for Development Studies, Thiruvananthapuram, affiliated to Jawaharlal Nehru University, New Delhi.

Sundeep Sahay is Professor in the Department of Informatics, University of Oslo. He has been studying global software work arrangements for over a decade and has examined such relationships involving organisations in North America, UK, Japan, Korea, Norway and India. He has also done policy level studies on how to stimulate global software exports in Iran, Costa Rica, Argentina and India. He has written more than thirty papers on this subject in international journals and conferences and has also co-authored a book on this subject.

Sonali Sathaye obtained her doctorate in cultural anthropology from Syracuse University, with a dissertation entitled 'Performing American Culture: Notions of Emotion and Self in Two American Theatres'. She conducted her fieldwork amongst actors in acting schools with differing performance philosophies. During 2004–2006 she was a Post Doctoral Fellow at the Centre for the Study of Culture and Society in Bangalore, where she continued her research into questions of emotion, language, rationality and science through a project that looked at changing notions of mental health in urban India.

Carol Upadhya, a social anthropologist, is currently Fellow at the School of Social Sciences, National Institute of Advanced Studies, Bangalore. Her research interests focus on contemporary Indian society and culture, globalisation, economic anthropology, the history of anthropology and sociology in India, and anthropological theory. Most of her recent work has been on work, workers and entrepreneurs in the Indian information technology industry. Earlier, she has written on the social impact of the Green Revolution and the emergence of a new business class in coastal Andhra Pradesh. She has a doctorate in social anthropology from Yale University and had taught sociology at SNDT Women's University in Mumbai.

A.R. Vasavi, a graduate of the Department of Sociology, Delhi School of Economics, holds a doctorate in social anthropology from Michigan State University, and is currently Professor at the School of Social Sciences, National Institute of Advanced Studies, Bangalore. She has taught at Michigan State University, Tufts University and the Indian Institute of Management, Kozhikode. Her early research work focused on the sociology of India and she is the author of *Harbingers of Rain: Land and Life in South India* (1999). In addition to coordinating a project on elementary education in Karnataka, she is working on an edited volume of translations of Kannada writings on society and culture and a volume of her collected writings on agrarian change in India. Her research interests also include the sociology of education and the new cultural economies of globalising India.

Index

absence, unauthorised, 243
absenteeism, 225
   and high labour turnover, 31
accommodation, rental, 94
accumulation,
   flexible, 12
   post-Fordist regimes of, 60
advertisements,
   employment, for BPO companies, 237
   vacancy, of call centre firms in India, 251
affluence, 85
agency, 38, 87, 212, 216, 224
agent,
   call centre, preferred profile of a, 237
   educational profile of, 238
   empowering the, 252
   engagement of, 242
   newly recruited, 238
   past track record of, 254
   regular, 242
alienation, 70
   from the capitalists, 60
   gendered, 67
   —, geographies of, 56
   of labour, 57
   from labour process, 57
   Marxian forms of, 57
   Marxist insights on, and software work, 57–60
   in the software industry, 33
   of software workers, 28
appraisal,
   annual, 199
   performance, 248–249
   —, commonly followed system for, 248
   —, daily, 248
   —, individualised, 25

—, individualised, system, 59
assembly line, global, 191
assignments, onsite, 94
attitudes,
   and behaviours required for the job, 249
   towards gender, 195
   positive values and, 251
   qualities and, 251
   shift in, 85
attrition,
   employee, in the Indian ITES industry, 32
   in the IT industry, 17–19
   push, 253
   rate, 17–18, 70, 208, 253
   —, of workers from call centres, 251
   voluntary and involuntary, 19
authoritarian managerial styles, 256
Automated Call Distribution (ACD), 246
autonomy,
   lack of, for individual engineers, 28
   worker, and techniques of normative control, 25
awareness, cultural, 115

back office,
   and customer service work, 29
   operations, 13
behavioural changes, 112
bodyshopping, 20
BPO (business process outsourcing), 13, 214, 237
   companies, 19, 30
   —, operations in, 242
   —, software and, 38
   firms, 238, 240–241, 250–251, 256
   in India, 240

industries, software and, 16
   prior experience in, 238
   workers, 14
brain drain, reverse, 96
break timings, inflexible, 256
bureaucracy,
   customer oriented, 249–250
   Indian redtapism and, 157
business, competitiveness of, in the
   global information society, 235

call,
   distribution, 246
   management, technology of, in Indian
     firms, 246
call centre, 221, 236, 243, 249
   agents, 10, 243, 245
   culture in India, 37
   Indian, 242
   —, and BPOs, 17
   —, software and, workers, 34
   —, worker, 39
   international, 13
   job, 19
   operations, 254
   organisation of work through, 244
   training courses, 241
   work, 16, 30–31, 242
   —, in India, 250–251
   —, organisation in, 246, 258
   workforce, profile of, 236–240
Capability Maturity Model (CMM) Levels
   of the Software Engineering Institute,
   182
   firms with, certification, 182
   Level 5, 28
   —, software services companies,
     123
capital,
   cultural, 69
   flexible, 38
   foreign, 50
   global, 51
   intersections between, and cultural
     identity, 103
   transnational, 21
   —, flows, 20
capitalism, 57, 78

Chinese, 128
   and consumerism, 229
   flexible, 229
   global, 52, 101, 129, 140
   —, advance of, 191
   —, cultural logics of, 128
   —, development of, 9, 12
   —, expansion of, 106
   —, history of, 102
   industrial, 60
   —, Marxist critique of, 51
   soft, 23
career,
   boundaryless, 79
   counselling services, 241
   growth, 90
   mobility, 33
   narratives of software workers, 76
   opportunities for execution workers,
     180–181
   options for the Indian youth, 11
   and professions, 89–92
caste,
   hierarchy, 87
   traditional, system, influence of, 86
certification,
   ISO, 183
   programme, 215
childcare, 204, 206–207

   support, 207
children, 35, 65, 84, 89, 94–96, 148,
   199–208, 224 and family responsibilities, 203
citizenship, new forms of, 77
client,
   foreign, 124
   international, 238
   needs and demands, 122
closed circuit cameras, 246
clothing, casual, 223
coders and testers, 173
codes of conducts, 253
Cognizant Technology Solutions (CTS),
   191
collectivism versus individualism, 140
collectivity and solidarity, 256

commerce, relationship between emotion and, 138
commitments, long-term, towards employees, 254
commodity chains, global, of service provision, 12
communication,
  across locations, 108
  cross-cultural, 15
  —, and collaboration, 105
  interaction and, 108
  inter-cultural, 115
  —, and cooperation, 105
  intranet, 249
  listening-skills and, workshops, 144
  mobile, technologies, 79
  skills training, 109, 219
  styles, 108
competency, 64
  behavioural, 64
competition, 12, 24, 33, 59, 146, 155, 240, 252, 257
inter-team, 223
computer,
  and information technology, extensive use of, 22
  networks, 246
  programming and software development, 12
  and telecom sectors, 13
  and telecommunication devices, integration of, 243
conference calls 108, 194
computer–telephony integration, 245, 258
consultancy, end-to-end software development, and knowledge process outsourcing, 14
consultative forums, 252, 256
consumer
  global, 211, 223–224, 228
  —, economy, 211
  —, industry, 211
  Indian, market, 80
  ultimate, 15
consumerism, 37, 220
  encouragement of, 224

global, 223–224
  and new sociality, 225
consumption, 32–34, 37–38, 50, 61, 65, 71, 84–85, 94, 220, 223, 229
contract,
  employment, 91
  for software services, 20
  temporary, 19, 62
  work, 206
contractual term, expiry of, 253
control,
  and coordination, traditional conceptions of, 235
  over costs and timelines, 28
  cultural and normative, 251
  deployment of subjective mechanisms of, 23
  direct (as well as indirect), employed in the Indian call centre industry, 30
  indirect, 25
  labour,
  —, managerial, 28
  —, totalisation of, 255
  management,
  —, and, of the labour process, 39
  —, over the work process, 31
  mechanisms, technology-aided, 246
  monitoring and, exacting systems of, 28
  organisational, 14
  —, techniques of, 30
  —, techniques of, direct and indirect, 29
  panoptical, and worker resistance in IT-enabled services, 29
  of software workers, 167
  and surveillance, 249
  —, panoptical systems of, 30
  systems, weaknesses in the organisation's, 258
  over the work process, 183
  work organisation, and empowerment, 235–259
coordination, problems in, 105
core values, changes in, 112
corporate practices, 55

cost reduction through rationalisation, routinisation and deskilling of professional work, 258
cost-efficiency, 222
creamy layer, 239
cultural communities, pre-existing, 103
cultural differences, 105, 109, 117–119, 122, 153
cultural difference, discursive constructions of, 117–119
cultural struggles, 103
cultural turn, 137
    in management practice and ideology, 25
culture, 26
    collectivist, 140
    consumerist, 35
    corporate,
        —, around the world, 111
        — differences between Indian and global, 112
        —, dominant global, 111
    elements of Indian work, 120
    extended family, 111
    global
        —, corporate, 15, 27, 111, 115
        —, corporate, model, 111
    feudal, 118
    hierarchical, 115, 150
    mmobilities of, 34
    Indian, 120, 139
        —, in a space warp, 139–141
        —, and tradition, 35
        —, and values, 140
        —, work, 118, 120
    labour and management in the global economy, 102–107
    management of, 101, 107
    managerial, 137
    managing through, 101
    meaning of, 137
    and organisation of large corporations around the world, 106
    pizza, 88
    feudal, 118
    hierarchical, 115, 150
    of the workers, 39

Western,
    —, and etiquette, 241
    —, work, 126
customer, 251
    cultural backgrounds of the agents and, 242
    norms and values of, service, 31
    offensive, 258
    orientation, 222
    related norms, 249
    service, 15
        —, norms, 221
        —, round-the-clock, 244
    support, 12
        —, in sales and helpdesk activities, 242

daily track/warning card, 248
data entry, 166
data processors, pink-collar, 191
dating, 220
deadlines,
    delivery, 63
    project, unrealistic 29
defect,
    transport, 248
    unscheduled, 248
delicensing, deregulation and, of the Indian economy, 55
deliverables, 90
    deadline, 199
delivery model, global, 28
demotion policies, 91
deskilling,
    Braverman's thesis on the, of work, 162
    invisible, of software engineers, 28
    of work, 176
    of workers, 57
despatialisation, 16
    implications of, and disembodiment of work in India's offshore economy, 20
deterritorialisation,
    of IT related work, 39
    of labour, 20
digitalisation, 21

discontent and tension between parents and ITES youth, 224
disintegration, vertical, of the production process, 12
disturbances in personal and social life, 254
documentation, 165, 182
dot com bust, aftermath of the, and '9/11', 19
downward shift, reason for a, 91
dress,
    alterations in 223
    code,
        —, HR policies on, 69
        —, strict, 253

economic forces, global, 13
economic restructuring, global, 11, 13
economies,
    advanced industrial, companies located in, 13
    formal, 53
    global, 9–10, 55
        —, cultural, 35
        —, informational, 12, 39
    India's,
        —, outsourced, 16
        —, visibility and reputation in the global cultural, 9
    industrialised, 12
    informational, India's, 38
    neoliberal, 52
    networked pattern of, 33
    new, 10–11, 13, 15, 22–23, 38, 51, 57, 73, 84, 130, 132, 157
    post-industrial, 10, 101
        —, informational, 102
        —, of the West, 9, 22, 38
    women's role in, 53
education,
    employment and entertainment, 222–226
    engineering, 17
    system, 216
educational choices and social trajectories, 11
electronic panopticons, 30–31
    deployment of, 222

elite professional class, 10
emotional exhaustion, 251
employability, 90
employee,
    corporate, 136
    development, 251
    empowerment and self-management, 116
    entrepreneurial, 29
        —, self-motivation of, 120
    European, 122
    in IT industries, 145
    performance, 30
    referral schemes, 241
    satisfaction, 106
    social characteristics of, 69
    subjectivities of, 15
    turnover, 62
    understanding of the self and the other, 26
employment,
    in BPOs, 253
    figures, 13
    flexible,
        —, arrangements, 18
        —, forms of, (contract labour and part-time jobs), 18
    insecurities, 253
    relationship, 23
    security, 90
    term, contracts, 254
    total direct, 13
empowerment, 252
    financial, 205
    through high earnings, 197
    ideology of, 34
    illusory, 29, 31
    opportunities, 258
    women's, 34, 201
        —, in IT, 196
end-to-end solutions, 55
engineers,
    onsite, 123
    software development, Indian, 107
English language, command over, 237
entrepreneur, IT, 152
    emergence of indigenous middle class, 13

equality,
    gender, at work, 195–200
    among individuals, 195
    as a right, 195
    women's individual, with men, 196
ethnicisation, internal, 27
ethnocentricism, , 111
    evils of, 113
ethos, managerial, 251
etiquette,
    coaching in, 109
    corporate, 110, 180
    inter-cultural and, training sessions,
        109
    training, 69
Europeans and Americans, individualist
    nature of, 140
e-workers, 36
expatriates, qualified, 96
exploitation,
    capitalist, of people, 51
    of labour, 244
    by mothers-in-law, 203
    of workers by capitalists, 60
export orientation, 80
    of the industry, 174
exposure, 197
    big, 198
    inside and outside the workplace,
        198
    to TV shows and Hollywood block-
        busters, 241

family, 34–36, 63–64, 66, 81–82, 84,
    86–89, 91, 93–95, 111, 118, 126, 137,
    148, 151, 190, 194, 197–208, 212–213,
    219–220, 225, 248, 254
    and career, 208
    and communities, compulsions of the
        social norms of, 36
    demands, 87
    relocation, 95
    values, Indian, 96
family-friendly policies, 208
feminisation, 53–54
    of labour, 52
financial freedom, 197

flexibilisation, 16
    concept of, 18
    trend towards, 19
flexibility, 62–64, 122
    concept of, 52
    corporations drive for, 52
    gendered notions of, 63
    gendering of, 63
    of the labour force, 56
    labour market, 18
    privileges of, 64
    promotion of, in labour relations,
        24
    with respect to labour processes and
        labour markets, 18
    in the work, 18
    valorisation of, 34
    of workers and workspaces, 52
flexi-time system, 204
flexi-timing, 63
Fordism, 52, 163
Fordist factory regime, 22
Fordist mass production, 12
foreign countries, desire to travel to, 217
freedom,
    to earn, 220
    and flexibility at the workplace, 253
    to take on-the-spot decisions while
        dealing with customers, 252
frustration, 254
    intense, 256
    stress and, 29
    at the workplace, 254

gated communities, 67
gender, 17, 21, 23, 32, 34, 37, 51–54,
    60, 63–67, 71–72, 102–104, 112,
    137, 190–191, 195–196, 198–200,
    206, 208
    inequalities, exacerbation of, 191
    gap, 206
    hegemonic, regimes, 51
    relations, 34
        —, in the high-tech workplace,
            63
gendering of IT work, 34
global best practices, 106

global software organisation, (GSO), 77
  mobilities in a, 81–84
global software professional, 107–117
global software work (GSW), 77
global youth workforce, India's, 211–229
globalisation, 78, 104, 112–213
  anthropological studies of, 38
  cultural logics of, 102
  cutting edge of, 36
  discourses about, 9
  of the economy, 38
  economic and cultural, 102
  and identity formation, 104
  in India, 11
  labour and cultural identity, 101
  models-of and models-for, 77
  products of, 39
  proponents of, 78
  of services, 12
governmentality, transnational, 224
graduates,
  engineering,
    —, or science, 17
    —, predominance of, 176
  harassment, sexual, complaints about, 194

HCL Technologies, 191
healthcare costs, 254
hierarchy, corporate, 93
high tech professional jobs, 12
human resources,
  management, 249, 258
  managers, 115
  skilled, 13

ID cards, electronic swipe, 211
identities,
  cultural,
    —, and narratives, 40
    —, within this group of upwardly mobile professionals, 35
  emergence of new work, among ITES employees, 37
  formation of a class-based, of high-tech service workers, 36
  gendered, 37

loss of, 126
national, 126
social, 111
working, of ITES employees as professionals, 37
IITs and IIMs, graduates from, 69
image,
  and branding, 85
  global, Indian software worker's, 122
immigration, impact of, 213
incentives and awards, 223
income, tax-free, 61
Indian companies, traditional, 18, 115
Indian engineers, hierarchical mindset of, 123
Indian firms, 55
Indian peasant, historical transformation of, 228
Indian software industry, growth of, 60
Indian workers, characterisation of, 122
Indian-ness, Western notions of, 139
Indians,
  collectivist nature of, 140
  professional middle-class, 148
individualisation, 18, 24, 26, 106
  and team work, 247
  worker, and self-management, 15
individualism, competitive, 18, 25
individuals, high performing, 223
industrialisation,
  19th century, 57
  export-oriented, 228
inflexibilities, 255
information and communication technologies (ICT), 77, 213
  modern, 12
information, 13
  economy,
    —, outposts of, 22
    —, post-industrial, 106
  panopticon, 28
  precisely scripted, 245
  processing and transfer, 242
information technology (IT), 9, 11, 13, 22, 37–38, 50, 77, 101, 136–137, 190, 211, 214, 230
  celebratory narratives about, 36

companies, 15, 194
—, corporate ideology of, 193
—, Indian, 195
—, Indian, large and medium size, 16
—, operating in India, 27, 105
education institutes, increase in, 80
and ITES,
—, companies, 9–11, 26, 40
—, companies in India, 25
—, expansion of, jobs in India, 41
industry, 14, 136
—, advent of the, in India, 34
—, boom in, 19
—, emergence and growth of India's, 13
—, globalised, 139
—, icons of success in the Indian, 86
—, Indian, 20, 80–81, 120, 137
—, Indian, history and political economy of, 11
—, leaders, 10
—, monetary rewards of working in, 33
—, outsourced, 38
—, political economy of the Indian, 11
—, social class and educational background in the Indian, 18
—, virtual and mobile workforces, 27
professionals, 10, 21, 85, 91, 94, 201
—, female, 200, 204
—, individual, 36
—, male, 202
rise of, 194
service,
—, companies, Indian-owned, 13
—, offshore, 13
work,
—, culture, 38
—, cultural consequences of global, in India, 35
workers, 82, 84
—, Indian, 26, 36

workforce, 16
—, Indian, production and control, 16–18
systems, 13
Infosys Technologies, 86, 191
innovation and creativity, 23
insecurities,
of representation, 255–256
and vulnerabilities, 253
intellectual unsuitability, 196
intensification, 77
interaction, customer–employee, 245
International Organization for Standardization (Geneva), 164
ISO 9000, 28
series of the International Organization for Standardization, 182
ITES (Information Technology Enabled Services),
brigade, 13, 211, 237
companies, 211, 222
and ICT training, 216
India's,
—, growing, 213
—, industry, 214
industry, 14, 215
—, and the government, 216
—, Indian software and, 25
—, Indian, 31
—, success of, 218
jobs, 219, 220
labour force, 216
market, 16
purchasing power of, salaries, 220
sector, 214
services, offshore, in the West Indies, 228
social circle of, persons, 225
synergies between IT services and, 16
work, 218, 222, 224, 228
—, as a lifestyle, 222–226
workers, 31, 36
—, Indian, 227
—, redressal of grievances among, 37
workforce, 19, 220
—, in India, 216

youth, 212, 227
—, as transnational information
    service subjects, 226–229
IT–ITES,
    companies, 10
    industries,
        —, emergence of the Indian, 11,
        13
        —, export-oriented nature of the,
        in India, 14
        —, history, growth and structure
        of India's, 10
        —, Indian, 24

job,
    advertisements of the BPOs, 241
    American and European, 10
    fairs, ITES, 218
    insecurity, 24, 33
    low-skilled routine, 176
    opportunities, 85
    tailored for youth, 217–219
    tempting, opportunities, 85
job-hopping, 24

knowledge, 13
    cultural, 197
    domain, specialised, 77
    economy, 61, 136, 153
    industries, 9, 23–24
    obsolescence of, forms and practices,
        33
    professional, 50–76
        —, in India, 14
    sharing sessions, 179
    work, 20
    worker, 14, 16, 26, 29
knowledge-self, 153

labour, liquifaction of, 20
labour,
    adaptability of, power, 24
    amnesty from normal emotional,
        258
    capitalist,
        —, control of the, market and
        work process, 57
        —, division of, 57, 163

cheap,
    —, costs, 53
    —, destinations, 235
cost arbitrage, 14
cost-effective and customer-oriented,
    214
demand, 251
    —, for ITES, 216
despatialisation, disembodiment and
    mobility of, 20
disembodiment of, 16
division of, 52
    —, into conception and execution
    tasks, 169
embodied, 50
emotional, 26, 30, 225, 250–251, 253
    —, empowerment, 250
    —, of workers, 31
flexibilisation of, 18–19, 21, 24
flexibility, 18, 33
force,
    —, culturally marked, 102
    —, segmentation of, 103
gender division of, 63
gendered and racialised, market, 54
global division of, 29
immobilisation of, 16
intellectual, 64
international division of, in the soft-
    ware production process, 184
market,
    —, flexible, 52
    —, supply conditions in, 239
mobile, 20
mobility, 16
neglect of Indian industry and, 40
organisation of, process, 14
physical, 64
pool, 53
pressures and pains of emotional,
    252
subjectivities in technology-mediated
    tertiary, 31
virtual, 34
women's role in the division of, 62
learning, constant online and on-the-
    job, 24
leave,

availing of,
—, without prior consent, 243
—, without prior permission,
    248
liberalisation, economic, 139
licences and quotas, preliberalisation
    days of, 87
life-cycle, changes in, of the IT person,
    92–93
lifestyle,
    altered, 223
    consumption-oriented, 220, 223
listening-skills, 148

management,
    characteristics of, and labour, 15
    cross-cultural, 26, 105
    —, or global, 104
    cultural, 26
    —, turn in, ideology and practice,
        23
    —, culturalisation of, 117
    global, 104–405
    of labour, 26
    new age, and the entrepreneurial
        employee, 105–107
    normative, techniques, 24
    organisation and, in the Indian soft-
        ware and BPO industries, 22
    panoptical, techniques, 29
    soft, 27, 30
    —, techniques, 25, 29
    of software projects, 108
    space, 253
    style, making fun of, 256
    theory, international, 104
    transnational, ideologies and prac-
        tices, 104
    of work and workers, 15
managers,
    of multi-sited or outsourced projects,
        122
    and the workers, 183
manpower,
    skilled, 14
    —, shortage of, 16
manufacturing,
    export-oriented, industries, 15

firms in India, 243
geographical dispersal of, 15
marketplace, global, 106
marriage, 35, 65, 87, 88, 200, 203, 212
arranged, 201–202
    —, conventional, 35
    —, traditional, 87
    love, 35, 201–202
mass production centres, 245
media,
    popular, 215
    —, in India and abroad , 50
medical transcription, 217
meetings, one-to-one, 247
mental and physical ill health, 254
messages, intranet, 247
middle class,
    educated, in India, 51
    new, 10
migration, virtual, 21
mobile phones, 79, 80
mobility,
    and individualisation, 70–71
    of knowledge work, 21
    multiple, 98
    periodic workplace, 34
    physical,
        —, or circulation of workers, 21
        —, and job, of workers, 18
    place, space and, 78
    rapid upward, 31
    social, 81
        —, upward, 61
    sociology of, 77
        vertical, of the agent in the firm,
            248
        work and workers flexibility,
            virtuality and, 14–22
modern corporation, structure of, 106
modernity, time–space configuration
    of, 78
modernisation, technological, push to-
    wards, 13
monitoring in real time, 30
monitoring, target-setting and, in real
    time, 30
monotony, strategies to lessen the, of
    the work, 223

Mother Tongue Influence (MTI), 219
mothers,
  full-time, 206
  working, 206
multicultural work teams, 127
multinational, 55
  companies,
    —, enterprises, 104
    —, foreign, 51
    —, opportunity to work in a, 220
    —, vertically integrated, 12
    —, Western, 105
multitasking, 63
Murthy, N.R. Narayana, 86
meritocracy, 50, 64
Myers Briggs Type Indicator (MBTI™),
  115, 139, 142–143, 149
  TA and, 148

National Association of Software and
  Services Companies (NASSCOM),
  16, 50
needs and demands, client's, 122
networking and personal ties, 58
networks, 12–14, 21, 35, 58–59, 67, 76,
  79, 94, 97–98, 104, 207, 212, 219,
  246, 256
  complex,
    —, production and services, 13
    —, transnational production, 12
  dispersed computer, 21
  informal, 67
  social, 59, 67, 89
normalisation, 199

occupations, IT-related, 14
office, low-end back, services, 12
offshore,
  industries high tech, in India, 9
  work,
    —, high end, in India, 96
    —, outsourced, 101
    —, service, 21
offshoring, 13
trend toward, 21
open market policies, 50
opportunities, high salaries and, 10
organisation, process and forms of, 18

Organisational Behaviour (OB), disciplines of, 142
outsourced projects, organisation of,
  121
outsourcing, 13, 39
  application management, services,
    81
  cultural logics of, 128–129
  Indian,
    —, software, industry, 107
    —, industry, 28, 124
  of IT services, 101
  offshore, 235
    —, hubs, 22
  requirements of, relationship, 15
  software,
    —, global, 20
    —, industry, 116
    —, projects, 125
    —, success of, projects, 108
    —, work, 85
  specificities of, business, 14
  of work to BPOs, 244
over-exertion, 254

parents, educational and occupational
  status of, 238
Parsonian modernisation theories, 105
performance,
  assessment, 254
  evaluation, 59
    —, in software firms, 59
  individual, 91
  linking, with incentives/punitive
    actions, 248
  quantitative and qualitative aspects
    of employee, 30
permanent transience, condition of, 33,
  92, 97–98
Personal Digital Assistants (PDAs), 79
personality,
  desirable, traits, 25
  development, 25
  linear active, 112–113
  multi-active, 112
placement,
  agencies, 240
  services, generic, 240

post-Fordism, 52
posthumanisation, 22
posting,
    overseas, 94, 202
    onsite, 94
Predictive Dialling Technologies, 246
process orientation, 28
processing, insurance claims, 12
production,
    and service, 20
    —, processes, 12
    internationalisation of, 13
    organisation of, 40
    post-Fordist networked flexible, 12
productivity, 90, 247
    and profits, 28
    improvement, 256
    quantum of work done and quality,
        248
professional priorities, 87
professionalism, 227
professionals, 29, 255
    empowered, 39
    upwardly mobile, 129
    young, from big cities, 84
programming, 12, 27, 54, 59, 60, 63, 68,
    77, 132, 164, 172, 182, 195
programmers, Indian, 55
project,
    management, 28, 90
    outsourced, 118
    participation of Indian workers in,
        174
    team members, 95
proletarianisation, technical, 185
promotions, 181
proprietary issues, 55
psychoneurotic disturbances, 255
punctuality and attentiveness, 247

qualifications, educational, 177
quality,
    of calls, 249
    certification,
        —, activities, 183
        —, procedures, 182
quantification and categorisation, 144
quitting, 254

rationalisation, 246
    and cost minimisation, 245
    of software production, 27
    virtualisation and, of the work pro-
        cess, 21
    of work, technology-aided surveil-
        lance and systems of control,
        245–249
recreation,
    and social activities provided by ITES
        companies, 223
    group activities for, 256
recruitment,
    agencies, 240
    campus, 218
    divisions, separate, 240
    through placement agencies, 240
    practices, followed by call centre
        firms, 240
reform,
    neoliberal, agenda, 51
    liberalisation, after 1991, 80
relationships,
    inter-organisational, 79
    subcontracting, with Indian firms, 55
    vending, 55
resistance,
    concept of, 31
    scope for, by workers, 31
restructuring, economic, 52
rewards,
    and treats, 223
    and recognition department, 223
    recognitions and, for work, 254
rights, individuals, 195
rosters, unreasonable, 256
routinisation, 32, 173
    of the production process, 29
    of software,
        —, production and techniques of
        direct control, 27
        —, work, 165
    of work, 165

sabotage and subversion, 31
salary, confidential, negotiations, 25
Sanskritisation, 87
Satyam Computer Services, 191

self-actualisation, 26
self-confidence, assertiveness and, 25
self-management, 15, 44, 106
self-motivation, autonomy empowerment
    and, 106
self-responsibility, demand for individual,
    24
self-surveillance, 26
service,
    conventional, sector, 243
    customer orientation of, 236
    industry, IT-enabled, 29
    IT enabled, 9
    provider, Indian, 124
service work,
outsourced, 15, 107
    —, high-tech, 38
Silicon Valley, 56
    —, model of the IT industry, 38
skills,
    behavioural/soft, 69
    communication, 108
        —, and inter-cultural, 108
    cultural sensitivity and communica-
        tion, training, 109
    experience and, of the workers, 183
    language aptitude and communica-
        tion, of the candidate, 240
    meritocracy, work culture and social
        construction of, 64
    operational, 149
    polarisation of, 52
    social, 197, 108
    soft, 51, 116
        —, global, industry, 157
    technical, 92
smoking, 255
social borders, relocation across physical
    and, 96
social circle of ITES persons, 225
social constructions, gendered, 63
social equality, 195
social exchange, 83
social gatherings, 95
social life, 89
sociality, 32
social rootedness, workers' sense of, 34
socialisation,

structured, 250, 252
    —, managements, 252
socialising, mixed-sex, 200
software,
    and computer services, 54
    and IT enabled services, 16
    companies, 17, 25, 51, 55, 59, 192.
        —, desire to encourage individual
        autonomy and innovation, 24
        —, Indian, 105–106, 108, 116–
        181
        —, Indian, of international quality
        certifications, 28
        —, large, 67
        —, products, 168
        —, working for, 191–194
development,
    —, centres, setting up of offshore,
    by MNCs, 13
    —, emergence of software factor-
    ies or assembly lines for, 27
    —, process, 172
    —, production process, 170
    —, structured programming, pro-
    cesses, 164
    —, waterfall model of, 168
engineering, 27, 63, 182–183, 194
engineers, 10, 14, 28, 33, 50, 58–59,
    70, 88, 125–126, 181, 192, 194,
    168
    —, emergence of the Indian,
    in the global cultural economy,
    101
    —, Indian, 19, 27, 103, 107–108,
    113–114, 117, 122–123, 125,
    127–128
    —, Indian companies and, 121
    —, Indian, working in multi-sited
    projects, 128
    —, offshore, and telematics
    workers, 15
    —, personalities of, 108
firm,
    —, organisational structure of a
    generic, 56
    —, Indian, 55, 183
    —, sample, 64
factories, advent of large, 28

industry,
—, academic literature on, 162
—, changes in the structure of, 69
—, cultural difference in the Indian, 128
—, early days of the, in India, 108
—, Indian, 18, 21, 25, 29, 50, 52, 54, 56, 62, 126, 168, 183
—, overview of the Indian, 54–56
—, spatial restructuring of the global, 56
low-level, workers, 163
outsourcing, 20
production,
—, and services, 54
—, process, 169
—, spatial relocation of, 54
—, transformation of, 28
professionals, 33, 55, 59
—, and BPO workers, 33
—, consumption practices of, 76
projects,
—, offshore, 105
—, outsourced, 107, 118
quality processes, 18–19, 27–28
rise of, and ITES industry in India, 101
services,
—, emergence of an Indian, industry , 50
—, Indian, business, 20
—, Indian, companies, 27, 122
—, Indian, industry, 116, 168
—, spectrum, 28
specially designed, 246
technology parks, 80, 83
work, 55, 60, 62, 76, 162–163, 166, 170
—, in India, 29, 162–185
—, module-based, 57
—, outsourced, 20
—, transformation of, 163
—, transformation of, from craft to industrial work, 164
workers,

—, in Indian, companies, 181
—, Indian, 181
—, Indian, in India and abroad, 19
—, oversupply of, 164
workspaces, 51
standardisation, 246
of the software development process, 164
standards and norms set by the companies, 222
subjective control, 36
subjectification, 32–33
superficial behaviour patterns, 112
supervision, continual scrutiny and, 252
surveillance, 28, 246–247
cultural capital and, 68–70
degree of, 246
digitilised systems of, and control, 30
electronic, 252
systems in IT companies, 91
techniques, 31

TA and MBTI™ trainers, 149
target, 247
daily, 247
meeting, 247
—, importance of, 247
task,
fragmentation, 167, 172
—, argument, 29
Tata Consultancy Services (TCS), 191
tax breaks for India's sunrise industry, 61
Taylor's scientific management principles, 163
Taylorism, 163
Taylorist strategies of dividing the work process into small parts, 28
Taylorist systems of direct management, 30
Taylorist techniques, 36
team,
activities, 199
performance, 199

teamwork and cultural management, 23

techie, 25, 58, 64, 69, 108–110, 115, 146, 148, 152, 218–219, 237, 240

Indian, 103, 114, 119, 122

—, cultural marking of, 121

technologies,

aided control, 246

and skills, 92

domination of, over labour, 246

mediating role of, 36

telecommunications,

advances in, industry, 53

digital information processing and, 235

telemarketing (IT-enabled services and business process outsourcing) , 12

tests, psychometric, 26

textualisation of work, 12

Tidel Park, 193

entry into, 193

time,

and space compression, 79

control over, 28

management, 25, 108, 118, 120

slavery, 120

track cards/warning cards, 248

trade unions, 256

lack of, 256

trainers, professional cross-cultural, 108

training, 221

behavioural, 26

sessions, continuous, 179

cultural,

—, and dress code, 70

—, programmes, 26, 113, 126

—, sensitivity, 108–110

—, sensitivity, and interaction, 35

—, sensitivity, programmes, 26

differential, 177–180

effective ICT and ITES related, 216

formal, programmes, 180

as inculcation of new dispositions, 220–222

in interpersonal and communication skills, 116

intensive, 17

manuals, 242

minimal, in the culture, 109

modes of recruitment and, 240–241

nature of, 179

non-technical, 179

on-the-job, 180

post-recruitment, 241

programme, 113, 180

—, corporate, 116

psychological, techniques, 26, 136

in-service, 177

skill-oriented, centres in India, 80

soft skills, 26, 108–109, 126, 145, 146, 154

—, programmes, 25, 108, 138

technical, 69, 137, 179–180

Transactional Analysis (TA), 115, 143

transfer of technology assignment, 125

transmission, satellite-based, processes, 58

travel,

city, and travails, 82–83

international, 89

overseas, glamour of frequent, 93

unionisation, among software professionals, 37

Unique Selling Proposition, India's, 140

value,

addition, 90

among candidates, 251

customer-oriented, 251

Indian, 138

video conferencing, 175

virtuality, 14, 223–224

virtual migration, 104

voice-based work, 255

Western fast food, availability of, 223

Westernisation, 224

Wipro Technologies, 191

women,

career-minded single, 201

commitment of, to their careers, 35

dependence on educated middle class professional, 50

emancipation of, IT workers, 34

empowered single, in IT, 202

English-speaking, middle class professional, 61
entry of,
—, into the IT industry, 51
—into the workforce, 34
in entry level programming positions, 60
ethnographic account of Barbados' offshore, workers, 37
focus on recruiting, 217
highly educated middle class, in Indian software, 54
household members, 94
imbrication of, within the circuits of global consumerism, 228
Indian, 208
IT professionals, 35, 202–203, 206, 208
ITES workers, 228
married, 200, 203
—, patients, 207
—, without children, 207
middle class, 34, 61
—, educated, 60
pink collar offshore, workers in Barbados, 36
poor, of colour and their marginalisation as workers, 53
professionals, 35
proportion of, in software firms, 51
single, 200, 201
—, position of, 207
social role of a, in the domestic sphere, 34, 65

working, 206
work,
boundary between, and non-work, 34
cultures of, 10, 22, 23, 121
despatialisation and virtualisation of, 39
devaluation of women's waged, 53
difference in, culture, 121
environment, 67
experiences, transnational, 102
high-tech, 54

in Indian BPOs, 243
Indian–European differences in, culture, 118
informatisation of, 236
monotony of, 223
odd, timings, 254
offshore,
—, and onsite, 107
—, IT and ITES, 21
organisation,
—, in BPOs, 243
—, of, in software outsourcing projects, 124
outsourced technology-based and mediated, 9
rationalisation, 245
redefinition of, 36
—, and the embodied experience of women, 57
regime, global high technology, 211
symbolisation of, 22
transnationalisation of, 37
worker,
Barbados pink collar, 37
consumers, 212
cyborg, 22, 30
division between conception and execution, 170
entrepreneurial, 24, 106
global,
—, a distinctive category of knowledge, 10
—, emergence of,
—, emergence of new categories of, 11
—, technical, 14
empowered, 115
entrepreneurial, 24, 106
geographical mobility of, across borders, 93
global technical, 14
higher-level, 179
high-tech nomadic, 20
immigrant, 54
Indian, 174
—, software, 121
individualised, 25, 39

industrial, in the global assembly
line, 103
informatics, 30
low- and middle-level, 180
low-level, 180, 179
migration of, 54
networked virtual, 21
newly emergent 'class' of, 36
in offshore factories in Malaysia or
Brazil, 15
offshore,
—, business process outsourcing,
21
—, ITES, 221
professional service sector, 54
qualified, 17
selected, 173
self-management of, 106
self-managing, 25
socio-economic background of, 176
sociological questions about IT, 32
subjectivity of, 15
supply of qualified, 16
temporary contract, 19
workforce,
composition of the software, in India
and the West, 176
culturally-defined, 113
flexible, 19
globally networked, 20
IT industry and its, 32
IT-based offshore, 15
IT–ITES, 16
—, in India, 20
mean and median ages of, 238
new,
—, global, 103
—, under capitalism and cultural
forms of resistance, 104
non-agricultural, 61
position of the Indian software, in the
labour process, 185
profile of the work and, in the BPO
sector, 239
ready availability of a large technical,
17

work and, in the Indian software
industry, 168–169
work–life balance, 120, 138
workloads, excessive, 256
workplace, 15, 18, 22–24, 26, 29, 31,
34, 36, 38, 40, 43, 50–53, 58, 60, 63,
65–68, 70, 74, 76, 80, 83, 87, 101–102,
104, 106–108, 110, 112–113, 116–117,
124, 126, 128–129, 136–137, 153, 163,
193, 198, 222, 225–226, 236–237, 244,
246–247, 252–258
corporate, 101
—, in the Fordist era, 23
cultures of work and organisational
control, 22
demands of the new, 15
design of, in call centres, 244
global, 108
interactions, 246
knowledge-intensive high tech, 116
managing in, 63
—, and assessment in, 32
new, 22, 106
and the new worker, 23
of the post-industrial information
economy, 29
unique design of the, in BPOs, 255
workspace, 51–52, 57, 60, 98, 193
workshops, cross-cultural, 127
training, 220
workstation, 83

youth,
emerging global, of the 21st century,
212–214
English-speaking educated, 14
global consumption-oriented, culture, 37
ITES,
—, personnel, 226
—, workers, 211, 227
middle-class, 31
population, 215
workforce, 32

For Product Safety Concerns and Information please contact our EU
representative GPSR@taylorandfrancis.com
Taylor & Francis Verlag GmbH, Kaufingerstraße 24, 80331 München, Germany

www.ingramcontent.com/pod-product-compliance
Ingram Content Group UK Ltd.
Pitfield, Milton Keynes, MK11 3LW, UK
UKHW020935180425
457613UK00019B/407